The Poetics of Historical Perspectivism

University of North Carolina
Studies in the Germanic Languages
and Literatures

Initiated by RICHARD JENTE (1949–1952), *established by* F. E. COENEN (1952–1968), *continued by* SIEGFRIED MEWS (1968–1980) *and* RICHARD H. LAWSON (1980–1985)

PAUL T. ROBERGE, Editor

Publication Committee: Department of Germanic Languages

For other volumes in the "Studies" see pages 149–50.

Number One Hundred and Fourteen
University of
North Carolina
Studies in the
Germanic Languages
and Literatures

The Poetics of
Historical Perspectivism:
Breitinger's *Critische Dichtkunst*
and the Neoclassic Tradition

Jill Anne Kowalik

The University of North Carolina Press
Chapel Hill and London   1992

© 1992 The University of North Carolina Press

Library of Congress Cataloging-in-Publication Data
Kowalik, Jill Anne.
    The poetics of historical perspectivism : Breitinger's Critische Dichtkunst and
the neoclassic tradition / Jill Anne Kowalik.
        p.   cm. — (University of North Carolina studies in the Germanic languages
and literatures ; no. 114)
    Includes bibliographical references and indexes.
    ISBN 0-8078-8114-7 (alk. paper)
    1. Breitinger, Johann Jacob, 1701–1776   Critische Dichtkunst.   2. Poetics.
I. Title.   II. Series.
PN1044.K66   1992
801'.951—dc20   91-23614
                                                                                              CIP

The paper in this book meets the guidelines for
permanence and durability of the Committee on
Production Guidelines for Book Longevity of the
Council on Library Resources.

Manufactured in the United States of America

96   95   94   93   92   5   4   3   2   1

For Hans-Hellmut and Hildegard Berthold, who
introduced me to the historical world, and for my
father, J. G. Warnecke, who made me curious about it

Contents

Acknowledgments

This book could not have been written without the advice and support of Wesley Trimpi, in whose brilliant seminars on ancient literary theory at Stanford University the idea for this study was first conceived. Since that time I have continued to benefit from his broad learning and painstaking scholarship as well as from his generosity as a teacher and friend. I am also grateful for the meticulous attention given my manuscript by the readers for the University of North Carolina Press. Their criticism was invaluable in helping me to address, successfully I hope, some of the inadequacies of my presentation. Thomas P. Saine read through an earlier version of the entire manuscript and made a number of useful suggestions for improvement. He also freely provided a great deal of technical assistance with the electronic processing of the manuscript. Hinrich C. Seeba kindly agreed to review my text after a major revision. Ruth (Angress) Kluger did me the dual favor of first suggesting that I try to publish this material and then ignoring my protestations that I shouldn't bother. Nicholas Vazsonyi did an excellent job with the galley proof. I would like to thank my husband, William S. Kowalik, and my friend, Gail K. Hart, for offering constant encouragement, and always when I needed it most. Finally, I am deeply indebted to my editor, Paul T. Roberge, for his patience and enthusiasm about my work when the final revising of the text was interrupted for reasons beyond my control.

A Note on Orthography

Most of the quotations of primary works in this study evince orthographic conventions that deviate from modern norms. Three aspects of these deviations deserve special comment. First, the spelling of the same word may vary within the same text, as when Breitinger writes for the dative plural both "unsren" and "unsern." Such discrepancies may reflect the printer's inconsistencies. Second, antiquated spellings may occur in texts in which the orthography appears to be otherwise fairly modern, as when Wegelin writes "Geschichtschreiber" instead of "Geschichtsschreiber." Third, the orthography of seventeenth- and early eighteenth-century French omits many of the diacritical marks that modern readers expect. Dubos has "reflexions" and not "réflexions"; Leibniz has "verités" or "veritez" instead of "vérités." Moreover, the letter *o* was often used in place of *a*. For example, the endings *-ait* and *-ais* appear as *-oit* or *-ois*. Thus Dacier's Aristotle was "traduite en françois." All quotations have been carefully examined for their fidelity to the editions cited in the notes and bibliography.

The Poetics of Historical Perspectivism

Introduction

The development of aesthetics in late eighteenth-century Germany coincided with a strong scholarly interest in language and with a new reflection on history. The apparently sudden progress in these three fields is usually attributed to the seminal work of a brilliant philologist, cultural historian, literary theorist, linguist, and art critic— namely, Herder. But the connections between aesthetics, the historical sciences, and the study of language, the reasons for the simultaneous attention given these disciplines in the eighteenth century, have yet to be explored adequately, primarily because scholars have often failed to examine in detail the origins of aesthetics in the early part of the century. This period was shaped by the Quarrel between the Ancients and the Moderns, which was intensely concerned with the interrelation of literary criticism, language, and history. My study is intended as a contribution to our understanding of this interrelation.

By using Breitinger's text as a focal point, I hope to delineate a specific aspect of aesthetic thinking in the eighteenth century: how it was that poesis and historiography could increasingly come to resemble each other in their assumptions, purposes, and methods of presentation. The concept that associates these two disciplines with each other in this period is "historical perspectivism." When applied to historiography, this notion holds that history is not accessible to us as an unrelated collection of "facts" or information, but only insofar as information can be placed in a context, a *Zusammenhang*.[1] The construction of a context, however, was viewed as an essentially poetic task. The historian no longer simply writes out chronicles but "represents" the past. History, now understood as narrative, is a *Gemälde*, an organized aesthetic whole that is not unlike the "Gemälde" that Breitinger says poets produce.[2] The historical representation was, furthermore, said to follow or be made possible by the adoption of a *Gesichts-Punkt*, a term that stood ready-to-hand in the poetic theory of the early Enlightenment. There the notion of perspectivism is manifest in the argument that the poet creates a literary work out of the perspective that he occupies vis-à-vis nature. When the term "historical perspectivism" is extended to poetic interpretation, it means that the critic must account for the historical and cultural "distance" between himself and the work. A central contention of my study is that historians learned to utilize the notion of perspective after its

1

development as an interpretive tool by the aesthetic thinkers of the early eighteenth century, of whom Breitinger is but one albeit highly significant example.

To be sure, a German version of the words "historical perspectivism" is nowhere to be found in Breitinger's oeuvre. Instead he relies on the term "Gesichts-Punkt,"[3] which he endows with a decidedly historical quality. His text therefore exemplifies a reflection on the relationship between historical consciousness, language, and literature that permeates the *querelle*. This has, however, not been generally appreciated. There are three reasons for this oversight. First, Breitinger's concept of language, his view of the historically changing nature of.languages, has remained curiously neglected. Second, the extent of Breitinger's reliance on French sources is not well understood. Dubos is most frequently mentioned *en passant* in interpretations of the *Critische Dichtkunst*, but Breitinger's appropriations from Dubos's text have never been carefully analyzed. Moreover, because Breitinger's work has been traditionally viewed as a "revolt" of sorts against neoclassic normative poetics, his use of other neoclassic critics, such as Le Bossu or Mme Dacier, has not been registered. Third, recent developments in *Germanistik*, including the disfavor into which *Ideengeschichte* has fallen, have discouraged attempts to interpret Breitinger's text from philosophic, poetic, and rhetorical perspectives at once. Although studies of Breitinger authored in the past decade, which usually avail themselves of rhetorical or semiotic concepts, have offered some novel explications of the *Critische Dichtkunst*, their interpretive aim (an elaboration of the Habermasian model of the literary public or an investigation of the relation between rhetoric and Wolffian psychology) sidesteps the issue of multiple influences.[4]

The question of influence is one of the thorniest issues to resolve in the interpretation of the *Critische Dichtkunst* because it is nearly impossible to establish with certainty what Breitinger actually read. He doubtless cited only some of the things that he knew, but he also quoted texts without citing them, and cited still other texts that he may have never seen. His commentary on chapter 7 of the *Poetics*, for example, includes extensive references to Aristotle's *Ethics* and *Politics*. Braitmaier, who in the late nineteenth century approvingly noted these citations, would have been less impressed with Breitinger's classical erudition had he known that the entire commentary was lifted verbatim from André Dacier's *La Poëtique d'Aristote avec des remarques*.[5]

Breitinger's rampant borrowing of passages from other critical treatises was of course not anomalous for neoclassic authors. Eventually the preoccupation with original genius, coupled with the desire for corporate profit, would manifest itself in publishing contracts and copyright laws, but in 1740 an author did not yet have to contend with such legal restraints. If he found a passage by another "Criticus" that was congenial to his meaning, he inserted it into his text. Often an insertion appeared not because it added to the sense of the work but because it added to its legitimacy. Hence, although it is important to recognize the source of Breitinger's words, it is even more crucial to grasp the function of his thefts within the entire presentation. "Qu'on ne dise pas que je n'ai rien dit de nouveau: la disposition des matières est nouvelle," Pascal had said, thereby designating exactly the neoclassic enterprise.[6]

An example of the naive handling of the problem of influence, in which the function of classical terms in the eighteenth century is not well understood, can be found in an essay by Wolfgang Preisendanz: "Selbstverständlich folgt Gottsched dem Aristoteles auch darin, daß die poetische Nachahmung der Natur Fiktion ist. Dichten heißt Ersinnen oder Erfinden von Möglichem, nicht Wiedergabe von Faktischem; Dichtung ahmt nach, was zu sein und zu geschehen pflegt, nicht was geschehen oder gewesen ist. Dichtung ist Verbindung von Wahrheit und Lüge, sie ist wahrscheinliche Fiktion."[7] This passage reflects a typical neoclassic distortion of Aristotle's distinction between history and poesis, a distinction I discuss in detail in the third chapter of this study. More to the point here, however, is Preisendanz's suggestion that Gottsched is actually following Aristotle, when in fact Gottsched's Aristotle had traveled through centuries of commentary before he finally came to rest on Gottsched's desk in Leipzig. Preisendanz has given us an accurate restatement of Gottsched's concept of "Fabel," but he errs in having accepted at face value Gottsched's contention (not quoted here) that his own "Fabelbegriff" is a faithful reproduction of Aristotle's concept of μῦθος or plot. Gottsched's definition of "Fabel" is a neoclassic commonplace, while Preisendanz takes it as a sort of direct emanation from the *Poetics*.

The problem with such misapprehensions is that many of the very interesting modern reconstructions or deformations of Aristotelian poetic concepts go unnoticed because there is no historical standard against which the eighteenth-century use of the *Poetics* can be measured. The purpose of such comparisons is not to establish which authors have "correctly" utilized The Philosopher's categories, but simply to inject some clarity into the discussion of what is at stake in the early eighteenth-century debates on poesis. A more recent interpretation of Breitinger's poetics in terms of the classical tradition, Gerlinde Bretzigheimer's *Johann Elias Schlegels poetische Theorie im Rahmen der Tradition*, is, like Preisendanz's essay, based on an insufficient grasp of the historical refraction introduced into Aristotelian poetics. [8]

Perhaps the most influential attempt thus far to situate Breitinger on the horizon of early eighteenth-century poetics is Hans Peter Herrmann's *Naturnachahmung und Einbildungskraft*, which appeared in 1970. [9] Herrmann's main—and laudable—objective was to excise Breitinger's work from the ideological context of *Genieästhetik* in which it had languished for nearly two centuries. Armed with a thorough knowledge of Baroque rhetoric and Wolffian philosophy, Herrmann set about analyzing many more passages than the usual six or eight places from Breitinger's text that had been used traditionally to construct the image of Breitinger as a "pre-Romantic," that is, as the defender of the "Entfesselung der Phantasie" in the face of the Enlightenment's supposed "Herrschaft der Vernunft." [10] But because Breitinger's text is so thick with quotation, citation, and outright plagiarism that it occasionally borders on indecipherability, Herrmann finally concluded that Breitinger did not possess the requisite insight and expository skill to develop a coherent literary theory. Such criticism recalls of course Goethe's statement that Breitinger's prose resembles an "Irrgarten." [11] Herrmann's observation that in the *Critische Dichtkunst* "es blieb bei der Aufgabenstellung" (264) suggests in fact a sort of "dialectical reversal" on Herrmann's part. For whereas he begins with a critique of the concept of "Genie," he ends with a radicalization of the "precursor" notion that had always been embedded in the genius cliché. Thus, while the value of Breitinger's work had been found traditionally in its anticipation of later, "Romantic," poetic theories, in Herrmann's account one senses the author's impatience that Breitinger was merely a precursor, that he did not know more. [12] The reason, Herrmann contends, that Breitinger failed to produce a truly innovative poetic conception lies in his failure to transcend the Baroque rhetorical categories of the seventeenth century. Breitinger himself, Herrmann suggests, remained entangled in the orthodox Protestant (i.e., Swiss patrician) political order. [13]

Precisely this aspect of Herrmann's interpretion is the basis of David E. Wellbery's reading of the *Critische Dichtkunst* that appeared in his 1984 study *Lessing's "Laocoon."* [14] Because this book contains the finest semiotic analysis to date of Breitinger's text, I want to discuss Wellbery's argument in some detail in order to clarify my own interpretive method and aims. Wellbery argues that Breitinger's work is "characterized by an overlapping of theoretical paradigms" (207), which he calls the "performance" and the "representational" paradigms (6, 207, etc.). Aesthetic experience and especially literary production and reception within the performance model is "intimately associated" (47) with rhetoric, from which it derives its "directives" (46–47) regarding successful presentation and appropriate appreciation. Such directives are eminently didactic and therefore similar to rules of social conduct (cf. 46). The world from which they emanate is utterly hierarchical; the purpose of art in such a system is *divertissement*, entertainment, or ornament, through which the existing structure of political, theological, and economic power is reinforced (cf. 45).

The representational model, by contrast, is based on the analysis of supposedly universal faculties of the mind and their interaction in the production of images that "move" rather than "entertain" (45–47). In this paradigm, language is "[extricated] from its place within the ceremonies of religious and absolutist authority" and "[transformed] into a medium of communication and debate among equal subjects" (36). Literary language, indeed all art, "is located entirely within the sphere of representations" (71). Its purpose is to evoke the "presence-to-mind of the [sensually absent] represented object" (71), and thereby to produce what was for the Enlightenment an essentially "specular" (11) experience: intuition or *anschauende Erkenntnis*.

As a follower of Wolff, Wellbery says, Breitinger understood the links between language, seeing, and cognition that are established by the representational paradigm. But Breitinger departs from this paradigm in that he subordinates poesis to the process of distinct cognition in Wolff's sense. The literary work is supposed to provide not *anschauende Erkenntnis*, or the illusion-of-presence, as for Lessing, but rather ever more detailed information about and interpretation of the discursive-conceptual order of reality, as opposed to the perceptual and sensual world of Lessing's aesthetic. For this reason, Breitinger remained indebted to the performance model in his distinction between poetry and ordinary language. Here he reverts to the "tactics of *elocutio*" (207). Poetry is reduced to the "use of ornaments, the deployment of verbal artistry in order to heighten or intensify the poetic message" (207). And this "message" invariably involves "spiritual-political hierarchies" (220) that Breitinger wants his reader to recognize and accept.

The distinction between ordinary language and poesis, however, is made by Breitinger not with reference to the presence or absence of ornament, but rather according to the use of metaphor (cf. my chapter 1). Furthermore, his theory of language, which is set forth in the second volume of the *Critische Dichtkunst*, is based on an explicit rejection of the ornamental function of the metaphor. In overlooking this rejection, Wellbery is able to consign Breitinger's work to the earlier performance theory type. Thus Breitinger is said to have a socially regressive desire to "[interpret] the text of nature for the reader" (220). I shall argue, by contrast, that Breitinger's poetics should be seen as a progressive investigation of the act of interpretation itself that seeks to free literature from its neoclassic preoccupation with didactic contents.

Wellbery's apparent oversight regarding Breitinger's concept of metaphor illustrates how persistent the view has been, ever since Gottsched's original condemnation of the Swiss concept of poetic language, that Breitinger intends metaphor merely as embellishment for the sake of heightened effect. Manfred Windfuhr, for example, had earlier claimed that the Swiss purpose with metaphor was "Emotionsausweitung," and that while Breitinger attempted to avoid the charge of "Maßlosigkeit," he nonetheless "entscheidet . . . sich meist für die Fülle."[15] And Eric Blackall, in what was for many years the standard work on German as a literary language, says nothing at all about Breitinger's concept of language per se. He merely provides a list of metaphors that he says Breitinger felt would enrich the German language. Although these three scholars have vastly different notions of language and literature, and thus should not be compared too strictly, their commentaries point to a recurring problem in Breitinger scholarship, namely, the failure to give Breitinger's second volume the careful attention that it deserves.[16] Had this occurred, one would have found there an early adumbration of the historicity of metaphor that is intimately connected to the emergence of historical poetics in the eighteenth century.

The most important differences between Wellbery's approach and my own may well lie, however, in our differing approaches to literary history, that is, in our use of semiotic versus hermeneutic models.[17] Wellbery says that he is in fact not writing literary history at all: this would imply for him the adoption of a quasi-teleological construct intended to reveal the "progressive unfolding" (6) of ideas. In the case of the eighteenth century, this has led to assertions of the historical development of "subjectivity," a term that has little explanatory value for him. He is interested instead in describing the "metasemiotic" (6) of the Enlightenment—its "attitude toward signs" (6)—of which literary discourse is merely one aspect. There remains nevertheless an implicit moment of progression in Wellbery's analysis in that he describes the sequential displacement of one paradigm by another over the course of the century.[18] History for Wellbery (at least, as he presents it in the book under consideration here) is a series of "metasemiotic" strata that sometimes overlap but are generally to be viewed in terms of their disjunction. Because Wellbery accepts and elaborates Lessing's critique of Breitinger, which he grounds in the representational paradigm, Breitinger must be forced "back" into an earlier, and by implication, more regressive, historical stratum.

While I share completely Wellbery's stated antipathy toward teleologically colored literary history and toward the term "subjectivity" in explanations of the intellectual developments of the eighteenth century, I prefer to think of this period in terms of multiple historical strands or currents that may run simultaneously through any given temporal stratum. My objective in this study is to describe that strand I have termed "historical perspectivism" as it cuts through the century beginning with the *querelle*. Wellbery prefers to focus on the field of discourse constituted by Wolffian philosophy and psychology; I have chosen to analyze Breitinger's use of multiple historical sources. As I have already indicated, however, in my remarks on "influence" and "function," this does not mean that Breitinger's text will be treated as the simple reanimation of, say, classical rhetorical notions or French neoclassic concepts of Homeric style. Here I agree with Wellbery that any given sign (linguistic, cultural, historical) must be interpreted within the system—I would say "context"—in which it appears. But whereas his semiotic, or metasemiotic, system is conceived of as a closed synchronic structure, the hermeneutic context can, and usually does, encompass complex and extensive diachronic traditions. For this reason an analysis of the historical elements at work in Breitinger's text is, in my view, inescapable if we are to understand it.

In my own attempt to draw the outline of Breitinger's argument, I have proceeded in the following manner: the first chapter contains an explication of Breitinger's theory of language in terms of the contemporary debate on both language and style. Here I want to show that Breitinger's use of the term "poetische Mahlerey" is based on an argument for the necessary relationship between concept formation and metaphor. The chapter then addresses the epistemological problem that any discussion of the relationship between words, thoughts, and things must inevitably produce, and it relates this problem to Gottsched's and Breitinger's differing approaches to practical criticism. Breitinger's notion of language as the historically determined evolution of conceptual differentiation is linked to his views on the interpretation of texts as historical documents. I argue that this is in fact the most significant difference between him and his antagonist.

The second chapter concerns creative process as poetic production, which in Breitinger's account is the depiction of possible worlds. The exposition there is an elaboration of the thesis presented in the first chapter, namely that Breitinger was interested in the relationship between historical perspective and poetic process. Perspective is analyzed in terms of Leibniz's notions of apperception, compossibility, and perfectibility. Breitinger's explication of creative process as the invention ("Erfindung") of possible worlds is then reviewed in the context of Wolffian logic and Leibniz's system of intellective integration.

The third chapter discusses creative process as poetic reception. Here I deal with Breitinger's deviations from Dubos by analyzing his many borrowings from the *Reflexions critiques*, the often-supposed source of his concept of poetic effect. I argue that there is a pattern in these deviations that shows Breitinger's attempt to establish, against the French neoclassic version of "vraisemblance," the act of poetic reception as itself productive. In this construction of analogous intellective functions for both author and reader one may locate an aspect of his poetics with potentially far-reaching implications. Literature is no longer an endeavor reserved for a cultural or artistic elite but initiates a general psychological process in which both poet and recipient participate. In this the *Critische Dichtkunst* indeed may be taken, with some qualifications, as an "anticipation" of later "Romantic" notions of the autonomous reader.[19]

The final chapter begins with Lessing's critique of Breitinger's notion of "poetische Mahlerey." I suggest that Lessing may not have grasped Breitinger's differences with Dubos, on which his defense of seeing as interpretation is based. Breitinger's "poetische Mahlerey" is then related to metaphors of historical interpretation in the eighteenth century: to the notion of "Sehe-Punckt" developed by Chladenius, and also to perspectivist theories of historiography proposed by Jacob Wegelin, who joined the Berlin Academy following his association with Breitinger's circle in Zurich.

In none of Breitinger's works is there an explicit assertion of identity or similarity between history and poesis such as we find in the later eighteenth century. But Breitinger's temporalization of poesis and his theory of perspectivist literary interpretation set the stage for the subsequent "poeticization" of historiography. This process should not be understood as a "making explicit" of something that was only "implicit" in Breitinger's work, but rather in a historically concrete sense as the adaptation of his interpretive paradigm to historical discourse.

1. *Ut pictura poesis*

Breitinger's designation of poesis as "Mahler-Kunst" is an often noticed but rarely examined adaptation of a sentence from Horace's epistle to the Pisos, or *Ars poetica*. The comparison of painting and poetry was a neoclassic preoccupation and not original to Breitinger, as the number of treatises on painting and poetry bears out: the essays by Dryden (1695), Richardson (1719), and Dubos (1719) are among the best-known examples. Breitinger's assertion that "was die Farben dem Mahler sind, das sind die Wörter und der Ausdruck dem Redner und dem Poeten" also could have been copied from any number of sources.[1] In view of the commonness of the comparison between painting and poetry, Breitinger's understanding of "poetische Mahlerey" is not readily apparent without analyzing his use of the Horatian simile in more detail than has thus far been attempted. This will be undertaken here first of all with respect to his concept of language. This analysis will be followed by an examination of the epistemological problem imbedded in Horace's comparison itself.[2] References to the *ut pictura* doctrine in secondary literature on the German Renaissance, Baroque, and Enlightenment appear to be universally indebted to a simplified notion of Horace's comparison. Horace is cast virtually without exception as the defender of strict mimesis, which in turn is defined as the notion that "art copies nature." Here scholars have been too willing to use one kind of neoclassic interpretation of Horace—the interpretation that equates imitation with the duplication of the object—as the basis of their own. But literary history cannot be written by unreflectively replicating the assumptions of the age that is being studied. The Horation simile is in fact much more complex than most critics would have us believe, and a careful scrutiny of what Horace actually says is essential for our understanding of neoclassic attitudes toward practical criticism.

Language and Metaphor

Breitinger opens his discussion of language by naming his sources: the French Cartesian Gerauld de Cordemoy and the English mathematician and grammarian John Wallis.[3] With apparent dependence on the terms of Cordemoy, whose treatise is marked by a radical division between mind and body, Breitinger defines language as "eine Kunst den Gedancken durch Thöne einen Leib und eine sichtbare Gestalt mitzutheilen" (2:13). Sounds and word meanings ("Bedeutungen") represent the material and the intellective ("geistlicher") aspects of language respectively. The union of sounds with meanings has arisen because of conventions created by human beings. This union is arbitrary ("willkührlich," 2:13, 44, 200, etc.), which means that there is not a natural or divine law according to which any given meaning adheres to a given sound. Breitinger does not mean here that words are derived by fiat, such as is the case in artificial languages, but that word meanings have arisen over time in a process of association carried out as a historical intellective activity. Because this process is historical, it is subject to vicissitude: meanings can shift over time, or words can die out altogether ("durch den Gebrauch etwann geändert oder abgeschaffet werden," 2:44), while new words are created in their place.

Yet Breitinger also maintains that just because words die, concepts do not die with them. In fact it is precisely the conventionality of language that allows other, new words to express the same concept captured in the previous word: "Denn so bald ein gewisser Thon, der in einer Sprache gebrauchet worden, einen gewissen Gedancken zu bezeichnen, abgehet, welches durch tausend Zufälle begegnen kan, so wird dieser Gedancke (denn auch die Seelen der Wörter sterben nicht) mit einem andern Thone aus seinem Cörper vereiniget, zumahl da mehrentheils die Gedancken nicht lange von einem Cörper abgesondert seyn können" (2:95–96). This definition reflects Breitinger's position within the modern debate on the "natural" or "conventional" origin of language. The proponents of natural language held that words proceeded necessarily out of the nature or essence of the things to which they referred, whereas the proponents of conventional language argued that words referred to things only because human beings had come to agree that certain sounds should signify certain objects (mental or physical).[4] It is interesting that Breitinger's source, Cordemoy, counts himself among the radical conventionalists ("ces signes . . . n'ont aucune conformité avec les pensées que l'on y joint par institution," 32), but in order to avoid complete skepticism, he subsequently avails himself of the occasionalist *deus ex machina* by arguing that words make sense at all only because there is a God-ordained (or "natural") exact correspondence between body and mind.[5]

On this point, however, Breitinger parts company with his source. Although he had begun his exposition with Cordemoy's terms, defining words as "angenommene Zeichen" (2:14) of thoughts, he now interjects, with a "Gleichwohl" (2:14), his own reflections on why signs should be accepted as expressions of thought. He begins by citing Cicero and Quintilian on euphony, and then explains the development of language—that is, the retention of some sounds rather than others to refer to specific thoughts—in terms of the auditory pleasure derived from certain expressions.[6] Language is thus a function of man's natural inclination ("natürliche Neigung," 2:18) to prefer one kind of sound over another. And yet this inclination is itself a kind of "natural convention" in that it varies from culture to culture.[7] His argument is different than Cordemoy's notion of a divine correspondence between sound and meaning. Breitinger emphasizes that euphony, not to be confused with the intellective content of words, is merely "eine Schönheit eines unbeseelten Leichnams" (2:35), and, in a reference to the proponents of Baroque "Klangmalerei," he criticizes those who exploit it to claim a sort of "metaphysical" bond between sounds and meanings by endowing euphony with "eine Magische Kraft" (2:37).

The conventional nature of language is responsible for the development of many languages. That two different sounds can represent the same concept, a phenomenon Breitinger calls equivalence ("Gleichgültigkeit," 2:139), is demonstrated by the fact that one culture has preferred one sound over another to express a given idea. Equivalence is manifested not only synchronically, across several language groups, but also diachronically within any given language: new words can replace old words, thereby preserving the concepts originally expressed.[8] This process requires constant, thoughtful effort by the users of a language. Breitinger therefore expresses his fear at a number of places that concepts will be lost because German "Scribenten" do not sufficiently attend to maintaining the broadest possible vocabulary; they "discard" some words through simple neglect before others have arisen to take their place, that is, before they can be technically called outmoded (cf. 2:211). This leads to the unfortunate state in which concepts and ideas ("Begriffe und Gedancken") become "verwahrloset und in Vergessenheit gesetzet" (2:204).[9]

There is, however, an infinite number of possible concepts that any given language can express (2:307). The richness of a language is determined by the number of vivid terms ("Machtwörter") it contains; these terms are responsible for the level of conceptual differentiation, that is, how precisely discrete concepts can be expressed by a language. The quality of a language is not to be found, Breitinger argues,

in the sheer number of terms, which are potentially redundant be-
cause synonymous, just as a library is better judged by the number of
titles and editions it has and not by its number of volumes (2:97). The
sources of new concepts for a language are located by Breitinger, first,
in the retention of "archaic" words and phrases whose concepts have
yet to be more adequately represented by newer terms (2:211–12)
and, second, in translation. Breitinger's model in both repects—the
use of archaic terms and successful translation—is Martin Opitz.[10]

The purpose of translation is not merely "eine Verwechselung
gleichgültiger Zeichen" (2:143)—that is, it is not a search for literal
correspondences. Literal translations are in fact not even possible,
for two reasons. First, a phrase in one language grew out of a histori-
cally determined set of circumstances ("verschiedene Gemüthes- und
Gedenckens-Art ungleicher Nationen," 2:144) that are not them-
selves transferable or translatable into the foreign context. Breitinger
gives as an example the French "faire la cour à quelqu'un" (2:343–
44), which, curiously enough for the modern reader, he hopes will
not enter the German language as "einem den Hof machen." Second,
the concept represented by some words may simply not exist in the
second (foreign) language. Here Breitinger mentions Leibniz's obser-
vation that the French have no word for the German reiten.[11]

The best translations, Breitinger says, will be carried out by those
who demonstrate equal competence in both the original language of
a text and the language in which it is to be rendered (cf. 2:142–44).
Competence, however, does not mean a simple command of vocabu-
lary and grammar, but rather the translator's ability to reanimate in
his own mind the conceptual relationships that the original language
expresses ("in eben solcher Ordnung, Verbindung, [und] Zusammen-
hange [der Begriffe]," 2:139). Only when he understands how words
express concepts can he attempt to find an equivalent form of expres-
sion for the language of the translation. The goal of the translation is
identical reception: "einen gleichen Eindruck auf das Gemüthe des
Lesers [machen]" (2:139). Breitinger's critique of the treatment of Ho-
mer by the modernes is based on this consideration, for he sees the
attempt to "modernize" Homer by La Motte and others as evidence
of their inability or unwillingness to reanimate the effect of Homer on
his original audience. Those who find Homer "primitive" do not un-
derstand the historical context of his language. I shall return to this
issue below.[12]

The growth of a language as it is fostered by translations means the
development of its ability to express concepts, which should not be
confused with the proliferation of words: to learn a new word for

every new concept "würde dem Menschen seine gantze Lebenszeit rauben" (2:308).[13] What needs to be increased, rather than the "Zahl der Wörter," is the range of word meanings, the "Gebrauch ihrer Bedeutungen" (2:309). How this should occur Breitinger explains with reference to John Locke's ideas on language.

Earlier in this same passage (at 2:308), Breitinger says Locke observes that abstract terms ultimately arise from the perception of "cörperlichen Dingen, die in die Sinne fallen." The section from *An Essay concerning Humane Understanding* to which he must have meant to refer his reader is 3.1.5, where Locke says that words "quite removed from sense" (one of Locke's examples is "spirit") may be traced to "sensible Ideas" (e.g., "breath"). Breitinger interprets Locke's point to be that all abstract concepts are ultimately figures of speech.[14] While this had been implicit in Locke's words, Breitinger extends his meaning by asserting that there is a necessary connection between concept formation and metaphor. Given, however, Breitinger's statement that metaphor, of all the figures, is the most "painterly" ("mahlerisch," 2:320), and therefore the most responsible for vividness in expression, it seems curious that he would propose it as the chief tool of abstraction. Here it is necessary to discuss what Breitinger means by "vivid."

In the opening chapter of the *Critische Dichtkunst*, Breitinger explains why he has chosen the term "poetische Mahlerey" to stand for the activity of poesis. Painting, he says, makes a swifter and more effective impression on the mind than speech because it works through the eye, the organ with the greatest power over the soul ("Macht auf die Seele," 1:15). He then refers his reader to what he calls Dubos's thorough explanation of the matter in chapter 40 of the first part of his treatise.[15] There the difference between poetry and painting is set forth as the difference between "des signes artificiels" and "des signes naturels." Dubos, whose argument Breitinger will use in part, goes on to explain that the difference between "des signes arbitraires & instituez" and painted images is that the signs a painter uses are in fact not really signs at all: "Je parle peut-être mal quand je dis que la Peinture emploïe des signes. C'est la nature elle-même que la peinture met sous nos yeux" (1.40.394).[16] Dubos then claims that the images of painting are immediately absorbed by the mind, whereas written representations have to be translated, as it were, by the mind "back" into visual images in order to be understood.[17] While Breitinger accepts some of Dubos's argument, namely, that visual images are stronger than verbal ones, he himself finds that one cannot be content simply with what is presented to the sight as a source of

artistic representation. Nature can be perceived under so many differ-
ent aspects ("Seiten," 1:18), and poesis therefore has the potential of
presenting a more complete imitation of nature than painting. Ideally,
it will do this by making those things not accessible to the sense of
sight nonetheless accessible as visions of the mind: the poet makes
"das unsichtbare sichtbar" (1:19).

Breitinger proceeds to argue that it is precisely because words are
"willkührliche Zeichen" that they, in certain cases, will have a direct
("unmittelbar," 1:20) effect on the mind, specifically, in those cases
where what is being depicted is an idea or quality that cannot be seen
("Begriffe und Bilder, die sich alleine dem Verstande vernehmlich
machen," 1:20). Such representational objects, were they first re-
quired to appear as pictures, would lose their immediateness, having
to be themselves "translated back" into qualities.

The goal of "poetische Mahlerey" is to create the immediacy of the
visual sense without restricting the representations to the merely pic-
torial. The way this is achieved is through the organization of the
reader's apprehensions: "der poetische Mahler [sammelt] das Auge
des Gemüthes aus der Zerstreuung" (1:22). The poet uses "alle
Kunst der Optick und Perspectiv" (1:26) to present a unified impres-
sion that can then be "in das Gemüthe des Lesers eingepräget"
(1:24). Most important to the poetic impression is that it be a repre-
sentative selection of particulars: it is drawn out of the poet's desire
to sift and weave them together ("aus dem Gemische so unzehliger
Umstände alleine diejenigen auszusuchen, und mit einander zu ver-
binden, die einen gewissen Eindruck auf das Gemüthe befödern kön-
nen," 1:27).[18]

At this point we can now understand Breitinger's interest in Locke.
For in the process of "Aussuchen" and "Verbinden" the poet engages
in exactly that process that Locke had called "the Workmanship of the
Understanding" (3.3.12–14), whereby the mind "combines several
scattered independent Ideas, into one complex one" (3.5.6). This is
Locke's definition of a "mixed mode," which he says arises when se-
lected simple ideas (sensations or reflections on sensations) are com-
bined to form a new idea, or "Notion" (2.22.1), that is, the concept of
a thing not apprehensible through sense impression alone. A meta-
phor is an abstraction for Breitinger in that it has isolated certain par-
ticulars of experience, which it then combines in such a way that the
nature of the connection can be perceived. Breitinger gives as an ex-
ample the phrase "das Haupt des Staats" (2:315), which he says
makes sense to us because the word "Haupt" has not yet lost its
"wahre Bedeutung . . . in Ansehung des Körpers" (2:315). The viv-

idness of the metaphorical expression derives from the fact that the reason for the connection is understandable in terms of things we already know through the senses, such as the function of the head with respect to the body. Hence Breitinger views metaphor as a remedy of sorts for the arbitrary nature of signs, for it is the vividness of the metaphorical expression that allows us to see the relationship between things and the words that describe them.[19]

As verbal constructs, however, metaphors remain arbitrary designations of our ideas and not designations of things; they represent merely a *perceived* similarity between two things in nature that can disappear at a later time. Metaphors can be "used up" ("abnutzen," 2:334), by which Breitinger means they lose their ability to evoke a comparison between two disparate objects because the objects, through the constant use of the metaphor, will eventually be associated "naturally" or spontaneously in the language (2:145 and 309). When a metaphorical expression becomes "naturalized" in a language, the insight is lost into its original nature as a comparison of two discrete objects, or as a relationship between particulars. The metaphorical expression becomes an "eigentliches Wort" (2:306), a common term, and not a figurative one. The meaning of such words is accepted without any awareness of the original mental construct that produced them, and they become viewed as arbitrary signs ("willkührliche Zeichen," 2:312) without any (understandable) connection to the object they describe (cf. esp. 2:308 and 312).

Breitinger's statements on metaphor are not a defense of rhetorical or poetic ornament. The purpose of metaphor is not to provide "kunstreiche Pinsel-Züge" for a description, but to create itself "neue Begriffe und Wahrheiten."[20] His guidelines for the appropriate use of metaphor (2:346–48) bear this out. He gives three conditions: (1) it should not be employed where the same concept can be just as clearly expressed literally; (2) it should be necessary—metaphors help to express new concepts in a language, but once such concepts have been integrated, a figurative expression to animate them is not needed; (3) a metaphor should be probable, that is, its words and reference should be understandable in terms of existing usage even as it introduces a new perspective on the already existing terms within a language, as it enhances the "Gebrauch der Bedeutungen."[21]

Metaphor in Breitinger's analysis of language is an operation of the intellect in which new concepts are presented (or "painted"). Vividness, for which metaphor is responsible, is as a stylistic category less the surface effect of literature in which the mind's interest is aroused, than an aid to the mind in the integration of new perceptions. It is interesting that Breitinger recognized this as a basic point of contention between himself and Gottsched. Gottsched would later write in the preface to the 1742 edition of his own *Critische Dichtkunst*: "Was war wohl von unserm Maler anders zu vermuthen, als daß er die ganze Dichtkunst in eine Kunst zu Malen, verwandeln, und von lauter poetischen Malereyen, und denen dazu nöthigen Farben handeln würde."[22] Gottsched is using "Farben" in the ancient pejorative sense of "deceptive elaboration" or "ornament." His criticism reflects what was to become a widespread notion of Breitinger's enterprise—not least of all because Lessing, in his famous critique of Haller and Breitinger, would later take the same dim view of Breitinger's defense of metaphor that Gottsched had, although for different reasons. But Breitinger had already anticipated such criticism when he defined the limitations of Gottsched's understanding of "Mahlerey" (cf. 1:12–13). Regarding, for example, Gottsched's criticism of some figurative expressions in Bodmer's Milton translation, he says: "Die Censur fällt eigentlich nicht auf die Redensart, sondern auf die Vorstellung einer gantz neuen und ungewohnten Sache selbst" (2:75). Breitinger thinks that Gottsched refuses to see metaphoric language in any terms other than ornament, and that he is offended when it is used for purposes other than reinforcement or elaboration of what is already known. Thus Gottsched is taken to task at another point (2:331–32) for rejecting metaphors not because they are bad, but because they are new and unusual. Breitinger also criticizes (2:338–39) those who reject out of hand all metaphors borrowed from foreign languages and translated into German—again, not because they are bad but because they are unusual.

Breitinger's analysis of language and metaphor in terms of the generation of concepts, and Gottsched's failure to provide any theoretical reflection on language in his own *Critische Dichtkunst*, would prove decisive for the development of their conflicting literary judgments. Breitinger and Gottsched were at odds because they were relying on different, and heretofore unrecognized, philosophical premises about the nature of literature. In order to explore this question further, we need to examine the problem of knowledge and representation as it was presented in Horace's comparison between painting and poesis. Following this examination, I want to suggest that Breitinger understood the issues raised by the Horatian lines in a more accurate way than Gottsched had, although he too demonstrates a characteristically neoclassic grasp of the question of representation. The comparison of Gottsched and Breitinger with reference to Horace's simile is important not only for an appreciation of Breitinger's work but because it allows us to "redraw the map" of the poetic issues separating them.

Epistemological Implications of Horace's Comparison

The passage under consideration from the *Ars poetica* is the following:

> A poem is like a picture: one strikes your fancy more, the
> nearer you stand; another, the farther away. This courts
> the shade, that will wish to be seen in the light, and
> dreads not the critic insight of the judge. This pleased
> but once; that, though ten times called for will always
> please.
>
> (361–65)

Traditional approaches to these lines, as I have already suggested, simply assume that Horace wants to equate poetry with painting in that both "copy" nature. But his real purpose here is to get at the problem of two different kinds of (pictorial or poetic) representation, each of which demands different modes of reception. Horace distinguishes these modes by using visual metaphors of distance and light to describe two fundamentally different ways in which representations are apprehended. In order to grasp his point, the *ut pictura* passage must be analyzed according to strict parallel construction.[23]

On the one hand there are works that are better seen "up close," that should be displayed in the shade, and that exhaust their appeal after being viewed only once. On the other hand there are works that ought to be seen from a distance, that require good (sun) lighting, and that will be enjoyed upon repeated examination. One may schematize Horace's comparison as follows:

Mode 1	*Mode 2*
Viewed "up close"	Viewed from a distance
Displayed in the shade	Displayed in bright sunlight
One viewing sufficient	Multiple viewings desired

The significance of this comparison is not immediately evident. In fact, its terms appear to be very nearly obscure. But the divisions of this schema make sense when one considers that Horace probably borrowed them from Aristotle, who had himself compared two styles of rhetorical performance to two different kinds of visual representation. Horace has apparently adapted Aristotle's distinctions to his own remarks on poetry. Hence in order to understand the Horatian simile, we need to review its probable origin in the work not only of Aristotle but also of Plato.

In *Rhetoric*, 3.12.1, Aristotle describes two broad categories of rhetorical style: "But we must not lose sight of the fact that a different style is suitable to each kind of Rhetoric. That of written compositions (γραφική) is not the same as that of debate (ἀγωνιστική); nor, in the latter, is that of public speaking the same as that of the law courts." Aristotle's general distinction, to which the Horatian division will be seen to correspond, is between written and oral discourse. (Within this latter category there is the additional distinction between public and forensic debate.) Aristotle continues: "The style of written compositions is most precise, that of debate is most most suitable for delivery. . . . When compared, the speeches of writers appear meagre in public debates, while those of the rhetoricians, however well delivered, are amateurish when read. The reason is that they are only suitable to public debates; hence speeches suited for delivery, when delivery is absent, do not fulfill their proper function and appear silly" (3.12.2–3). In other words, there is a scale of refinement appropriate to three types of audience: the crowd before whom civil questions are debated, the judge of the law court, and listeners who attend to stylistic excellence and accuracy during an epideictic performance. The style of spoken oratory, according to Aristotle, should be less precise than speeches composed for epideictic display, which themselves, if delivered before a large and miscellaneous crowd, would not be sufficiently impressive.

One method of impressive oral delivery, Aristotle suggests, employs repetition of phrase, and he cites some lines from the *Iliad* as an example. The designation of Homer's works as a paradigm of the oral style will be repeated by Horace, within the context of his own comparison, by marking Homer as the type of poet whose works need not be examined for precision, or which are best "viewed" from a distance.[24] Aristotle's and Horace's identification of Homer with the oral rhetorical style will play an important role, as we shall see, in neoclassic discussions of the Horatian comparison.

Aristotle then describes oral delivery with a metaphor significant to Horace's eventual comparison: "The deliberative style is exactly like a rough sketch (σκιαγραφία), for the greater the crowd, the further off is the point of view; wherefore in both too much refinement (ἀκριβῆ) is a superfluity and even a disadvantage" (3.12.5). In the ancient Greek context, σκιαγραφία denoted a boldly drawn sketch done on a white background using a single, usually dark, color to achieve various levels of shading. Such a sketch was distinguished from σκηνογραφία, that is, a painting displaying subtle compositional effects achieved through the complex use of color—effects, however, that would be lost if displayed in bright sunlight far away from the viewer's eyes. The σκιαγραφία, by contrast, because of its size and rough outline, could only be appreciated ("made out") from a distance. Getting closer to it would in fact prevent one from recognizing what is depicted, whereas the σκηνογραφία requires the viewer to assume exactly the right position from which the many complexities of the composition can be discerned.[25]

Horace's *ut pictura poesis* thus may be compared with Aristotle's metaphorical distinction between oral and written styles of oratory. Horace has simply transposed it into his own Augustan setting: written rhetorical performances are found in the "shaded" halls of the schools of declamation where the rhetor would have the leisure to develop his argument (with its many rhetorical flourishes, its "colors") before an audience that would be "close" to the speaker by virtue of both physical position and sympathetic attention.[26] Because such carefully crafted oratorical compositions were likely also to be somewhat precious, they would "please but once." They are exercises only and of no lasting significance. The orally delivered rhetoric of the forum, on the other hand, forces the speaker to contend with a large and perhaps unsympathetic crowd, and challenges his strength and endurance in the heat, dust, and noise. Such a speaker "dreads not the critic insight of the judge" because his aim is not to produce carefully turned phrases for the inspection of his listeners but to be heard. He can only achieve his goal through forceful delivery and with arguments that impress his listeners. His performance, moreover, will please when repeated because its emotional power arises in part from the fact that it deals with matters of great concern to all members of the state.

Yet Horace, however critical he may have been of the schools of declamation, is not interested in defending the oral style at the expense of the written, for he was himself a master of the finely crafted phrase.[27] Further on in the epistle, he cautions his readers, the Pisos, against turning their backs on the principles of careful composition (385–90), just as he had begun by advising them to take "care in weaving words together" (46). Indeed the point of the comparison between written and oral styles for both Horace and Aristotle is not the juxtaposition of "well-wrought" prose against "spontaneous creation," for even the skiagraphic style, Aristotle emphasizes (*Rhetoric*, 3.12.3–5), is an art. Horace says: "Often it is asked whether a praiseworthy poem be due to Nature or to art. For my part, I do not see what avail is either study, when not enriched by Nature's vein, or native wit, if untrained; so truly does each claim the other's aid, and make with it a friendly league" (408–11).

While these words would become a neoclassic cliché, to be repeated more from habit than from understanding or conviction, Horace uses them in a decidedly Aristotelian sense that refers to his distinctions in the *ut pictura poesis* passage. In order to appreciate this link, it is necessary to cite one additional passage from his epistle: "Take a subject, ye writers, equal to your strength; and ponder long what your shoulders refuse, and what they are able to bear. Whoever shall choose a theme within his range, neither speech will fail him, nor clearness of order" (38–41). The key to successful composition is the ability to discern what subjects can be best represented by one's native wit in conjunction with one's acquired skills. Not all authors may hope to treat the same kinds of topics. Poets have to decide what kind of topic is appropriate to their own inclinations and abilities. They must also choose what to represent based on their particular position with respect to the total range of possible matter. But such an evaluation carried out by poets toward their own production is also analogous to the critic's ultimate estimation of what the poet (or painter) has created. The critic must recognize that some forms of discourse are meant to be scrutinized from close up, while others are intended to be appreciated from a distance, with an eye less to minute detail of execution than to the total psychagogic effect of the statement.

Underlying Horace's observations on the right choice and right judgment of poetic subject matter is a philosophic issue that, although not pursued rigorously by Horace himself, nonetheless is crucial for understanding the neoclassic interpretation of his *ut pictura poesis*. Critias in Plato's dialogue of the same name expresses the problem as follows:

> All statements made by any of us are, of course, bound to be an affair of imagery and picturing. Now, suppose we consider the ease or difficulty with which an artist's portraiture of figures divine and human, respectively, produces the impression of satisfactory reproduction on the spectator. We shall observe that in the case of earth, mountains, rivers, woodland, the sky as a whole, and the several revolving bodies located in it, for one thing, the artist is always well content if he can reproduce them with some faint degree of resemblance, and, for another, that since our knowledge of such objects is never exact, we submit his design to no criticism or scrutiny, but acquiesce, in these cases, in a dim and deceptive outline (σκιαγραφία). But when it is our

own human form that the artist undertakes to depict, daily familiar observation makes us quick to detect shortcomings and we show ourselves severe critics of one who does not present us with a full and perfect resemblance. Well, we should recognize that the same is true of discourses. Where the subjects of them are celestial and divine, we are satisfied by mere faint verisimilitudes; where mortal and human, we are exacting critics.[28]

Critias makes two points. First, he observes that the exactness of our knowledge will vary with the objects of knowledge. Those things subject to "daily familiar observation" are more clearly recognized than the distant divine creations. Second, he maintains that we judge the representation of knowledge in accordance with the level of exactness fairly to be expected of the artist given the nature of the object represented. We tolerate, Critias says, the dim and deceptive sketch, the σκιαγραφία or rough outline, because some knowledge about divine things, however inadequate it may necessarily be, is nevertheless desirable in view of the superior importance of the objects themselves. Moreover, the most valuable or "divine" things are paradoxically precisely those objects that cannot be known exactly to us, or "possessed" by the mind via its own perceptions. There is, in Critias's account, an inherent conflict between what we most want to know, and what we are most capable of knowing.

The σκιαγραφία is a "deceptive" picture of the object because our knowledge of the divine is necessarily incomplete. But such a representation—this is the crucial point—will nevertheless be *accepted* as "complete" insofar as the viewer's possible knowledge is concerned. Similarly for Aristotle, σκιαγραφία had meant, in the passage from *Rhetoric*, 3.12, a representation of things about which certain knowledge was neither possible nor expected, such as questions concerning the future of a community that are debated in the forum. The object represented in the skiagraphic image cannot be known more exactly by "getting closer" to it, that is, by more precise representation, because its "knowability" is not a function of its representation. The degree to which the object can be known is determined by the nature of the object itself. The value of the σκιαγραφία is not that it acts as a complete and accurate representation when viewed from afar, but that it provides some knowledge about things that are *not subject to* precise representation. Yet because of the compelling importance of the skiagraphically represented object, the viewer will be impressed and overwhelmed.

This Aristotelian concept of rhetorical (agonistic) effect is a major influence on Pseudo-Longinus's treatment of the sublime, a document that acquires enormous significance in neoclassic discussions of poetic effect. Thus before we return to a discussion of the fate of the *ut pictura* passage in the eighteenth century, it may be useful to mention briefly the relationship between the issues of reception that Horace raises and those found in the Longinian statement. (A fuller examination of the sublime appears in the discussion of Homer in the final section of the present chapter.) In the opening paragraph of his treatise, Longinus describes the sublime in terms that recall the Aristotelian distinction between epideictic craftsmanship, which Longinus calls "persuasion," and what he calls "transport," which corresponds to agonistic performance. Longinus then observes that "inventive skill and the due disposal and marshalling of facts do not show themselves in one or two touches: they gradually emerge from the whole tissue of the composition, while, on the other hand, a well-timed flash of sublimity scatters everything before it like a bolt of lightning and reveals the full power of the speaker at a single stroke" (1.4). He is careful to add, in keeping with Aristotle's and Horace's positions, that such effects are produced not by ignoring art but by concealing it. The sublime representation is not simply the result of "spontaneous" insight, or artlessness, but rather of appropriately conceived figures of thought and speech that produce the desired (overwhelming) effect: "Although [natural genius] is rather a gift than an acquired quality, we should still do our utmost to train our minds into sympathy with what is noble and, as it were, impregnate them again and again with lofty inspiration" (9.1). Elsewhere he affirms: "Above all we must remember this: the very fact that in literature some effects come of natural genius alone can only be learnt from art" (2.3).[29] And like Aristotle and Horace, Longinus views the works of Homer as the primary locus of sublime composition.

Although Περὶ ὕψους is mainly a discourse on style, Longinus does not neglect the philosophic dimension of the problem. "Nature," he says, "from the first breathed into our hearts an unconquerable passion for whatever is great and more divine than ourselves" (35.2). The sublime aims at "Nature . . . the prime cause, the great exemplar" (2.2) and not at what is "correct" but "mediocre" (33.1), terms recalling Horace's distinction between the precise but ultimately less important composition of the shaded schools, and the striking skiagraphic image.[30]

Neoclassic readings of Horace's comparison tend to eliminate his crucial distinction between the skiagraphic (the not completely knowable/representable) and the skenographic (the exactly representable). To see how this reduction occurs, we can turn now to Gottsched's interpretation of the Horatian passage in his translation of and commentary on the *Ars poetica* that stands in place of an introduction to his *Critische Dichtkunst*. I first give his rendering of the passage, and then his relevant textual notes.

Ein Vers ist Bildern gleich, wo manches uns gefällt,
Wenn mans genau besieht und nah vor Augen stellt;
Indem sich andre nur von ferne trefflich zeigen.
Dem einen ist die Nacht und Dunkelheit fast eigen.
Das andere liebt den Tag und volles Sonnenlicht,
Und scheuet dergestalt die schärfste Prüfung nicht.
Dieß mag man einmal kaum; und jenes zehnmal leiden,
Denn man erblickt es stets mit neuer Lust und Freuden.

Ein Vers ist Bildern gleich. Dacier erklärt dieses auch
von lauter guten Gedichten, und meynt, daß mancher guter
Vers bey genauer Prüfung Stich halte, ein andrer aber nur
obenhin angesehen werden müsse: nicht anders, als wie
Bilder von gewisser Art ihre gewisse Stellung oder
Entfernung erfordern. Von Gemählden hat dieses seine
Richtigkeit: aber von Versen ist es ganz anders. Ein
Gedichte, das nicht die Prüfung eines Richters aushält,
taugt so wenig, als das Gold, welches nicht Strich hält.
Das Gleichniß Horatii muß von solchen Bildern verstanden
werden, die im Dunkeln oder von weitem schön zu seyn
scheinen, aber in der That schlecht sind: da hingegen
andre desto mehr Schönheiten zeigen, je länger und genauer
man sie betrachtet.

Dem einen ist die Nacht. Das sind die schönen Werke der
Poeten, die bey dem Pöbel so viel Beyfall finden; Kennern
aber nicht gefallen. Man muß sie gleichsam nur bey
neblichtem Wetter lesen; sonst gefallen sie einem nicht.
Ich will sagen, man muß einen finstern Verstand haben,
wenn man sie bewundern will. Bey dem Lichte einer
gesunden Critik verschwinden alle ihre Schönheiten. Daher
fürchten auch ihre Urheber nichts mehr, als die Prüfung
eines scharfsichtigen Kenners.

(96–97)

In anticipation of my argument later in this chapter concerning Gottsched's arbitrary handling of texts, it is worth noting here that his version is not a close translation of Horace's poem. In the preface to his translation Gottsched admits, but does not seem to regret, that "aus fünfhundert lateinischen Versen habe ich mich genöthiget gesehen, fast 700 deutsche zu machen" (34).[31] More important for our discussion at this point, however, are the two typically neoclassic distortions that his commentary introduces into the Horatian text.[32] First, Gottsched reads the passage as a chiasma. Horace's parallel construction is ignored and his comparative terms are reversed, in the following manner:

Mode 1	Mode 2
Viewed up close	Viewed from a distance
Displayed in bright light	Displayed in darkness
Multiple viewings desirable	One viewing sufficient

Second, based on this chiasmic reading, Gottsched changes the descriptive metaphors of distance and light, with which Horace had distinguished between *kinds* of representation, into *evaluative* terms. This change allows Gottsched to speak, for example, of the "finsterer Verstand" of those who read bad literature in "Nacht und Dunkelheit." Horace's term here was *obscurum*, "shade." Moreover, Gottsched's reversal of Horace's distinction means that works read in "Dunkelheit" are for the crowd, which Gottsched views as the unenlightened "Pöbel," not for the sophisticated recipient sitting in the shaded halls of the school.

For Gottsched, precise scrutiny of poetic works—up close under bright light—is the only method of appreciating their beauties because poetic works are themselves precise and exact imitations of the beauties of nature. The poet must produce his work such that it provides, "bey dem Lichte einer gesunden Critik," a completely clear or obvious correspondence to nature. It should replicate the natural order, "Fuß vor Fuß" (141)—a phrase one finds repeatedly in neoclassic definitions of imitation. Of course, Gottsched's frequent references to nature as the poet's "einziges Muster" cannot in themselves express his conception of poesis; "nature" and hence the product of its imitation can have a range of meanings that will require definition. His insistence, however, that poesis in some sense *copies* nature (which can, but need not, imply simple naturalism) belies the important fact that for Gottsched there is no fundamental uncertainty about what kind of representation might be appropriate for what kind of object. The object ("nature") is completely knowable and therefore completely representable to the poet with sufficient insight.

Such certainty vis-à-vis the representation is most apparent in Gottsched's definition of "Witz," which he says is equivalent to *ingen-*

ium: "Dieser Witz ist eine Gemüthskraft, welche die Aehnlichkeiten der Dinge leicht wahrnehmen, und also eine Vergleichung zwischen ihnen anstellen kann. Er setzet die Scharfsinnigkeit zum Grunde, welche ein Vermögen der Seelen anzeiget, viel an einem Dinge wahrzunehmen, welches ein andrer, der gleichsam einen stumpfen Sinn, oder blöden Verstand hat, nicht würde beobachtet haben" (152). Gottsched's definition of "Witz" reflects traditional Renaissance notions of "wit" as the faculty responsible for seeing resemblances between things in nature.[33] What is interesting about this definition (and what is clear from the context at 152–54, which cannot be quoted here in full) is that Gottsched does not propose a representational form that might correspond to this faculty of the mind ("Vermögen"). The representation of similarities is for him entirely unproblematic; all that is required of poets is that they recognize them. The poetic realization then follows almost "automatically" out of this recognition itself.

It may be helpful at this point to compare Gottsched's remarks with those of Aristotle on similarities and genius in the *Poetics*: "By far the greatest thing [in diction] is the use of metaphor. That alone cannot be learnt; it is the token [σημεῖόν] of genius. For the right use of metaphor means an eye for resemblances."[34] Elsewhere (at 21.8–14) Aristotle defines metaphor as a logical operation: "the application of a strange term either transferred from the genus and applied to the species or from the species and applied to the genus, or from one species to another or else by analogy." (Various examples follow.) He then explains metaphor-by-analogy as the transfer of a term from one analogy to another similar analogy. For example: "Old age is to life as evening is to day." Hence, the poet will call old age "the evening of life."

Gottsched's passage on similarities recalls Aristotle's. But there is the crucial difference that for Aristotle genius is not the ability to be impressed or imprinted by nature via the "discovery" of its similarities. It is not the equation of mind and nature, but rather the ability to recognize similarities, and then to "translate" this recognition into a representational form, the metaphor. Aristotle, unlike Gottsched, preserves essential distinctions between mind (genius), the object it perceives (similarities), and the representation of that perception (metaphor).[35]

These distinctions, however, are nowhere maintained by Gottsched. His assumption that the poetic representation can be an exact copy of nature means he has assumed as well (following not only Wolff but also the Stoic tradition) the exact coincidence of human *ratio* and cosmic φύσις, or the identity of the mind, the object it contemplates, and the representation. This in turn accounts for the highly normative aspect of his poetic evaluations, because the judgments of human reason then can be put forth as "natural law."[36] The conflation of *ratio* and φύσις means that no "distance" or discrepancy exists between them, that no relationship is possible because they are identical.

Hence Gottsched's interpretation of the Horatian simile: poetic imitations of nature are legitimate only when they can be contemplated without any intervening "distance" between them and the "viewer." That is, there is no fundamental difference, expressed in the metaphor of distance, between contemplation (an activity of the mind) and representation. Imitations must bear out, under scrutiny, their perfection, which means for Gottsched their adherence to the "laws of nature": "Die Regeln nämlich, die auch in freyen Künsten eingeführet worden, kommen nicht auf den bloßen Eigensinn der Menschen an; sondern sie haben ihren Grund in der unveränderlichen Natur der Dinge selbst; in der Uebereinstimmung des Mannigfaltigen, in der Ordnung und Harmonie" (174). Gottsched renders logical categories ("Uebereinstimmung," "Ordnung") as ontological categories, that is, as aspects of nature. Criticism becomes thereby merely a vehicle for establishing that the work has produced an exact replica of natural order, such that rules are not decided upon by individuals (cf. "Eigensinn") but only "discovered" in nature.

Gottsched's neoclassic reading of Horace's comparison assumes that all objects of poetic depiction are completely knowable; it eliminates the skiagraphic side of the comparison altogether. Another neoclassic reading of the analogy disposes of the skiagraphic aspect in a slightly different fashion by claiming that the degree to which objects can be known and represented is a function of the distance between them and the viewer. This is not to say, with Gottsched, that objects are better perceived the "closer" they appear (the more exactly they are represented), but that the viewer, to use a term of Alexander Pope, must assume a "Due Distance" between himself and the object or the work. This is the second kind of neoclassic distortion of Horace's passage, which is Breitinger's.[37] (The term "distortion," which may be used normatively to imply "betrayal" or descriptively to designate "variation," means here the latter.) This second interpretation, however, more closely resembles Horace's original sense than the first distortion had because it does not assume—as in Gottsched's version, for example—that precise poetic representation of nature is possible as a result of careful scrutiny of nature. Although it proposes that the object ("nature") is knowable according to our perspective on it, the interpretation also holds that this perspective requires constant read-justment relative to the object if the object is to be correctly perceived. Thus the existence of the object independent of the beholder is maintained, although it is subject to complete representation under the appropriate circumstances or, as Breitinger says in a number of places, from the proper "Gesichts-Punkt" or "in ihrem rechten Licht."

Breitinger's terms indicate a reliance on optical perspective to provide the most valuable representations of nature. This means that the "ontological" assertion of the skiagraphic comparison, the unknowability of the object, becomes the "psychological" assurance of skenographic perspective, the intimate and complete experience of the object. The compelling effect of the bold general outline, which acquires its power due to the importance of the object it represents, will be transferred to the "design," the careful organization of particulars in the clearly "focused" image of nature. In the skenographic representation, the emotional power of the image will derive not from the ultimate value of the object, as in the σκιαγραφία, but from the vividness of the representation itself. Such a shift in psychological function from the σκιαγραφία to the σκηνογραφία will prove to be of critical importance in Breitinger's discussion of vividness and "poetische Mahlerey."

The function of poetic language for Breitinger, as outlined in the first section of this chapter, is to provide a different perspective on objects than nonfigurative language would, and hence to tell us more about them: "Der figürliche und verblühmte Ausdruck läßt uns die Gedancken nicht bloß aus willkührlichen Zeichen errathen, sondern machet dieselben gleichsam sichtbar; er stellet uns die Sachen nicht gerad in ihrer nackten Blösse vor das Gesicht; sondern zeiget uns dieselben in ihrem besten Vortheil, in dem angenehmsten Gesichts-Puncten, und der vortheilhaftesten Entfernung" (2:316).[38] The concept of "vortheilhafteste Entfernung" was foreign to Gottsched, but it is the central category for Breitinger in both poesis and the evaluation of poesis. Because the following chapters of my study seek to define how Breitinger conceived of the "Due Distance" between the poetic object, nature, and the poet or reader of the poetic work, the epistemological problem (i.e., the problem of what kind of knowledge is possible and desirable in poesis) will be pursued at a later time. Suffice it to say that "poetische Mahlerey" for Breitinger is depiction—but not copying—and that he understood the process of "depicting" in a manner analogous to Leibniz's model of conceptual activity, whereby for both men the notion of "Gesichts-Punkt" plays a

determining role. Here the term "focusing" on nature should be re-
membered as a metaphorical expression that will figure in the entire
subsequent exposition. Now, however, we may proceed to the notion
of "vortheilhafteste Entfernung" as it relates to Breitinger's practical
criticism, for here lies perhaps the most interesting—and hitherto ne-
glected—point of conflict between Breitinger and Gottsched.

Issues of Practical Literary Criticism

The single most important critical issue of the period in which Breitin-
ger wrote was the debate over the value of Homer's works, which had
been the focal point of the *querelle des anciens et des modernes*.[39] Al-
though this literary feud was largely resolved (or at least had fallen
silent) by the time Breitinger published his work, it plays a role in his
poetics because the German language was at that time still developing
as a literary medium, that is, at a relatively late date in comparison to
other European vernacular literatures. This process involved, as it
had in the seventeenth century in France, the integration or rejection,
on a selective basis, of the poetic theories of antiquity. The debate over
Homer (itself the result of Plato's banishment of the poets and the
many "defenses of poetry" that his banishment aroused) became a
topos of literary critical discourse. Breitinger therefore opens his *Cri-
tische Dichtkunst* by commenting on this very problem.[40]

The controversy had five major aspects: (1) the possibility of trans-
lating Homer's works; (2) the evaluation of his style; (3) the proba-
bility of the epic scenes and events; (4) the morality of Homer's gods
and heroes; and (5) Homer's identity as a poet. I have already indi-
cated Breitinger's position on the first of these issues with reference
to La Motte in the opening section of this chapter. It may be added
here that La Motte's "modernization" of Homer, which Breitinger
found so questionable, is based on what was termed in the previous
section the first distortion of the Horatian comparison. The applicabil-
ity of the comparison to Breitinger's critique of La Motte requires,
however, a brief clarification.

Horace uses metaphors of distance and light to explain that poems
are subject to different criteria of evaluation based on the different
kinds of perception they involve. One traditional distortion of this
simile, as we have seen in Gottsched's interpretation, holds that no
discrepancy exists between what the "viewer" (the reader) knows
about the object of consideration (either nature or the work) and what
the object is. Now, the discrepancy might also be conceived in tem-
poral terms: the "distance" between the reader and the work would

then be due to the distance in time between the production of the work and the reader's own opportunity (in time) to read it.

Such a neoclassic temporalization of the Horatian simile, at work in Breitinger's evaluation of La Motte, would understand "discrepancy" in skenographic terms, that is, as a function of the viewer's, or reader's, historical knowledge of the object (the poetic work), and not as a function of the value of the work in itself. For there is no "objective" reason why old works should be *eo ipso* more (or less) valuable than recent works, arguments of the *anciens* (or the *modernes*) notwithstanding. "If poems are like wine which time improves," Horace had mused, "I should like to know what is the year that gives to writings fresh value. A writer who dropped off a hundred years ago, is he to be reckoned among the perfect and ancient, or among the worthless and modern?"[41]

The differences between Breitinger and La Motte with reference to "temporal distance" illustrate how Breitinger, despite the absence of an authentic skiagraphic category in his poetics, nonetheless comes closer than Gottsched had to preserving Horace's (Aristotelian) intention. For whereas Gottsched viewed all "distance" as undesirable, arguing for the necessity of precise scrutiny "up close" of literary works, Breitinger argues that the distance between the reader and the work should not be destroyed but traversed. In the case of Homer's works, temporal distance requires that the reader explore the historical conditions of Homer's language and culture in order to understand Homer's epic poem.[42]

La Motte's desire, by contrast, to clothe Homer's language in a modern idiom, whereby the original syntax and word choice are ignored, is based on the assumption that there should be no distance, meaning historical distance, between the perceiver and the object perceived. The attempt to make Homer more "accessible" to the modern reader leads La Motte to claim that he is "improving" Homer's work: "C'est un usage immémorial parmi les Traducteurs, de relever l'excellence de L'Auteur qu'ils traduisent. . . . Je traduis moins que je ne l'imite."[43] One might say that La Motte is carrying out the final destruction of distance between the poetic painting and its viewer: the artist's work is simply appropriated by the interpreter and the "painting" is made to conform to the viewer's expectations and desires rather than being allowed to confront the viewer with something new for eventual acceptance or rejection.[44] The destruction of distance, of ontological discrepancy, between the viewer and the object was a goal shared by La Motte and Gottsched. It is therefore not surprising that Gottsched simply repeated many of La Motte's criticisms of Homer.[45]

Breitinger's position on the second and third aspects of this controversy, the evaluation of Homer's style and the probability of his epics, derives from a remarkably consistent argument with respect to vividness. Both vivid (metaphorical) terms, or "Machtwörter" (the nature of which has already been discussed), and vividness in style (or depicted epic event) are dependent on the poetic production of images, "poetic" here in the root sense of "making." The process as Breitinger conceives it involves a high degree of intellective participation by both poet and audience, in which particulars are organized into a compelling design. This is a thoroughly Horatian concern, albeit in the context of the neoclassic transformation of the skiagraphic into a skenographic metaphor. Breitinger found this appreciation of the intellective nature of vividness in Alexander Pope's interpretation of Homer, and his own evaluation of Homer thus is based to a great extent on what Pope said. The words "Due Distance" and "vortheilhafteste Entfernung" are not an accident of terms.

One of Breitinger's most important borrowings from Pope is his famous comparison of Homer and Virgil: "Jede von diesen beyden Arten zu mahlen hat ihren besondern Werth. Die Homerische hat einen Original-Character, und machet sich dem mehreren Haufen angenehm; die Virgilische hat viel mehr Kunst, und ist gelehrter. Homer war der größte Genius, Virgil der beste Künstler" (1:43). Breitinger does not tell his readers that these words at the beginning of his book are drawn from Pope's preface to the *Iliad* translation.[46] Near the end of the first volume, however, Breitinger returns to his source with an explicit reference: "Der Herr Pope" has said that "Homer macht uns zu Zuhörern, Virgil läßt uns Leser bleiben" (1:494–95).[47] And on the second to last page of this same volume, Breitinger says that "ein vortrefflicher heutiger Scribent" has given us the true observation that "Virgil habe zwar wenig schlechte und gemeine Gedancken, aber er habe auch bey weitem nicht so viele herrliche und erhabene" (1:502).[48]

What is interesting about these borrowings is not their frequency but their theme: Breitinger has chosen those passages from Pope's preface that are congenial to the Aristotelian distinction between agonistic and epideictic styles.[49] Thus Homer's skiagraphic style is for matters of general concern, those addressed to "dem mehreren Haufen," whereas Virgil's precision is suited to experts, those who are "gelehrt."[50] Homer's work provides immediacy, it makes us listeners, while Virgil's asks for reflection and scrutiny from readers. Finally, the absence of both mean and sublime thoughts in Virgil recalls Longinus's admonition regarding correctness and mediocrity, which was itself a restatement of the Horatian distinction.

The distinction that Breitinger, following Pope, draws between Virgil and Homer becomes then his own general distinction between two kinds of "poetische Mahlerey." He expresses this difference as that between "erzehlen" and "zeigen." Here the neoclassic shift from the skiagraphic to the skenographic depiction is especially evident. The careful design of the epideictic piece is made to assume the impressive (psychagogic) function that the agonistic display had had in the original Aristotelian context. Thus, the distinction between bold general outline on the one hand and complex and subtle design on the other is transformed into a distinction between vivid design versus exhaustive collection of particulars without regard to their organization. "Erzehlen" in this account occurs when the poet "bloß historisch beschreibet" (1:470), in which case a number of particulars are simply brought together in accordance with completeness rather than according to the organization inherent in the skiagraphic-turned-skenographic representation. Such an amassing of particulars (instead of the careful organization of detail in the "focused" design) results in frigid ("frostig") works wherein "die starckgezeichneten Züge und die Heftigkeit würden verschwinden" (1:470). But Breitinger's attempt to reanimate an agonistic kind of poetic effect, as evidenced in this last quotation, is carried out with epideictic methods.[51] In a distinction between "poetische Schilderey" and didactic "Beschreibungen," the criterion is design rather than collection. The purpose of "Beschreibungen" is "alle Umstände und Merckmahle einer Sache . . . sorgfältig auf- und zusammensuchen" (1:47–48). By contrast, the "poetisches Gemählde" whose purpose is "zeigen" relies on "auslesen" and "verbinden" of particulars in order to create its special effect on "das Gemüthe" (1:48). Aristotelian epideictic form is realized in Breitinger's conception by the appropriate use of metaphor, the very function of which is to join together isolated particulars into a new image: "Der wahre Verdienst eines Poeten [bestehet] im wenigsten darinn, daß er ohne Wahl und Unterschied alles schildere, was in der Natur vorkommt . . . die Poesie empfängt ihre größte Stärcke und Schönheit von der geschickten Wahl der Bilder" (1:84).[52]

The comparison of representations lacking compelling design to the style of Virgil, who was the "better artist," is an apparent contradiction that is understandable in terms of Breitinger's and Pope's use of the Horatian simile. Virgil's work is like the kind of painting viewed in the shade, where boldly drawn patterns (which for Breitinger means *vivid* patterns!) are not to be found. Hence he quotes the passage from Pope's preface where Virgil's characters are said to resemble each other to such a degree as to be indistinguishable. They are a collection, an amassing, of similar figures, rather than a representation of clearly drawn individuals. The sometimes sententious speeches could be given by any of them, whereas Homer's characters are easily distinguishable in that their personalities stand in stark contrast to one another.[53]

Homer's value lies in his ability to set something before the eyes, in his talent with "zeigen." This is what would later be called the Longinian ability to bring about "transport": Homer "ziehet uns fort" (1:43), whereas Virgil merely entertains and persuades (1:43). At another point in his exposition, Breitinger says, referring to chapter 15 of Περὶ ὕψους, that transport comes about as a result of the most intensely vivid images produced by the imagination and imparted to the reader: "Der aufgebrachte, und durch eine strenge anhaltende Leidenschaft erhizte Phantasie wird öfters so sehr verzücket, daß sie ihre lebhaften Einbildungen von den Empfindungen gegenwärtiger Dinge nicht wohl unterscheiden kan; der Poet, der das Wort für sie führet, wird daher in währender Entzückung von solchen als von würcklich gegenwärtigen Dingen reden, und sie dem Leser gleichsam mit dem Finger zeigen" (1:321–22). Breitinger is in fact so enamored of the notion of transport that he copies out Quintilian's entire description of it into both of his own volumes in Latin (1:334–37 and 2:362–63).[54] It is interesting that for the line (6.2.32) reading: "From such impressions arises that ἐνάργεια which Cicero calls illumination and actuality . . . " Breitinger has in his second volume the word ἐνέργεια. The passages differ in a few instances of punctuation but are otherwise identical. Whether he was quoting from two separate editions is impossible to determine. The confusion of the Greek terms was, however, a common one in late antiquity and had been utilized, for example, by the Neoplatonist Proclus in his literary theory.[55] Ἐνάργεια or "vividness" was then taken in the Renaissance to stand for ἐνέργεια or "effectiveness" (of discourse). Breitinger is here repeating a philological "mistake" of the rhetorical tradition—probably without even realizing it—because he views these terms in analogy: the poet's vividness coincides with the receptivity of his audience to the vivid representation.[56]

Like Longinus, Breitinger views the phenomenon of "transport" as an art, and he criticizes those "Scribenten, die von dem Enthusiasmo reden" (1:329). Readers should not be deceived about the quality of what such enthusiastic writers offer: "Sie kommen mit lauter prächtigen Wörtern von einem heiligen Rausch, einer göttlichen Raserey, Licht, Verzückungen des Gemüthes, Aufwallungen, aufgezogen, welche neben einander gesetzet vortrefflich klingende Sätze

machen, aber in dem Gemüthe keinen deutlichen Begriff hervorbrin-
gen" (1:329–30). The passage recalls Longinus's criticism of "emotion
misplaced and pointless" produced by authors "as if they were
drunk" (3.5). The truly sublime is not achieved by assuming that
"sublimity and emotion [are] the same thing, and that one always
essentially involve[s] the other" (8.2). Sublimity for Breitinger is the
result of vividness, and vividness is the result of careful design ("Ver-
binden") of particulars to produce the "Gemüthes-Bewegung" *and*
the "deutlichen Begriff." Although Breitinger clearly prefers poesis
when produced according to the emotionally compelling "Homer-
ischen Geschmack" (1:45), he does not equate this with "spontane-
ous" or "artless" creativity. This point, however, has been completely
obscured in discussions of the "Romantic" Breitinger—perhaps be-
cause Breitinger himself contributed to this misunderstanding with
his evaluation of Homer the man.

The identity of Homer as a poet and the morality of his gods and
heroes were two issues on which Breitinger took a particularly con-
servative position: "Was konnte Homerus anders thun, da er mit sehr
abergläubigen Götzendienern lebte, die sich ihre Götter nicht an-
derst, als unter menschlichen Gestalten vorstelleten, als sich nach
ihrer Schwäche richten, wenn er gleich mehr Erleuchtung gehabt ha-
ben mag, als andere" (1:161). Homer's "Erleuchtung," he goes on to
say, is nothing but a historical variation on Christian wisdom because
the more acceptable Christian vocabulary was not available to him.[57]
Further, Breitinger makes the astounding claim that Homer himself
was aware of the limitations ("Schwäche") of his own audience. The
most important point to be made about this passage is that Breitinger
did not always subscribe to it. For in his actual interpretations of Ho-
mer, there is not a single justification of Homer's heroes or the proba-
bility of their actions on the grounds of Christian theology. Breitin-
ger's Homer was Pope's, and Pope saw Homer as a poet.[58]

Breitinger's defense of Homer's "Christian" genius is one of those
annoying neoclassic inconsistencies caused by the need for legitimi-
zation of the critical text. It appears in a conservative German envi-
ronment that was only just beginning to come to terms with Christian
Wolff's attempt to separate philosophy from theology. Breitinger's de-
fense of Homer's work, on the other hand, is a defense of vivid lan-
guage as it was preeminently developed in the *Iliad* and the *Odyssey*.
It is in fact a striking anomaly in his work that he would list (1:162–
63) a series of commentators on Homer who support, he says, the
view that Homer was a brilliant framer of allegories, given the fact
that he himself does not resort to allegorical interpretations. The list

is headed by Porphyry and Proclus, Homer's Neoplatonist defenders, and includes Palephatus, Heraclides, Ponticus, Eusthathius (a favorite of Anne Dacier's and Pope's), Mme Dacier, André Dacier, and Pope. Breitinger follows the Neoplatonist tradition in that he views Homer as an original source of wisdom, but he casts his praise in the modern form. Homer is an "Original-Geist" who is credited with "die Erfindung aller dieser Gleichnisse" that make his work so powerful; he is "ohne einen Vorgänger," and has "unbeschränkte Wissenschaft."

But these phrases, which appear in the *Gleichnis-Abhandlung* (277), were influenced no doubt by Pope's preface, where Homer is credited with "the utmost Stretch of human Study, Learning, and Industry" (7:3) and where Virgil is said to have "scarce any Comparisons which are not drawn from his Master" (7:9), a sentence Breitinger quotes (1:35). All of these statements were, however, commonplaces by Pope's time.[59] They derived ultimately from the Neoplatonists, who had relied heavily on allegory to defend what was held to be Homer's privileged access to divine knowledge.[60] This particular debt of Breitinger to the Neoplatonic tradition—his conception of Homer the poet—has not been recognized.[61] When Breitinger's "Neoplatonism" is discussed at all, it is confined to his supposed theory of the poet as *alter deus*, as was suggested by Oskar Walzel, and more recently by Hans Blumenberg, whose study is philosophically more sophisticated than Walzel's but nonetheless fails to account for the effects of Neoplatonic categories on literary studies.[62]

Interpretations of Breitinger's work throughout the nineteenth century and up until recently in the present century tended to focus on the conservative strain in his thinking, by locating his contribution to poetics in the defense of the "genial" creative individual. This in turn was judged, quite mistakenly as I shall argue in the next chapter, a progressive attitude, while the truly progressive aspect of his poetics has been disregarded, namely the willingness to confront the literary work as a historical object requiring interpretation on its own historical terms. In this respect his poetics constitute a significant attempt to reconstruct, against the system of his antagonist Gottsched, the independence of the work, and it is here that his notion of "vortheilhafteste Entfernung" will prove to have significant positive consequences for the study of literature.

An example from Breitinger's later publications and an edition produced by a member of Gottsched's literary circle will illustrate the difference between the two critics. Partly as a result of Breitinger's prodding, the German literary milieu in the early eighteenth century became interested in bringing out editions of the work of Martin Opitz. Breitinger and Bodmer produced one such edition themselves, which they published in 1745. One year later, a student of Gottsched's, Daniel Wilhelm Triller, also brought out an edition of Opitz's poems. A comparison of the two prefaces provides a good example of the fundamentally different attitudes toward literature fostered in Zurich and in Leipzig.

Breitinger and Bodmer, for their part, explain that their text derives from "der letzten Auflage von einem jedweden Gedichte, die von dem Poeten selbst und unter seinen Augen besorget worden."[63] In addition, there are a number of "Lesearten" of the poems that they have analyzed and included in their annotations. These "Lesearten" are not to be confused, however, with the "Variantibus der Classischen Ausleger" because they contain the various versions that the poet himself produced. The "Variantibus," by contrast, is more the product of a copyist's "Begierde . . . neue Meinungen in einem Scribenten zu entdecken . . . damit man die eitle Freude habe, solche zu erklären." Their responsibility, they say, is to supply their readers with "den Opitz aufrichtig, rein, und vollständig."

Triller also claims to offer Opitz's poems in a form that is "genau, treulich, rein, sauber, verständlich." Nevertheless there have appeared, he says, in all existing editions of Opitz's poems a number of "fehlerhafte Stellen" that he (Triller) has "verbessert" according to his own "wahrscheinlicher Mutmassung." The reader will also be spared what Triller finds to be the very confusing "Wortfügung, Construction, Sylbenmaß . . . [und] allzuharter Reime" of Opitz's juvenilia, which the editor has corrected with "leichte Versezung der Worte . . . Veränderung des Reimes, und dergleichen geschwinde Hülffs-Mittel."

Breitinger's philological standards are not a curiosity of his later career; they are directly linked to his theories of language and literature. For if "poetische Mahlerey" is to allow the reader to reanimate the conceptual relations expressed in the language of a particular historical period, a process that can contribute to the development of his own linguistic consciousness, then he must have the literary document as it was originally created. Triller, however, following Gottsched, does not see that poesis contributes to the generation of ideas; it only acts as an illustration of existing knowledge, and those aspects of the text that do not reinforce present conceptions are manipulated or destroyed.[64]

Breitinger's introduction of historical distance between the poetic painting and the viewer allows interpreters to assume a relationship to the work by defining their exact position with reference to the object. In terms of the now temporalized Horatian analogy, they "step back" from the "painting" by removing themselves from the moral and aesthetic criteria of their own time, which allows them to bring the many apparent improbabilities and imperfections of the work into historical focus. Breitinger says, following Dubos, that the more one knows about a period and its customs, the better one will be able to provide an appropriate interpretation of the literary works produced at that time (1:477–82). But this is not to agree with the *modernes* that the work is merely an archaeological artifact that at best can only illustrate the crudeness or primitiveness of the period in which it was created, nor is it to agree with the *anciens* that such primitiveness should be glorified as a "Golden Age." Historicizing the poetic work, which means that viewers acknowledge their own historical distance from it, is the act of "stepping back" that is equivalent to viewing poesis from the "vortheilhafteste Entfernung," the position that places it in the most likely spot from which it can be understood or assimilated on its own terms. For Gottsched and his students, by contrast, the appreciation of poetry as painting meant "stepping closer" by examining exact likenesses of a nature already fully known. For Breitinger it is the focusing on otherwise obscure or remote, that is to say, *wondrous* mental images of nature by setting them in "ihr rechtes Licht."

2. Poetic Production and Breitinger's Notion of Possible Worlds

In his *Gleichnis-Abhandlung* Breitinger criticizes Gottsched for overlooking the ambiguity inherent in the term "Nachahmung der Natur": "Er [Gottsched] antwortet: Man darf nur auf die Natur sehen; alleine da wisset ihr nicht, was vor eines Dinges Natur gemeint ist; und das Wort Natur, wenn es so lediglich gesetzt wird, ist viel zu weitläufftig und unbestimmt, als daß es euch einen deutlichen Begriff geben könnte."[1] Thus, while Gottsched's chapter on imitation is called "Von den dreyen Gattungen der poetischen Nachahmung," Breitinger's corresponding chapter in his own *Critische Dichtkunst* discusses imitation per se: "Von der Nachahmung der Natur." Nevertheless, their statements seem to be in neoclassic harmony with each other. Breitinger defines poetic production, "das eigene und Haupt-Werck der Poesie," as "Nachahmung der Natur in dem Möglichen" (1:57). Gottsched defines "das Hauptwerk der Poesie" as the "geschickte Nachahmung der Natur" (141). Their statements differ only because Breitinger qualifies the term "Nachahmung" with a reference to "das Mögliche," which was itself a Renaissance commonplace.[2] Yet commentators assumed for decades that Breitinger's treatise represented an aesthetic adaptation of Leibniz's concept of possible worlds because Swiss allegiance to Leibniz is mentioned in the preface to the *Critische Dichtkunst* and in the first chapter (1:9).

In 1970, Hans Peter Herrmann pointed out in his important study of early eighteenth-century poetics that Gottsched had also relied on the notion of possible worlds and that in fact both critics were indebted not to Leibniz but to Christian Wolff.[3] Herrmann also took Breitinger to task for a muddled exposition—for example, in his equation of "Wahrheit," "Wahrscheinlichkeit," and "Möglichkeit" (an equation that is grounded in the Neoplatonic context discounted by Herrmann). Had Breitinger understood the true meaning of ideas such as internal consistency and organic structure, which Herrmann finds implicit in the Wolffian definition of possible worlds, Breitinger would have—indeed *should* have—produced the concept of form peculiar to German Classicism. Therefore, Herrmann concluded, Breitinger cannot be said to have availed himself of a "hochmetaphysischer Begriff," as traditional commentaries assert. Breitinger's references to possible worlds were, like Gottsched's, nothing more than a legitimizing device intended to add a philosophic veneer to his Protestant didactic poetics.[4]

The salient feature of Herrmann's critique—Breitinger's failure to arrive at the principle of classical form because of his theological bias —was not new. Ernst Cassirer had already presented a similar argument in 1916 in his study *Freiheit und Form*.[5] Because the main points of Cassirer's influential interpretation recur in almost all twentieth-century interpretations of the Swiss, it is useful to restate his position briefly. This will help to clarify the question of Breitinger's relation to Leibniz and Wolff, and his difference from Gottsched with respect to the notion of possible worlds.

Cassirer bases his interpretation on the distinction, fundamental to Leibniz's system, between necessary truths (*vérités nécessaires* or *vérités éternelles*), and factual truths or truths of experience (*vérités de fait*).[6] Truths of the former kind are independent of empirical verification, and are based on the principle of identity or of noncontradiction ($A = A$, or $A \neq$ non-A). Such propositions are necessary because their opposites are impossible. In truths of reason, possibility and necessity converge: by demonstrating that the sum of the angles of a triangle can equal 180 degrees, one shows as well that it can equal nothing else. Leibniz assigns to the class of necessary truths mathematical, logical, and metaphysical propositions and definitions.

Truths of fact are those things known to us either *a posteriori* through sense experience, or *a priori* through reflection on the observed order of nature.[7] They do not derive their validity from simple possibility but rather from existence. Truths of experience are observable, which does not mean, however, that they need be actually observed to be true. Leibniz uses the example: "I will write tomorrow." The opposite of this statement ("I will not write tomorrow") is equally possible, that is, it involves no contradiction. The truth of the statement rests therefore on what actually happens tomorrow (whether or not there is a witness, including a writer conscious of his own actions).[8] Included in factual truths are the laws of nature, for example, the laws of motion.[9]

Necessary truths exist in the mind of God, yet it is not within his power to create or destroy them.[10] Rather he is bound by them in his creation of the natural order. Thus, while all necessary truths are possible, not all possibles are necessary.[11] The possibles represented in necessary truths are eternally true, that is, they are independent of realization in time and space. Truths of experience are the realizations of only some of the many options, or possibilities, God has available to him within the constraints of necessary truth.[12] Their existence, which follows out of the Creation, is based upon the principle of sufficient reason, that is, God's goodness and omnipotence.[13]

Cassirer says that Breitinger's poetics are an attempt to open the realm of necessary truths to poetic representation. When the poet depicts possible worlds, he is not representing factual truths but rather the timeless truths of necessity, which he grasps with his imagination guided by the understanding ("Verstand"). The identification of Breitinger's possible worlds with Leibniz's *vérités nécessaires* caused Cassirer to seek in Breitinger's poetics a new principle of form that might have allowed the *Critische Dichtkunst* to count as a significant anticipation of the aesthetics of German Idealism. Breitinger did not deliver this new idea of form, Cassirer suggests, because it would have involved establishing the poet as an autonomous "second maker" who created new worlds out of the infinite possiblities presented by the necessary truths. The prospect of the poet as *alter deus* was apparently unacceptable to Breitinger's conservative and pious character. Hence Breitinger is said to have contented himself with confining his poetics to the safer territory of selection and recombination of that nature already provided by God. Breitinger is credited first with a great insight and then with a failure of nerve.

Cassirer had included in his interpretation the often cited passage from the *Critische Dichtkunst* in which the notion of possible worlds is set out. "Alle diese möglichen Welten, ob sie gleich nicht wirklich und nicht sichtbar sind, haben dennoch eine eigentliche Wahrheit, die in ihrer Möglichkeit, so von allem Widerspruch frei ist, und in der allesvermögenden Kraft des Schöpfers der Natur gegründet ist."[14] Because the quotation refers to both the principle of contradiction and the principle of sufficient reason ("in der allesvermögenden Kraft . . . gegründet"), we cannot properly identify Breitinger's possible worlds with Leibniz's *vérités nécessaires* because such truths were not grounded, according to Leibniz, in divine omnipotence. That is, God does not have the power to decide what shall count as a contradiction.[15] Moreover, in an earlier passage of the *Critische Dichtkunst* (1:54) that Cassirer does not cite but that he must have seen, Breitinger expressly excludes from poetic representation all those truths that are independent of empirical verification ("die alleine dem reinen und von den Sinnen gantz abgekehrten Verstand vernehmlich sind"): that is, truths of logic ("Vernunft-Lehre"), of geometry ("Meß-Kunst"), of metaphysics ("Lehre vom Wesen der Dinge") and of arithmetic ("Rechen-Kunst")—in other words, the necessary truths as Leibniz defines them.

Breitinger's exclusion of the necessary truths from poetic represen-
tation was apparently based not only on what he read in Leibniz and
Wolff, but also on what he took from Muratori.[16] This passage corre-
sponds to another apparent borrowing from Muratori in which Brei-
tinger distinguishes between "das Wahre des Verstandes," which
does indeed capture the necessary truths, and "das Wahre der Ein-
bildung."[17] It has often been argued (following Cassirer) that Breitin-
ger anticipated, but did not achieve, the classical-Idealist "poetics of
autonomy" with his notion of "das Wahre der Einbildung." Breitinger
is always seen to revert to "philosophic truth," or Enlightenment ra-
tionality, to which the poetic representation is made subservient and
which guarantees its ultimate validity.[18]

The discussion of "Verstand" and "Einbildung" has been particu-
larly distorted by the nearly universal tendency, even among recent
critics of *Genieästhetik*, to compare Swiss poetics to later developments
in German aesthetics. The proper historical context, however, for un-
derstanding this issue is not the latter part of the eighteenth century
but rather the late seventeenth century. This period witnessed an
enormous expansion and diversification in the mathematically based
natural sciences, as well as a consolidation of the philological disci-
plines initiated in the Renaissance. The Quarrel between the Ancients
and the Moderns, in the literary sphere, was precipitated, in part, by
a sense among the *modernes* that ancient literary artifacts were no
longer valuable, having been created in the prescientific phase of
Western culture. Only present-day authors (or present-day "transla-
tors" of ancient works), writing in the age of rational exactitude,
could be credited with universal, timeless insights into human na-
ture. As a debate over the value of literary historical texts, the *querelle*
was a conflict between universalists, whose methodological model
was mathematics, and historists, whose model was philology.[19] In
Germany, this debate manifested itself, among other places, in the
controversy between the universalist Gottsched and the historical
philologist Breitinger.[20]

Breitinger's adoption of the historian Muratori's distinction be-
tween imaginative and rational truth (the theft is too rarely recog-
nized) has been generally viewed as an example of a polarization in
his thinking between "feeling and reason" or "intuition and reason"
or "Sinnlichkeit und Verstand" (as a recent book title suggests). By
casting Breitinger's project in such Kantian terms, the historical posi-
tion of his poetics cannot be grasped. His work should be interpreted
instead as the reflection of a distinction, emerging out of the *querelle*,
between the kinds of knowledge provided by the exact sciences and

the human sciences (a question that was, to be sure, not resolved when Kant began to write his first *Kritik*). In both the *Critische Dichtkunst* and in the *Gleichnis-Abhandlung*, Breitinger expresses his fear that modern authors are failing to produce new knowledge—hence his reformulation, examined earlier, of the task of metaphor. In these passages Breitinger holds up the progress made in the natural sciences to the lack of comparable achievements among German poets.[21] While Gottsched responded to this crisis in the humanities by attempting to assimilate his poetics to the exact sciences, Breitinger proposes that poesis be viewed as a historically evolving field of knowledge. This is his fundamental link to Leibniz, whose philosophy is the preeminent statement of the problem of knowledge and representation at the end of the seventeenth century. Leibniz's concept of possibility therefore needs to be examined in detail in order to understand Breitinger's enterprise. Breitinger's primary philosophic source was of course Christian Wolff, who took his notion of possible worlds directly from Leibniz.[22]

Leibniz's Concept of Possibility

Leibniz's system is founded on two essential types of distinction, one metaphysical (or ontological), the other epistemological. The epistemological distinction—between *vérités nécessaires* and *vérités de fait*—has already been discussed. The metaphysical distinction involves a fourfold division (Figure 1). In his own version of the ontological argument, Leibniz argued that the Cartesian proof of God's existence was inadequate because it assumed God's possibility. The Leibnizian version, stated briefly, holds that the idea of a thing's existence cannot be true unless the possibility of that thing can first be demonstrated. The idea of a possible is not simply that which is thinkable, for we can conceive of any number of things that are impossible, such as the idea of the most rapid motion. A wheel, for example, that spins at the fastest possible rate could have a spoke protruding from its outer rim that would move faster than the rim itself. Hence the idea is absurd (impossible).[23] An idea is possible only when it involves no contradiction. In the case of our idea of God, there is no contradiction between a perfect being and an existing being. Therefore God is possible. Further, because (following Descartes) existence is a kind of perfection, God exists necessarily.[24] (This version of the proof manifests of course the same circularity as its scholastic and Cartesian predecessors.) God's necessary existence also is proved by Leibniz *a pos-*

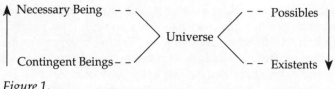

Figure 1.

teriori: there are contingent beings, all of which are caused by something rather than nothing. Contingents are caused by anterior contingents, but an infinite regress is not possible because there then would be no reason for the chain of contingents itself. Thus there is necessarily a self-caused cause that stands outside contingency.[25]

According to Leibniz's form of the ontological argument, God is the only being whose possibility necessarily involves existence.[26] (The parallel epistemological formulation, already outlined, is that necessary truths are rendered true by their possibility.) No other possible being exists necessarily. The existence of contingent beings is determined not by their simple possibility but rather by divine will[27] (just as the truths of fact require more than possibility to be true). Hence some contingent beings remain merely possible, "existing" only in the divine mind, while others become real, that is, actualized. Moreover, Leibniz posits this distinction not as a disjunction but as a continuum: "Les possibles pretendent à l'existence à proportion de leur perfections."[28] The difference between possibility and existence is a matter of degree, not of kind. The universe appears to be constructed in completely Plotinian terms as an "upward" scale of reality (as the arrow to the left in Figure 1 indicates), whereby God is posited as the most real being and the contingents as less real. Unlike the Neoplatonists, however, Leibniz assigns greater reality to the existents than to the possibles, whose relative perfection determines their degree of reality or existence (which is shown by the arrow on the right).[29] Both arrows in Figure 1 therefore refer to value. The existing world is contingent, as are all possible worlds, of which group indeed this world is the most perfect member. By definition the contingents realize themselves in time and space and are represented by the truths of fact. Because their existence (or nonexistence) is based on divine will, which "decides" on their existence based on their perfection, the possibles are not necessary. Had they been necessary, they could not have been the object of divine choice because even God is bound by necessity.[30]

There is an infinity of possibles, such as, Leibniz suggests, those depicted in the novels of Mme Scudéry that may never become real (actual), but that are not therefore impossible.[31] Some possibles that have not yet manifested themselves in time and space may still become actualized. But Leibniz also distinguishes in the *Théodicée* (8–9) between those possibles of the existing world that have still to be realized and the possible worlds rejected by God at the Creation. Whether or when the actualization of any given possible occurs is based on the preestablished harmony of the universe. Some possibles will never harmonize with the existing world, therefore will never be actualized. God, unlike all other existents, can envision at once the connection of all of the possibles to each other and thus their position in the unfolding universe.[32] The *intellectus divinus* alone distinguishes between the possibles chosen for existence and those forever rejected.

The actualization of the world does not occur according to necessity. Leibniz's argument goes as follows: divine prevision of the world does not account for the truth of those contingencies that are subsequently actualized. Actualization follows not from prevision but from the actions of individual existents, all of which are indeed divinely ordained but carried out nonetheless in time. Their possibility does not automatically result in their actualization.[33] Their existence is "certain" or "determined" but not necessary. This distinction between necessity and determinacy was, and remains, one of the most disputed aspects of Leibniz's thought. Lovejoy, for example, remarked that it "is manifestly without logical substance; the fact is so apparent that it is impossible to believe that a thinker of [Leibniz's] powers can have been altogether unaware of it himself."[34]

However that may be, the difficulty appears to stem from the fact that Leibniz is using "possible" in two completely different senses— one logical, the other metaphysical. The logically possible is necessary; the metaphysically possible is contingent. Because Breitinger expressly rejects the (logically) necessary truths as objects of poetic representation, that is, those truths that follow necessarily out of their possibility, we must assume that the possibles he means are metaphysical, that is, those things whose existence may or may not follow from their possibility. And because some of these possibles were rejected by God at the Creation, this would appear to leave Breitinger in the theologically embarrassing position of recommending inferior worlds as aesthetic objects.

Yet this would hardly be the correct approach for a critic attempting to stimulate increased respect for literature among a presumably pious public. What seems more likely is that Breitinger meant literature to depict those metaphysically possible worlds that have not yet been actualized. The new epistemological significance that Breitinger assigns to literature lies in its role as an agent of contingent truth, that is, as the means by which contingent truth is realized in time. In order to understand this process, which is the basis of Breitinger's poetic conception, it is necessary to execute a digression into Leibniz's metaphysics.

Leibniz's Concept of Substance

"La Substance est un Etre capable d'Action." The sentence opens one of Leibniz's last metaphysical essays, *Principes de la Nature et de la Grâce, fondés en raison*, and expresses an axiom of his system. In place of the Cartesian division of substance into *res extensae* and *res cogitantes* Leibniz sets the concept of activity or force.[35] This new concept of substance, developed primarily during the course of Leibniz's mathematical and physical studies in Paris,[36] refers to the unifying activity that constitutes form in both the physical and mental spheres—which are not, however, oppositional dimensions as in the Cartesian system. With his concept of substance Leibniz shows how the physical and the mental are aspects of the continuum of Being such that the physical becomes increasingly mental, or better, the phenomenal becomes ideal in proportion to its degree of unifying, form-creating activity. Both corporeal and incorporeal things have the capacity to act, but substance (force) is that which is incorporeal in the corporeal.[37]

The phenomenal world consists of the multiplicity of bodies acting upon each other such that the force of one (A), when transferred to another (B), is "felt" or registered by all bodies (Cx) impinging on (B), also by those bodies impinging on (Cx), and so forth ad infinitum. But each body (B) so acted upon is also the center of its own field of forces, such that the quantity of force it receives from any one source (A) will be determined by the force received from all other sources, "sources" meaning here not just the immediately impinging bodies but all those bodies impinging on them. The phenomenal realm is a web of an infinite number of forces (efficient causes) acting upon each other in accordance with the laws of motion.[38]

Force transferred from one body to another is not a mystical "quality" moving through passive receptors. Force transferred becomes force *exerted*, unless hindered by an opposing force. Thus each body is a center of both reception and generation of activity. The generation of force Leibniz calls the "immanent action" of substance. The notion of immanence is what makes Leibniz's concept of force a meta-physical idea rather than a mechanistic one. Primary matter, as distin-guised from bodies, cannot generate action; it is not spontaneous. Secondary matter (bodies), by contrast, has a "vital principle" that is a soul, or "something analogous to [it], a first entelechy."[39] Hence matter is substance insofar as it is dynamic form. In the case of mo-tion, form is the acting out from a center-point determined by the web of forces registered or "represented" at this point.[40] Each action or movement represents the unification of a multiplicity of forces, resulting in a new motion. Motion is, however, only one species of action.[41] The more general term for the unifying activity of substance is "perception."[42]

The term has caused considerable difficulty among those students of Leibniz who conceive of perception in the Lockean sense as the imprinting of the multiplicity of the phenomenal world on a passive mind. The problem is intensified when the perceiving beings, or monads, are said by Leibniz to be without windows.[43] The confusion was intended. Leibniz's point is precisely that the notion of percep-tion needs to be reconceived as the spontaneous (i.e., self-generated) organization of disparate elements, an organization furnished not by the outer environment, but by a "principe interne" called "appe-tition."[44] Indeed a monad does not "have" perceptions at all; it *is* perception.

Perception occurs in various degrees of clearness and distinctness, forming an infinite continuum that ranges from the divine intel-lect—the continuum is closed at the top—downward to the most ob-scure and confused perception. The reality or perfection of each mo-nad is a function of the degree to which its perceptions are clear and distinct. Distinctness is a function of the level of multiplicity that has been organized.[45] In the monad with the highest perfection (God), the entire multiplicity of the universe is grasped with absolute clarity, unhindered by the confusion inherent in mere physical existence. All other monads are united in some degree to matter (the source of con-fused or disorganized perception), which is recognizable in the force of their perception, that is, in its level of distinctness. Those beings more subject to physical existence necessarily have less intellective capacity, or ability to integrate a multiplicity in their perceiving.[46] This integrative function makes for the *activity* of the monad, whereas its failure to do so means the dominance of the multiplicity, the domi-nance of matter in its representation, hence, its passivity.

An example from the *Monadologie* (§§ 26–29) will illustrate the point. Animals, Leibniz says, have a memory based on successive

events in the phenomenal world. The memory causes them to antici-
pate certain events and to act out of this simple anticipation, such as
when a dog is shown a stick with which it has been beaten and runs
away. Similarly we may expect the sun to rise because it has always
done so in the past. But rational beings (such as astronomers) as dis-
tinguished from "Empiriques"—who Leibniz thinks rather resemble
animals in their thinking—are able to recognize the cause of events,
that is, the necessary connection between all such successions of
events in the future. Both reasoning beings and empirics observe the
same phenomena, but they make different sense out of what they see.
The phenomena themselves cannot be said to "cause" reasoning in
the one and a conclusion based on habit in the other. Thus lesser
monads are not "more affected" by phenomena (which would imply
a causality); rather, their existence shows a privation of activity, that
is, the absence of intellective integration of multiple events in a unity.
In this case the insight into the cause of all future similar events uni-
fies more phenomena than the simple anticipation of one additional
similar event in the future.[47]

I have thus far used "perception" as a generic term. Leibniz em-
ploys in fact a hierarchy of designations, availing himself of Cartesian
language, to express the activity of perception, the lowest level being
"confused" and the highest "distinct." Because perception is the ac-
tivity of substance rather than simply a state of the human mind,
these terms have metaphysical significance insofar as substance is the
intellective process of the ordering of a multiplicity.[48] "Petites percep-
tions" or "perceptions confuses" are representations unnoticed by
the monad. (More will be said about them.) "Perception," similar to
sensation, consists of clear but confused representations of (but not
imprints from) the outer world,[49] such as color or coldness, whereby
a quality is recognized independently of its causes. Leibniz gives the
example of green pigment, which is a mixture of two very fine pow-
ders, one blue, the other yellow, whose existence in the color green
cannot be discerned.[50] "Apperception" is reflexive perception, that is,
the state in which the monad is aware of its own perceiving, thus
aware of its own Self.[51] Leibniz illustrates the difference between per-
ception and apperception as that between sleeping and waking, or
even between life and death, which is only an apparent cessation of
all life, because perception never ceases.[52] Simple monads perceive;
souls apperceive. Finally, there is "la Raison" or *Intellectus*, in which
the connections of all things to each other are established.[53]

The universe in the Leibnizian system is given as a field of force in
a state of flux. There are continual shifts in position on the Chain

of Being ("[les]substances . . . changent continuellement leur rap-
ports"),[54] whereby some monads lose while others gain in perfection.
These shifts, proceeding according to the law of continuity, are meant
to be qualitative, not quantitative. Monads or souls do not have parts
to be lost or acquired when they undergo changes in state. They do
not lose or gain perceptions. Instead, their perceptions decrease or
increase in force, that is, in the level of integrative activity.[55] Such
activity, however, never sinks "below" the level of the "petites per-
ceptions," which continue to inform or "incline" the monad even
though it is unaware of their existence.[56] Nor can the monad ever rise
completely above "petite perception"; only the divine intellect is ca-
pable of this.

Perception occurs according to a "principe interne," the individ-
ual's vital force driven by appetition.[57] This principle makes for the
individuality of the monad in that new perceptions are generated
strictly out of the specific history of perceptions of that particular mo-
nad, which is the basis for Leibniz's famous statement "le present est
gros de l'avenir."[58] Thus it is curious that Leibniz would claim, as he
does in the *Monadologie* (§ 17), that perception can never be explained
mechanically. What he means is not that the perceptions are not con-
nected, but that they are not connected as in the phenomenal realm
of motion by efficient cause, that is, by the direct transfer of the force
of one perception to another. Perceptions are linked together instead
purely by spontaneity, which is a final cause, namely, the divine
choice of what is best.[59] And this choice has determined in what order
perceptions shall evolve, through appetition, into new constellations
of perceptions.

The development of individuality in the ideal realm may be viewed
in analogy with the phenomenal dimension of motion. In the phe-
nomenal realm, continuity is manifested as the law of the conserva-
tion of energy. When any body (B) is acted upon by another body
(A), it receives not only the force of (A), but, in different degrees
according to its own position, that of all other bodies that have acted
on (A). In the metaphysical-epistemological context, all monads are
said to represent the entire universe, though with differing degrees
of distinctness based on their individual perspective, those things
"closest" to them being perceived more distinctly. Continuity justifies
the importance of confused and obscure perceptions (the "petites
perceptions"), which cannot be excluded by fiat from substance, or
from the mind's activity. Instead, the "petites perceptions" provide
the possibility for the intelligibility of the universe. For Descartes, and
later for Locke, the only admissible mental entity was the clear and

distinct idea. Leibniz directed some of his sharpest words against this doctrine, accusing the Cartesians of denying the possibility of the soul's immortality (which Leibniz grounded in the unceasing nature of perception), and ignoring the true commonality of humans with other beings.[60]

While the theological issue of immortality is less interesting for us today, the model of the intellect that Leibniz proposed was of major consequence, not only for the exact sciences but also for the historical disciplines. In defending the significance of the lesser perceptions, Leibniz did not merely point out their usefulness but rather their necessity in the formation of all thought. For although God created the best possible of all worlds, populated by beings with infinite degrees of intellective power and perfection, he created it as a universe that finds itself in continual motion. And since the motion of intellection is thought, which is the movement from one perception to another,[61] all intellective activity is appetition, which integrates the "petites perceptions." Leibniz seems to have been less concerned, in his concept of plenitude, with the continual production of new individuals within the Chain of Being,[62] than with the spontaneous development of substance out of its own ground, a process involving the integration, as a unity, of ever more perceptions into an increasingly differentiated whole. This is not, however, the "acquisition" of new perceptions, but a process of focusing on that which is already in the soul. The activity of substance is the movement from potentiality to actuality. The ontological goal, or *telos*, of Leibniz's system, the greatest possible variety coeval with the greatest level of order,[63] is also an epistemological goal, in that an increase in Being means an increase in intelligibility.

Leibniz's notion of spontaneity preserves the problematic distinction between contingency and necessity that he attempted to resolve with the word "determinacy." In the assimilation or integration of ever more perception by the monad or soul,[64] not all "petites perceptions" are chosen—Leibniz says they "compete" with each other—and some remain unnoticed. The final cause that governs the selection is the principle of appropriateness ("convenance"). Only those perceptions that contribute to the unifying activity of the larger perceptual process are integrated. The ability to be integrated is called "compossibilité." Thus the competition among the perceptions is the conflict ("le combat") among the possibles for existence. The possibles, striving toward existence in proportion to their perfection, are actualized according to their "intelligibilité," which is the definition of perfection.[65] The best possible world is getting better because it is

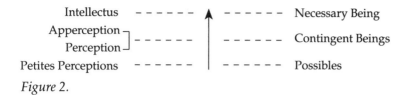

Figure 2.

becoming more intelligible. The increasing intelligibility of the world, founded as it is in the continual absorption of previously unrecognized (but not previously unreal) perceptions, is not a sequential revelation of individual necessary truths. Rather, intelligibility unfolds on a scale of increasing probability (or increasing certainty), such that the determinacy of the world *tends* in the direction of necessity, but never becomes identical to it. Stated in terms of human knowledge, no scientific theory is necessarily true, but subject to constant revision as more evidence is collected and integrated.

Based on the foregoing discussion of substance, the position of the possibles within Leibniz's metaphysical divisions can now be redrawn (see Figure 2). Contingent beings are *like* necessary being insofar as their perception rises to the level of intellection; conversely, their souls sink to the level of possibility (potentiality) when the unifying activity of perception is greatly reduced. The divisions are not static categories, it must be remembered, but "regions" on a continuum. No contingent being can ever become identical to pure *intellectus*. As in Figure 1, the arrow represents increasing value. It should be noted that increasing value (increasing reality and intelligibility) means for Leibniz also increasing pleasure,[66] a point that will become important in the subsequent discussion of Breitinger's poetics.

Although it is true that the possibles are less perfect than the existents, they become, when seen in context with the "petites perceptions," the very source of all that is valuable in the monads or souls. They are the condition of possibility for the greatest variety next to the greatest order. For without them there can be no multiplicity, whose integration makes for increased order and distinctness, which is the apprehension of the relationship of parts to each other. Because the individual substances shift "up" and "down" in their level of activity, new perception is brought into the system and the universe as a whole progresses "upward."[67] To discount the importance of the possibles as potential actuality, to view them simply as logical possibility, is not only to ignore Leibniz's own application of the principle of plenitide, but also to miss completely the basis for his critique of Descartes. By arguing for the potential intelligibility of the less certain and confused, Leibniz was aiming for the destruction of the Cartesian fascination with absolute certainty that he believed might destroy the development of knowledge. In this respect he embodies the spirit of Aristotle, whom he greatly admired, and who also defended the value of probable knowledge when certainty was not to be found. Whereas Aristotle's distinction between probable and certain was, however, primarily a logical issue, in Leibniz's system it is also a metaphysical issue.[68] His system is cast in Neoplotinian imagery that describes perception moving upward toward intellect as the development in time of increasing probability. The process of Being is the universal movement toward necessary truth that is grounded in the vitality and spontaneous development of the individual ordained by divine will.

It should now be clear that the question of Breitinger's adherence to Leibniz's concept of possible worlds is only incompletely answered by referring to Leibniz's theological reflections. In that context the possible worlds indeed have less value than the existing world and "exist" only in God's understanding as purely logical entities. In the context of Leibniz's metaphysics, however, "possibility" and "possible worlds" are given the status of dynamic potentiality. The possibles are those things that are realized as the world becomes more perfect, which it does ceaselessly. Indeed they are the precondition for the world's perfection. Breitinger's choice of "the possible" as the prime object of poetic representation means that when literature depicts the possibles, it contributes to the continuing perfectibility of the world.[69] Yet this is not to say that poesis reveals necessary truths, as Cassirer suggested, because the metaphysically possible only tends or inclines toward necessity and cannot be identified with it.

Breitinger, Gottsched, and Wolff

Breitinger's reading of Wolff was augmented by his study of Muratori, so that the dynamic concept of nature as emanation peculiar to Neoplatonism and preserved in Leibniz's metaphysics reappears in Breitinger's literary theory.[70] A critic such as Gottsched, who proceeded from a concept of nature based on static and timeless geometrical relations, was bound to read Wolff differently than Breitinger did. There is now a widely held assumption that Gottsched and Breitinger, because of their mutual indebtedness to Wolff, used the concept of possible worlds in nearly identical senses. An examination of how the concept functions in their poetics will clarify this issue.

It has already been established that Breitinger's poet depicts nature and all that lies "in ihren Kräften verborgen." Stated in Leibnizian terms, poets do not confine themselves to actualized being, but represent potential being: "Denn ich darf vor gewiß setzen, daß die Dicht-Kunst, insoferne sie von der Historie unterschieden ist, ihre Originale und die Materie ihrer Nachahmung nicht so fast aus der gegenwärtigen, als vielmehr aus der Welt der möglichen Dinge entlehnen müsse" (1:57).[71] The traditional interpretation of passages such as this (to review briefly) is that Breitinger thought of the poet as an *alter deus*. As the creator of possible worlds, the poet becomes a quasi competitor with God by bringing to realization the possibles that God has not chosen to actualize. In this context, critics often point out Breitinger's supposed indebtedness to Addison, who had written in no. 419 of the *Spectator* that "the Poet quite *loses sight of Nature, and . . . has no Pattern to follow. . . .* Poetry . . . has not only the whole Circle of Nature for its Province, but makes new Worlds of its own, shews us Persons who are *not to be found in Being*" (3:570–73, my emphasis). Invariably, however, critics return to Breitinger's religious side and discount "his" *alter deus* as underdeveloped.

This interpretive cul-de-sac should be avoided altogether by substituting the Leibnizian monad for the *alter deus*. For the latter term, although already widely used in the Renaissance, is nonetheless laden with the Promethean overtones of German Idealism. Leibniz's monad, by contrast, was never meant to displace but only to represent, imperfectly, the divine mind. It stands at its own center of intellective integration of perception. The creative task of the poet *qua* monad is to absorb the "petites perceptions"—that is, that which lies hidden in nature's forces—by moving them "up" to the level of apperception in the act of *re*-presentation that is "poetische Mahlerey." Poets make "das unsichtbare sichtbar" (1:19) by focusing on and integrating the normally unnoticed manifold particulars of the empirical world into a poetic image that embodies their own artistic purpose. "Die Natur hat denen Künsten des Poeten und des Mahlers alle ihre Schätze, auch die verborgensten vor den äusserlichen Sinnen, eröffnet, und ihnen ohne Maßgebung überlassen, die Wahl unter denselben nach ihren Absichten einzurichten" (1:78). Unlike the Addisonian "make[r] of new Worlds," Breitinger's poet uncovers the possibles hidden in nature itself that emanate out of the already existent: "Kennet der Poet die Gesetze, nach welchen alle Würckungen und Veränderungen in der gegenwärtigen Welt der würcklichen Dinge erfolgen, und verstehet er die Natur der Dinge genau, so kan ihm nicht verborgen seyn, was bey jeder veränderter Absicht und

Umstand nach diesen Gesetzen und vermöge dieser Natur der Dinge möglich ist, und erfolgen muß" (1:271–72).

Breitinger does, however, appear to follow Addison's reference to allegorical figures when he says (1:143) that the poet "durch die Kraft seiner Phantasie gantz neue Wesen erschaffet," which he lists ("die Tugenden, die Arten des Lasters, die Welt-Theile, Königreiche . . . die Künste, die Winde, die Jahreszeiten, und so fort"). Addison's "another sort of Imaginary Beings" arises "when the Author represents any Passion, Appetite, Virtue or Vice, under a visible Shape" (3:573). But these allegorical figures do not constitute Breitinger's possible worlds; indeed they are said to have become so much a part of our literary tradition that "sie haben so zu sagen bey den Menschen das Bürgerrecht erhalten" (1:143–44).[72]

The poet's creative activity therefore does not "improve" nature by adding a new world. The poet merely acts as an agent of nature in the process of actualization. "Die Natur hat in der Erschaffung dieser gegenwärtigen Welt nicht alle ihre Kräfte erschöpfet, wenn also der Poet etwas vorstellet, das die Natur zwar noch nicht zur Würcklichkeit gebracht hat, aber doch an das Licht zu bringen vermögend ist, so kan dieses wieder keine Verbesserung der Natur, sondern nur eine Nachahmung derselben auch in dem Möglichen selbst, geheissen werden" (1:268).[73] We recall that the monad neither lost nor gained perceptions but simply represented them with a greater or lesser degree of clarity. The continual reordering of perceptions means that each monad mirrors the universe in accordance with its own perspective.[74]

This limited perspective of the monad is the basis of Wolff's explanation of perfection. "Keine Creatur kan den größten Grad der Vollkommenheit erreichen. Denn woferne dieses geschehen sollte / müsste ihr Wesen in das Wesen GOttes verkehret werden" (*Metaphysik*, § 1088). And because, in the Leibnizian system explicated by Wolff, being and perceiving (or representing) are identified with each other, the limited degree of perfection attainable by any one monad corresponds to the limited ability of nondivine beings to apperceive the perfection of the universe. "Wenn . . . die Anzahl des mannichfaltigen / so mit einander übereinstimmen soll / sehr groß ist / fället es schweer von der Vollkommenheit des gantzen zu urtheilen. *Und dieses ist die Ursache, warum die meisten sich betrügen, wenn sie von der Vollkommenheit der natürlichen Dingen urtheilen wollen*" (§ 171). Moreover, Wolff envisions a specific application of the monad's perspectivism to the problem faced by the artist. The passage continues: "*Ja, es gehet ihnen auch wol in den Wercken der Kunst nicht besser. Ist aber die*

Zahl grösser / als daß wir sie zu überdencken vermögend sind; so stehet gar nicht in unserer Gewalt / die Vollkommenheit des gantzen zu beurtheilen" (§ 171).[75]

Precisely these formulations are to be found in Breitinger's discussion of artistic judgment. "[Es] ist ein blosser Betrug der menschlichen Unwissenheit, wenn wir würckliche und mögliche Dinge mit einander vergleichen, und uns einige davon, ausser ihrem Zusammenhange betrachtet, von grösserer oder geringerer Schönheit und Vollkommenheit zu seyn beduncken lassen. Dieses rühret alleine daher, weil wir den Zusammenhang und die Uebereinstimmung aller Theile, als worauf die Vollkommenheit des Gantzen beruhet, nicht vermögen auf einmahl zu übersehen" (1:269). Breitinger's poet therefore faces a dilemma. On the one hand, he wants to compare his artistic representation of the possible with actuality (holding his work up to nature is a source of pleasure),[76] but he will never be able to grasp sufficiently the total structure of nature ("Zusammenhang") against which such a comparison must be carried out. Breitinger attempts to resolve this dilemma by suggesting that although poets can never assume the position of the divine intellect, they can replicate its activity in their own creative process. "Ich sehe den Poeten an, als einen weisen Schöpfer einer neuen idealischen Welt oder eines neuen Zusammenhanges der Dinge, der nicht alleine Fug und Macht hat, denen Dingen, die nicht sind, eine wahrscheinliche Würcklichkeit mitzutheilen, sondern daneben so vielen Verstand besitzet, daß er seine Haupt-Absicht zu erreichen, die besondern Absichten dergestalt mit einander verknüpfet, daß immer eine ein Mittel für die andere, alle insgesamt aber ein Mittel für die Haupt-Absicht abgeben, müssen" (1:426).

The passage was apparently synthesized from two different paragraphs in Wolff's *Metaphysik* that explain divine omniscience and omnipotence. At § 1048 Wolff has: "GOtt erkennet vermöge seiner Allwissenheit alle Absichten / die möglich sind / und alle Mittel / wodurch man sie erreichen kan (§ 972). Weil er nun nichts anders als das beste will (§ 985); so muß er auch die besten Absichten haben / und die besten Mittel dazu erwehlen. Derowegen weil er auch seine Absichten so einrichtet / daß immer eine ein Mittel der andern wird / insgesammt aber alle endlich als ein Mittel seiner Haupt-Absicht anzusehen sind (§§ 1034, 1044); so hat er die allervollkommenste Weißheit" (§ 920). And at § 1053 he writes: "GOtt hat Dingen / die durch seinen Verstand bloß möglich waren / auch durch seine Macht die Würcklichkeit gegeben (§ 1020). Diese Würckung GOttes wird die Schöpffung genennet: von welcher wir keinen Begriff haben / weil wir keine Krafft haben etwas zu erschaffen. . . . Denn wir bringen alsdenn Dinge hervor in Gedancken / in denen Wahrheit ist / und die zuvor nicht da waren / nach unserem Wohlgefallen / und erhalten sie durch die Krafft der Seele gegenwärtig / so lange wir wollen: jedoch können wir ihnen keine Würcklichkeit ausser der Seele geben / welches doch GOtt in der Schöpffung thut / und darinnen eigentlich die Schöpffung bestehet."

Wolff's point had been that divine creation occurs according to a set of infinitely complex yet organized purposes ("Absichten") whose ultimate interconnection the limited human mind is incapable of grasping entirely. Since all creation flows from these purposes, products of the human imagination are but a part of the overall divine plan for the realization of the world. God's "Rath-Schluß," rather than our own creativity, is responsible for the existence of "Wercke der Kunst." And "wir müssen ihm unwissende zu Ausführung seines Rathes dienen" (*Metaphysik*, § 1031). Artistic service in this divine project of realization of the world means continual albeit imperfect cognition of the interconnection of all things to each other. Thus Breitinger's poet seems to be a somewhat limited "Schöpfer" insofar as he merely reproduces a limited version of the universal "Verknüpfung" of purposes in his own work. It is tempting to view the passage at 1:426 simply as a discourse on the poet as the creator of a microcosm. The topic under discussion there is not, however, the limited ontological status of the poetic *product* but rather the psychological *process* of "Erfindung" as he understood it according to Wolff.

Wolff defines invention as "die Fertigkeit unbekandte Wahrheit aus anderen bekandten heraus zu bringen" (*Metaphysik*, § 362).[77] He then distinguishes (*Metaphysik*, §§ 362–67) between two methods, or "Arten der Regeln": invention *a priori*, which relies on "Witz," and invention *a posteriori*, which relies on "Verstand." The *a priori* method is the faculty of analogic thought, the ability to transfer arbitrarily, through "Verkehrung," something that is known to something unknown, which is nonetheless perceived to be equivalent ("gleichgültig"). Invention *a posteriori* is the method of drawing new conclusions ("Schlüsse") based on what is already known. Because "Verstand" is defined (*Metaphysik*, § 277) as the ability to recognize distinctly what is possible, invention *a posteriori* produces statements or truths that are *compossible* with existing knowledge. That is, new conclusions are reached by analyzing the "Verknüpfung" of known statements or facts to each other.

The inductive process of "Verkehrung" ensures that "man in den Stand gesetzet wird einen Anfang im Schlüssen zu machen" (*Meta-*

physik, § 364). But invention *a priori* must always be conducted in tandem with invention *a posteriori* (*Metaphysik*, §§ 367, 861). Wolff posits a continual interplay between "Witz" and "Verstand," or the *a priori* and *a posteriori* methods. We can see why this interplay is essential if we look at what Wolff has to say about imagination. Although he does not explicitly equate "Einbildungskraft" and "Erfindung," they operate in analogous ways.[78]

Invention uses two methods and imagination operates according to two "Manieren." The first "Manier" Wolff calls "die Krafft zu erdichten" (*Metaphysik,* § 242). This is the ability of the imagination to combine two previous perceptions into an image that is impossible in the real world ("nicht möglich ist, und daher eine leere Einbildung genennet wird"). Wolff gives as examples "die Gestalt der Melusine / so halb Mensch und Fisch ist; die Gestalt der Engel / wenn sie als geflügelte Menschen gemahlet werden; die seltsame Gestalten der heydnischen Götter und dergleichen" (§ 242). Such imaginative products belong to the class of notions Wolff elsewhere calls "willkührlich formirte Begriffe": "Allein wenn wir nach unserem eigenem Willkühre etwas determiniren, können wir nicht wissen, ob dieselbigen Begriffe möglich sind, oder ob wir nur leere Worte gedencken. Denn unser Wille kan nichts möglich machen. Derowegen müssen wir in dergleichen Fällen beweisen, daß die erlangten Begriffe etwas mögliches in sich fassen. Es ist auch nicht genung, daß die Determinationes an sich möglich sind, sondern es wird zugleich erfordert, daß sie nebst denen übrigen bestehen können."[79] Wolff makes two important points. First, the human mind can bring forth many things that are not possible. (This recalls Leibniz's distinction between nominal and real definitions.) Second, even if a concept contains no internal contradiction (if it is "an sich möglich"), it must still be possible within the context in which it functions. Concepts that are not compossible thus cannot contribute to the formation of new knowledge; invention *a posteriori* cannot be circumvented in this process. "Erdichtung," therefore, is "Erfindung" carried out without regard for compossibility.

The second "Manier" of the imagination is dependent on the principle of sufficient reason (*Metaphysik,* § 245). Its product is not merely logically possible, but also capable of actualization. This kind of imaginative work (Wolff mentions at § 246 the architect's image of a building) has been brought forth according to the rules of certain arts (e.g., "Baukunst"). Such an image can be actualized into an object because it has been conceived according to the principles of production whose possibility in the real world has been demonstrated by the construction of other buildings.

Wolff's distinctions between "erfinden" and "erdichten" form an essential background to his discussion of poesis and possible worlds. (We must remember here that "erfinden"/"erdichten" are, like "Kunst," generic terms, and that poesis is merely a specific kind of invention.) At §§ 570–73 in the *Metaphysik*, he had compared the possible worlds with the "erdichteten Geschichten, die man Romainen zu nennen pfleget." He begins by noting that the real ("würcklich") world, that is, that which is described by the *vérités de fait*, is in constant flux. For example, he says, I am now sitting, but a new world could come about in which I would have occasion to stand up. So it is with novels. What is narrated may not have happened, but it might happen if the world were in a different configuration ("in einem anderen Zusammenhang"). Wolff seems to have restated fairly Leibniz's notion of possibles that are not yet but still could be actualized. But whereas Leibniz's point in referring to books by Mme Scudéry had been that not all possibles need *necessarily* be actualized, Wolff's use of Leibniz's example makes a different statement. Wolff concludes that novels depict neither what has been, nor what is, nor what will eventually develop in this world; they only show what is possible in another, completely separate world that cannot be actualized in the present world.[80] This means that Wolff identified the possible worlds represented in the literary work with the *logical* possibles rather than with the compossibles striving for actualization in this world. In other words, Wolff believed poesis operates merely according to the principle of invention *a priori* but not according to invention *a posteriori*.

In Wolff's restriction of poesis to one aspect of the process of "Erfindung," namely, to what he called "Erdichtung," the ability of poesis to contribute to the development of new knowledge is considerably weakened. While Gottsched borrowed Wolff's limited notion of the poetic possible, Breitinger wanted to appropriate Wolff's entire process of "Erfindung" for his own concept of literature. (The subtitle of Breitinger's book is, after all, "worinnen die Poetische Mahlerey in Absicht auf die Erfindung im Grunde untersuchet . . . wird.") It is therefore misleading, as has been so often done, simply to point out that both Gottsched and Breitinger were indebted to Wolff. They used his work in different ways in keeping with their own purposes. Let us examine first how Gottsched defines possible worlds:

> Ich glaube derowegen, eine Fabel am besten zu beschreiben, wenn ich sage: sie sey die Erzählung einer unter gewissen Umständen möglichen, aber nicht wirklich vorgefallenen Begebenheit, darunter eine nützliche moralische Wahrheit verborgen

liegt. Philosophisch könnte man sagen, sie sey ein Stücke von
einer andern Welt. Denn da man sich in der Metaphysik die Welt
als eine Reihe möglicher Dinge vorstellen muß; außer derjenigen
aber, die wir wirklich vor Augen sehen, noch viel andre der-
gleichen Reihen gedacht werden können: so sieht man, daß ei-
gentlich alle Begebenheiten, die in unserm Zusammenhange
wirklich vorhandener Dinge nicht geschehen, an sich selbst aber
nichts Widersprechendes in sich haben, und also unter gewissen
Bedingungen möglich sind, in einer andern Welt zu Hause ge-
hören, und Theile davon ausmachen. Herr Wolf hat selbst, wo
mir recht ist, an einem gewissen Orte seiner philosophischen
Schriften gesagt, daß ein wohlgeschriebener Roman, das ist ein
solcher, der nichts Widersprechendes enthält, für eine Historie
aus einer andern Welt anzusehen sey. Was er nun von Romanen
sagt, das kann mit gleichem Rechte von allen Fabeln gesagt
werden.

(204)

This extended quotation comprises very nearly Gottsched's entire
treatment of possible worlds. His sole criterion for poetic possibility
is drawn from Wolff's (Leibnizian) definition of logical possibility:
"möglich sey / was nichts wiedersprechendes in sich enthält" (*Meta-
physik*, § 12). Nowhere does Gottsched refer to the actualization of the
possibles represented in the literary work; his possible worlds are not
meant to be integrated into the configuration of this world. This is
borne out by his definition of poetic probability.

Gottsched says that "Wahrscheinlichkeit" is "die Aehnlichkeit des
Erdichteten, mit dem, was wirklich zu geschehen pflegt" (255). He
later revises this initial determination because it cannot explain what
is for him the most valuable poetic genre, the didactic Aesopian fable,
in which the presence of talking plants and animals manifestly does
not accord with "was wirklich zu geschehen pflegt." For this special
case Gottsched introduces the notion of "bedingte" or "hypothe-
tische Wahrscheinlichkeit," which relies, not surprisingly, on the con-
cept of logical possibility. In order to make the fable seem probable,
the poet need merely establish the hypothesis that in another possible
world, animals and plants could talk. The probability of such a world
is based on the absence of self-contradictory elements *within* the con-
fines of that hypothetical configuration. Of course, Breitinger had
also defined the probable, like Gottsched, as that which has "keinen
Widerspruch in sich" (1:134), but he immediately goes on to say that
our judgment of this must be based on "eine Vergleichung mit unsren

Meinungen, Erfahrungen, und angenommenen Sätzen," a qualification Gottsched would never have admitted.

Although Gottsched undoubtedly believed he had correctly applied Wolff's concept of possible worlds to his poetics, the circularity of his definition demonstrates, ironically, precisely that tendency Wolff had described for *a priori* constructions of possibility to deteriorate into "leere Worte" (or Leibniz's nominal definitions). Hence poesis, as we have already seen in the context of Gottsched's notion of metaphor, can have no role to play in the formation of new knowledge, a process Wolff explains in his discourse on "Erfindung." The function of poesis for Gottsched is merely to reinforce the "nützliche moralische Wahrheit." Breitinger's notion of probability is also based on the concept of contradiction, but it is the *work itself* that must not contradict what is generally perceived to be true or thought to be possible. "Da nun die Poesie eine Nachahmung der Schöpfung und der Natur nicht nur in dem Würcklichen, sondern auch in dem Möglichen ist, so muß ihre Dichtung, die eine Art der Schöpfung ist, ihre Wahrscheinlichkeit entweder in der Uebereinstimmung mit den gegenwärtiger Zeit eingeführten Gesetzen und dem Laufe der Natur gründen, oder in den Kräften der Natur, welche sie bey andern Absichten *nach unsern Begriffen* hätte ausüben können" (1:136–37, my emphasis).

In the second chapter of the *Critische Dichtkunst*, "Erklärung der poetischen Mahlerey," Breitinger says (1:47–48) that the task of the poet is to bring together distinct but previously unnoticed qualities of discrete objects in such a way that the resulting image moves the mind ("Gemüthe in . . . Bewegung setzen [und] . . . rühren"). The poet exercises his "Kraft zu erdichten" by taking known qualities and extrapolating them into a previously unknown image that is new, unusual, or wondrous. As a result, "der wahre Verdienst eines Poeten [bestehet] im wenigsten darinn, daß er ohne Wahl und Unterschied alles schildere, was in der Natur vorkömmt, und es ist bey weitem nicht das vollkommenste Lob, wenn man gleich von seinen Wercken sagen kan, daß sie wahr, natürlich und ähnlich seyn; die Poesie empfängt ihre größte Stärcke und Schönheit von der geschickten Wahl der Bilder" (1:84). Although selection and recombination were of course well-established mimetic techniques in Breitinger's day, they do not in his poetics serve the purpose of the idealization of nature as they had, for example, in the Renaissance. Instead, Breitinger is following the principle of analogic transfer of the known to the unknown outlined by Wolff in his discussion of *a priori* invention. The poetic effect is heightened whenever the analogy is strained to its apparent limit.

At that point the image is wondrous, that is, it appears to stand in actual contradiction to the presently known: "Folglich hat das Wunderbare für den Verstand immer einen *Schein* der Falschheit; weil es mit den angenommenen Sätzen desselben in einem *offenbaren* Widerspruch zu stehen *scheinet*," (1:131, my emphasis). Breitinger stresses the apparent nature of the contradiction because he wants to claim, in keeping with Wolff's insistence on the *a posteriori* aspect of invention, that "das Wunderbare muß immer auf die würckliche oder die mögliche Wahrheit gegründet seyn, wenn es von der Lügen unterschieden seyn und uns ergetzen soll" (1:131).[81] In Breitinger's view, unlike in Gottsched's, the poetic conception is not mere "Erdichtung" alone; it must always refer back to the existing configuration of knowledge, even as it advances beyond it.

The application to poesis of this Wolffian process of invention is most evident in a passage from the chapter "Von dem Wunderbaren und dem Wahrscheinlichen," where Breitinger sets forth how probability is recognized when confronting the wondrous image:

> Das widersinnige Aussehen einer solchen [wunderbaren]
> Vorstellung ziehet unsere Aufmercksamkeit nothwendig an
> sich, und verheisset unserer Wissens-Begirde eine
> wichtige und nahmhafte Vermehrung: Die nachfolgende
> Beschäftigung des Gemüthes, da es die Vorstellungen mit
> seinen Begriffen und angenommenen Sätzen vergleichet, da
> es durch den Schein der Falschheit durchdringet, und in
> dem vermeinten Widerspruch eine Uebereinstimmung und
> Vollkommenheit entdecket, muß nothwendig angenehm und mit
> Ergetzen verknüpfet seyn; zumahlen da diese Entdeckung die
> unschuldige List des Poeten recht verwundersam machet, und
> unsere Eigenliebe und vortheilhaftige Meinung von unserer
> eigenen Geschicklichkeit speiset.
>
> (1:141–42)

Through a process of comparison with the presently known ("Begriffen und angenommenen Sätzen"), the probability is established of the apparently impossible ("vermeinter Widerspruch") that has been represented in the work. During such an analysis ("Beschäftigung des Gemüthes"), the wondrous comes to be apprehended not as a possibility in itself but as a possible part of a larger series of assumptions and concepts. By working out this probability, one establishes compossibility.[82]

When the compossibility (i.e., probability) of the vision presented by the poetic work is recognized, it is held to be compatible with the existing intellective structure or with existing "attitudes." Compatibility with the present world does not mean, however, that the work simply reproduces existing knowledge, for the wondrous vision is a new vision.[83] It is a glimpse into the possible and the future ("das Mögliche und Zukünftige," 1:61)—the realization of probable reality. As the assimilation of new perception into our consciousness, it is an act of apperception in Leibniz's sense of the term: the process of focusing that is continually underway in the system of monads as they assume varying perspectives.

The "Gemüthes-Bewegung" (1:83, 85, etc.) that accompanies every encounter with the wondrous represents a pleasurable increase in knowledge in that "Wissens-Begierde" is satisfied. "Wissens-Begierde" is the need for new visions that flows out of the *principe interne*, our innate desire ("angebohrene Begierde," 1:61) for possibilities, novelty, and things of the future. Its parallel concept in Leibniz's system is appetition, the source of new perceptual integration. The new and unusual therefore exerts by itself a special power over the mind: "Ist die Materie, die der Poet erwehlet hat, mit einer eigenthümlichen verwundersamen Neuheit begabet, so wird sie das Gemüthe durch ihre eigene Kraft, auch ohne die Hülfe der Kunst, einnehmen und entzücken" (1:293). But these "new things" belong to the possible worlds: "der Verdienst eines Poeten [besteht] vornehmlich in der . . . Erfindung solcher Materien . . . welche vor sich selbst gantz neu, fremd und wunderbar sind, und ohne die Hülfe der Kunst durch ihre eigene Kraft die Gemüther einnehmen und entzücken, von welcher Art alle diejenigen sind, die der Poet aus der Welt der möglichen Dinge mittelst der Erdichtungs-Kraft nach den Regeln des Wahrscheinlichen herholet" (1:294–95). The rules of probability are important because they ensure that the wondrous possibles will not just flash before our eyes as an entertaining diversion but will also be integratable into the existing structure of consciousness. "Was die Erdichtung und Aufstellung gantz neuer Wesen und neuer Gesetze anbelanget, so hat der Poet dießfalls eine grosse Vorsicht und Behutsamkeit zu gebrauchen, daß das Wunderbare nicht ungläublich werde und allen Schein der Wahrheit verliehre. Er muß darum, seine Freyheit zu erdichten, wenigst nach dem Wahne des größten Haufens der Menschen einschräncken, und nichts vorbringen, als was er weiß, daß es schon einigermaaßen in demselben gegründet ist" (1:137). As a Wolffian writing in a period in which a German literary critical terminology was only just emerging, Breitinger uses "Erdichtung" and "Erfindung" interchangeably, but the process he describes is what Wolff had called "Erfindung," the constant interplay between *a priori* intuitions and *a posteriori* comparisons, between "Witz" and "Verstand," between the wondrous and the probable that occurs in the mind of the poet and the recipient alike.

Breitinger takes his possibles more seriously than Gottsched does, because he envisions a more serious and significant function for literature than Gottsched had. In Breitinger's poetics, the confrontation with possible worlds involves the development (*Bildung*) of individual and communal consciousness in the assimilation of probable visions of truth. In Gottsched's system, hypothetical worlds are vehicles for conveying *sententia*. Breitinger is interested in the dynamic relation between poesis and the perfectibility of the world, Gottsched in the replication and transmission of an already existing universal perfection. Breitinger's linking of poetic probability to the "Wahne des größten Haufens der Menschen" has been viewed as an abandonment of poetic truth to relativity. But his reflection on probability is in fact an elaboration of Wolff's "Kunst zu erfinden" in terms of the complex relation between possible truths and established truth, new experience and existing intellective structures, and finally, between poets and their audiences. Hence we turn now to the problem of poetic reception.

3. Poetic Reception and
la vraisemblance historique

German literary historians have tended to view the *Critische Dicht-kunst* exclusively as a "Wirkungspoetik." Breitinger is said to be particularly indebted to Dubos, from whom he adopted the primacy of "feeling" or "sense experience" in aesthetic reception. Wolfgang Bender, author of the "Nachwort" in the Metzler reprint of the *Critische Dichtkunst*, says Breitinger takes from Dubos "die Lehre vom Rührenden," and notes Breitinger's appropriation ("wörtliche Anlehnung") of Dubos's sentence: "S'il est permis de parler ainsi, l'esprit est d'un commerce plus difficile que le coeur" (1.8.63).[1] But Bender is too timid in his estimation, for a considerable portion of the first six chapters of the *Critische Dichtkunst* was—to use the eighteenth-century expression—"stolen" from Dubos.

The precise nature of Breitinger's reliance on Dubos has in fact never been thoroughly examined. In the following pages I attempt to show not only how Breitinger absorbs the neoclassic ideas of Dubos, principally his notion of *la vraisemblance historique*, but also how he transforms them. Neoclassicism, as we have seen in the case of Gottsched, conceives of the recipient as a medium on which nature, or the work, imprints its images. Although Dubos has a far more sophisticated concept of the recipient than Gottsched did, he nonetheless holds to the recipient's essential passivity. Breitinger, on the other hand, envisions a productive role for recipients that is grounded in their intellective participation in the poetic experience. How he arrives at this conception, however, can only be understood by reviewing some of the assumptions of Neoclassicism proper.[2]

Neoclassic Distortions of Aristotle's *Poetics*

The neoclassic concept of reception, that is, the relation between the work and its audience, was determined by the concept of *vraisemblance*, or probability.[3] The popular notion of this relation is based in part on the criticism of the *modernes* (Figure 3). For both the neoclassic *anciens* and the *modernes*, art was the imitation of nature. At issue

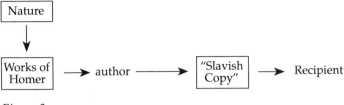

Figure 3.

between them was the definition of nature: the *modernes*, such as Corneille and his nephew Fontenelle, believed that the *anciens* confused "nature" with its depiction by ancient authors, and that the poet would do better to imitate *le vrai* rather than "pagan fictions" or the "merely probable."[4] The conflict is summed up by Boileau in a famous gibe at Corneille in his *Art poétique*:

> Jamais au spectateur n'offrez rien d'incroyable
> Le vrai peut quelque fois n'être pas vraisemblable.[5]

A modernist restatement of this rhyme would have it claim that a believable representation based on convention is preferable to an unbelievable but accurate representation. Indeed the *anciens* also defined the probable as convention, as "tout ce qui est conforme à l'opinion du public."[6] But Boileau is interested less in convention for its own sake than in believability, of which convention can be a means. Credibility is important because without it the poem will miss its (didactic) effect. Thus Boileau continues his rhyme:

> Une merveille absurde est pour moi sans appas:
> L'esprit n'est point ému de ce qu'il ne croit pas.
>
> (339)

For the recipient to be affected, he must believe that what he sees is probable, or like the truth, that is, verisimilar. Neoclassic decorum is based on this:

> Quiconque voit bien l'homme, et, d'un esprit profond,
> De tant de coeurs cachés a pénétré le fond;
> Qui sait bien ce que c'est qu'un prodigue, un avare,
> Un honnête homme, un fat, un jaloux, un bizarre,
> Sur une scène heureuse il peut les étaler,
> Et les faire à nos yeux vivre, agir et parler.
>
> (372)

In addition to the "correct" drawing of character, decorum also in-
cluded the use of historical realism, a notion that French Neoclassi-
cism inherited from Scaliger.[7] Boileau writes:

> Conservez à chacun son propre caractère.
> Des siècles, des pays étudiez les moeurs:
> Les climats font souvent les diverses humeurs.

(347)

Because, however, the overriding concern of the *anciens* was the
probable, and not the true, what could only be at issue in such a
"realism" was whether the poetic depiction appeared to conform to
"les moeurs et les climats"; whether such images actually conformed
to historical reality would be irrelevant. The poetic representation
therefore would not present historical information about a given
country or period but would tend rather to reinforce the recipient's
already defined view of the time and place in question, which he
likely simply viewed as analogous to his own.[8] Any attempted fidelity
to historical truth was of interest not because of the desire to preserve
the integrity of a given epoch, but to assure the acceptance by the
audience of the poet's vision. Such acceptance would follow if the
audience believed that the poet had made a faithful copy of "nature,"
that is, "les temps et les moeurs des personnages."

The essential circularity of this position points out the crux of the
neoclassic concept of *le vraisemblable*. Probability means that recipients
see in the work what both they and the author see in "nature" (how-
ever this latter term may be defined). The corresponding term on the
level of poetic production is "imitation of nature," which assumes an
act of *precise seeing* in which both author and recipient participate.
Reception becomes, in the neoclassic context, a category for explain-
ing the relationship (i.e., functional identity) between poets and their
audience. This relationship is diagrammed in Figure 4.

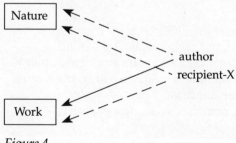

Figure 4.

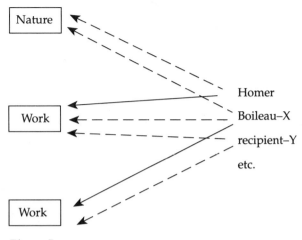

Figure 5.

It should be noted in passing that this identity of position vis-à-vis nature and work also explains, in a somewhat fairer way than in Figure 3, the neoclassic interest in literary models. Such interest is based on the belief that authors are also recipients. The dotted lines in Figures 4 and 5 refer to seeing, or "reception"; the solid lines refer to seeing that ends in production. Both the author and the recipient are in an identical position from which to compare the work (the "imitation of nature") with nature itself. The author's relation to the work is active, the recipient's is passive, but both are engaged in a process of comparing one with the other. A work produced in imitation of another "imitation of nature" (i.e., *imitatio* instead of *mimesis*) could be compared with both nature and with the model, whereby poets would be both the recipient of a previous work and the creator of their own work. To reflect the authorial role of the recipient, Figure 4 could be modified to produce the diagram in Figure 5.

The neoclassic concept of probability, which assumes the mutual participation of author and recipient in an act of precise seeing, was not only shared but radicalized by the *modernes*. This neoclassic version of probability in turn informs Breitinger's notion of "das Wahrscheinliche" and poetic reception. It is therefore necessary to examine in more detail the "original" neoclassic concept of probability in order to trace its subsequent transformation.

The author of *Les Réflexions sur la poétique de ce temps et sur les ouvrages des poètes anciens et modernes*, René Rapin, believes he is faithfully adhering to Aristotle in his discussion of probability:

La vray-semblance sert . . . à donner aux choses que dit le poète un plus grand air de perfection que ne pourroit faire la vérité mesme, quoique la vray-semblance n'en soit que la copie. Car la vérité ne fait les choses que comme elles sont; et la vray-semblance les fait comme elles doivent estre. La vérité est presque toujours défectueuse, par le mélange des conditions singulières, qui la composent. Il ne naist rien au monde qui ne s'éloigne de la perfection de son idée en y naissant. Il faut chercher des originaux et des modèles, dans la vray-semblance et dans les principes universels des choses: où il n'entre rien de matériel et de singulier qui les corrompe. C'est par là que les portraits de l'histoire sont moins parfaits que les portraits de la poésie: que Sophocle qui représente dans ses tragédies les hommes, comme ils doivent estre, est au sentiment d'Aristote, préférable à Euripide qui représente les hommes comme ils sont.

(41)

Nowhere in the *Poetics*, however, does Aristotle say he "prefers" Sophocles. In fact, he says precisely the opposite: Euripides is "the most tragic of the poets" because of his ability to construct plots (cf. *Poetics*, 13.10). Rapin makes this mistake because he (or the tradition out of which he is writing) has conflated two entirely different passages from the *Poetics*: the comparison of Sophocles and Euripides in chapter 25, and the distinction between history and poetry in chapter 9. In chapter 25, Aristotle gives three possible sources for poetic representation: "things as they were or are; or things as they are said and seem to be; or things as they should be" (25.3). Since all of these alternatives are equally usable in poetry, they may all be treated according to probability. Later in chapter 25 Aristotle identifies Euripides with the first, and Sophocles with the third alternative, whereby no judgment is made, contrary to Rapin's assumption, as to whether Sophocles' plots were "more probable" or "more perfect" than those of Euripides.

Rapin likely thought Aristotle was carrying forth his argument from chapter 9, an argument that Rapin nevertheless also fundamentally misunderstands. There Aristotle says that poesis is more "serious" or "philosophic" ($\sigma\pi o\upsilon\delta\alpha\iota\acute{o}\tau\epsilon\rho o\varsigma$), not "more perfect," than history because poesis tells what might happen and history what actually happened (9.3). "What might happen" means what a given sort of man would probably say or do. "What has happened" means what a particular individual has actually said or done (9.4). This does not mean, Aristotle continues, that historical actions may not be used in poesis: "For there is nothing to prevent some actual occurrences being the sort of thing that would probably or inevitably happen, and it is in virtue of *that* that he the [poet] is their 'maker' [ποιητής]" (9.10, emphasis in original). Rapin, however, assumes that Aristotle intended a radical break between historical "things" ("les choses comme elles sont") and poetic "things" ("les choses comme elles doivent estre"). Moreover, Rapin endows his distinction with a sort of metaphysical cast, implying that "la copie" actually "returns" the object of poetic representation to its more perfect original "ideal" form, which it lost through its birth into the world. Yet the notion that singular material objects are "corruptions" of universal forms is a thoroughly Plotinian concept and has nothing to do with Aristotle's distinction in the *Poetics* between the particular and the general.[9]

It is significant that Rapin's interpretation of chapter 25 does not represent an idiosyncratic reading of the text. André Dacier, for example, has this to say about the passage in question:

> C'est à mon avis, le sens de ce passage qui est tres remarquable, en ce qu'il nous apprend, que du temps même de Sophocle & d'Euripide, il y avoit des gens qui trouvoient que le premier flatoit trop ses principaux personnages, & que l'autre les flatoit trop peu. En effet Sophocle tâchoit de rendre ses imitations parfaites, en suivant toûjours bien plus ce qu'une belle Nature étoit capable de faire, que ce qu'elle faisoit. Au lieu qu'Euripide ne travailloit qu'à les rendre semblables, en consultant d'avantage ce que cette même Nature faisoit que ce qu'elle étoit capable de faire.[10]

Although Dacier does not mention the "vray-semblable" in Rapin's sense (Dacier's "semblable" means something like "copied naturalistically"), his understanding of chapter 25 matches Rapin's in two respects. First, Sophocles' imitations were "parfaites" because they copied the ideal ("la belle Nature") rather than the existent. Second, and most important, the categories "things-that-might-be" and "things-that-are" refer to two—separate—states of Nature (which can be copied), and not, as in Aristotle, to two kinds of representation (i.e., history or poetry) whose objects may, but need not, coincide.

The most important implication of the radical break between historical "things" and poetic "things" is the transformation of probability from a quality of the representation into a quality of the "thing" represented. Whereas for Aristotle probability results from the way the plot is constructed, for Rapin it is a quality inherent in a particular object that renders it appropriate for poetic depiction. Rapin's syntax betrays as much: "la vray-semblance sert à donner *aux choses*. . . ."[11]

But his deviation from Aristotelian probability is most clearly revealed in a later passage of his *Réflexions* in which he discusses what he finds to be "ce qu'il y a de plus grand et de plus noble dans la poésie" (71), that is, the epic.

Although Rapin had earlier declared "vray-semblance" to be that which gives poesis "un plus grand air de perfection," he curiously neglects probability when discussing the abilities of authors of epic, "des plus parfaits génies" (72). They have, he says, "un discernement si exquis, une si parfaite connaissance de la langue . . . une méditation si profonde . . . "—the list continues for about six to eight lines—but nowhere are they said to have the ability to make plots. In fact, plot and probability are totally divorced in his conception:

> Le prix de la poésie heroique est encore plus grand par sa matière et par sa fin, *que par la forme*: elle ne parle que de rois et de princes; elle ne donne des lecons qu'aux Grands pour gouverner les peuples; et elle propose l'idée d'une vertu bien plus parfaite que l'histoire laquelle ne propose la vertu qu'imparfaite, comme elle est dans les particuliers: et la poésie la propose sans aucune imperfection, et comme elle doit estre en général. Ce qui a fait dire à Aristote que la poésie est une meilleure école de la vertu que la philosophie mesme: parce qu'elle va plus droit à la perfection, par la vray-semblance, que la philosophie n'y va par la vérité, parce que le poète ne rend jamais raison de ce qu'il dit, comme fait le philosophe, mais il la fait sentir, sans le dire.
>
> (74, my emphasis)

Rapin here again probably has in mind the sentences from chapter 9 of the *Poetics*, in which Aristotle states that poetry is more philosophic than history because poetry reveals the causes of events, whereas history (i.e., chronology) can only record the sequence of particular moments and not their connection (cf. 9.11). Rapin correctly associates Aristotle's notion of philosophic activity with the study of causes, but he confuses completely the point of Aristotle's comparison of history and poetry. He therefore locates the general not in the articulation of causes, that is, not in the plot, but rather in the identification between poet and recipient, in which the recipient feels ("sentir") the poet's "raison," or meaning.[12] In view of Rapin's already demonstrated misapprehension of chapter 9, one must wonder whether he was merely trying to "improve" on Aristotle's text, or whether he understood that he was asserting the exact opposite of what Aristotle meant. At any rate, his departure from the Aristotelian concept of probability could hardly be more profound.

Whether Rapin "violates" the Aristotelian meaning is less interesting than how he modifies the earlier concepts for neoclassic purposes. When probability ceases to be the essential element of plot, and becomes instead a quality of the objects of poetic representation, its definition becomes arbitrary, and its presence or absence in the poetic work a matter of individual preference. Rapin defines the probable as "tout ce qui est conforme à l'opinion du public," whereby "public" is of course not to be confused with "peuple" (39). "L'opinion public" defers to the example set by the "Anciens," who knew best how to depict "de grandes pensées et . . . de grands sentimens" (46). That Rapin did not appreciate the arbitrary nature of this definition is clear from his attempt to ground the rules of decorum in what he viewed as an ultimately inscrutable universal: "le coeur de l'homme." [13]

The modernist attack on the neoclassic position did not challenge the conception of the probable itself, but only its content. That is, the *modernes* continued to view the probable as a quality of the objects of poetic representation, but they defined this quality differently. In his *Réflexions sur la poétique* of 1691, Fontenelle echoes Aristotle's history-poesis distinction, but his interpretation departs as much from Aristotelian thinking as had Rapin's. "Le vrai et le vraisemblable sont assez différens. Le vrai est tout ce qui est; le vraisemblable est ce que nous jugeons qui peut être, et nous n'en jugeons que par de certaines idées qui résultent de nos expériences ordinaires. Ainsi, le vrai a infiniment plus d'étendue que le vraisemblable, puisque le vraisemblable n'est qu'une petite portion du vrai, conforme à la plupart de nos expériences." [14] Fontenelle substitutes "nos expériences" for Rapin's "l'opinion public," with the important result that the object of poetic representation (i.e., not the purpose but the thing), the probable, becomes historicized. This means that Rapin's abstract idealized universals, "les choses comme ils doivent être," become a series of "concrete" (i.e., already seen and felt) particulars: "ce qui . . . peut être." Fontenelle then identifies the probable with the possible, by simply leaping from one term to the other, whereby "possible" is also historicized. Thus, for the possible he very nearly repeats the definition he had just given the probable. The possible is that which we have already seen (experienced), and therefore believe can happen again: "Il faut, pour être reçu, que [le vraisemblable] se rapporte à nos idées communes. Incertains que nous sommes, et avec beaucoup de raison, sur l'infinie possibilité des choses, nous n'admettons pour possibles que celles qui ressemblent à ce que nous voyons souvent" (22). [15] The most rigorously probable representations are "extrêmement connu" (23).

Fontenelle's poetics introduce a "quantification" of probability: the most probable literary representation describes events that we have seen the most often, and therefore determine to be the "most possible" or lifelike.[16] Moreover, Fontenelle does not limit "nos expériences" to what any given individual has witnessed. The term is applied as well to the cumulative experience of an entire culture manifest in its historical record. "Nos expériences" then takes on the double meaning of "how much of the historical record (i.e., witnesses of past events) has been witnessed (i.e., read or heard) by present individuals." The best candidates for poetic representation are "des sujets connus," such as the life of Pompey. Less satisfying but still acceptable objects are the stories "peu connu," which should nonetheless be "du moins vrais et historiques, comme le Cid et Polyeucte." As a last resort, the poet should use stories where at least the names are historical, if nothing else (22).

Fontenelle's use of "nos expériences" (or history) as the criterion for evaluating poetic probability could not destroy, as he undoubtedly hoped it would, the attachment to literary convention among the *anciens*. His critique was not fundamental, and his notion of probability merely replaces ancient with modern convention, as is evident from his definition of decorum: "si les personnages ne sont pas connus par l'histoire, les charactères doivent être pris sur l'idée que l'on a communément de leur condition, de leur âge, de leur pays, etc." (23). On its face the statement is simple enough: if no specific historical information is available on which to base the poetic characterization (or if the characters are fictional, which means the same thing for Fontenelle anyway), one should draw them according to generally held views about their class, period, country, and so forth. What Fontenelle fails to discuss, but which is already implicit in his own definition of probability, is the source of this "l'idée que l'on a communément." The syntax of the passage suggests that the characters are drawn either historically or according to a vague "l'idée," whereby the idea appears almost *ex nihilo*. Indeed when this passage is taken in context with the entire essay, Fontenelle does not seem to realize, in the truly "modern" sense, that the idea can only be a product of history, even if it is ultimately based on information that is inaccurate or incomplete. Thus he eventually reverts to a completely neoclassic conception of decorum, based on a "timeless" standard, namely that of the present.[17]

A far more radical historicization of probability than Fontenelle himself attempted was carried out by Dubos and, later, by Breitinger. The *Reflexions critiques sur la poësie et sur la peinture* of 1719 attacks

Fontenelle at certain specific points (though his name is usually not mentioned). These occasional disagreements with Fontenelle do not hinder Dubos, however, from conducting his discussion of poetic probability with the same terms that Fontenelle had used. "La premiere regle que les Peintres & les Poëtes soient tenus d'observer en traitant le sujet qu'ils ont choisi, c'est de n'y rien mettre qui soit contre la vrai-semblance. Les hommes ne sçauroient êtres gueres touché d'un évenement qui leur paroît sensiblement impossible" (1.28.236). In keeping with the neoclassic tradition, Dubos does not refer probability to the plot but to the "thing" (in this case, "un évenement"), which is "put into" the work ("y mettre"). Dubos's full definition of the probable-possible reveals his points of contact and his differences both with Fontenelle and with the Aristotelian base of ideas that is ultimately his source. "Un fait vrai-semblable est un fait possible dans les circonstances où on le fait arriver. Ce qui est impossible en ces circonstances ne sçauroit paroître vrai-semblable. Je n'entens pas ici par impossible ce qui est au-dessus des forces humaines, mais ce qui paroît impossible, même en se prêtant à toutes les suppositions que le Poëte sçauroit faire" (1.28.237). Dubos appears to define probability in terms of a (vaguely Aristotelian) set of circumstances, or plot. But unlike Aristotle, the poet in Dubos's account is not making the circumstances, but placing ("fait arriver") the poetic event ("un fait") within a set of already existing circumstances. The passage continues: "Comme le Poëte est en droit d'exiger de nous que nous trouvions possible tout ce qui paroissoit possible dans les tems où il met sa Scene, et où il transporte en quelque façon ses Lecteurs: nous ne pouvons point, par exemple, l'accuser de manquer à la vrai-semblance, en supposant que Diane enleve Iphigenie au moment qu'on alloit la sacrifier, pour la transporter dans la Tauride. L'évenement étoit possible, suivant la Theologie des Grecs de ce tems-la" (1.28.237–38).

The statement might be construed as simply one more neoclassic reference to decorum based on "les temps et les lieux" such as can be found in Boileau, Rapin, Pope, and any number of others. Dubos, however, means here something rather different. Neoclassicism in its more trivial form (Rapin) locates probability in "l'opinion public" (which usually means "l'opinion des Grecs" as intepreted by the French critic); Fontenelle's version of neoclassic probability is based on what we think is possible given what we have ourselves seen or what we know about the past. Probability for Dubos is based on what the *past epoch itself* (or the foreign culture) thought was possible or usual.

For example, when Dubos takes his turn with one of the *topoi* of early eighteenth-century criticism, the issue of whether Homer was "right" to show Hector conversing with his horses, Dubos fills six pages of his book (2.37.546–52) with anecdotal historical evidence showing that conversations with animals, and especially with horses, were completely unexceptional in Phrygia, where Hector was raised, and in "l'Asie" (Dubos's term is a bit general here), where the horse conversation in the *Iliad* is set. In an earlier passage, Dubos had countered another criticism of Homer with the same kind of argument. "Si les Heros d'Homere ne se battent pas en duel aussi-tôt qu'ils se sont querellez, c'est qu'ils n'avoient pas sur le point d'honneur le sentiment des Gots ni de leurs pareils" (2.37.542).[18]

Dubos creates a new category of probability, which one might call the relative probable, and which Dubos himself refers to as "la vraisemblance historique" (1.28.242; 29.253; etc.). In effect, he has superimposed Aristotle's concept of plot onto history itself. In order to decide on the probability of a given part of a work, "un fait," we do not refer this part back to the structure of the work but to the historical "plot," the historical context of which it is supposed to be a partial depiction.

> Je sçais bien que le faux est quelquefois plus vrai-semblable que le vrai. Mais nous ne reglons pas notre croïance touchant les faits sur leur vrai-semblance métaphysique, ou sur le pied de leur possibilité: c'est sur la vrai-semblance historique. Nous n'examinons pas ce qui devoit arriver plus probablement, mais ce que les témoins necessaires, ce que les Historiens racontent; & *c'est leur récit & non pas la vrai-semblance qui détermine notre croïance.* Ainsi nous ne croïons pas l'évenement qui est le plus vrai-semblable & le plus possible, mais celui qu'ils nous disent être veritablement arrivé. *Leur déposition étant la regle* de notre croïance sur les faits, ce qui peut être contraire à leur déposition ne sçauroit paroître vrai-semblable.
>
> (1.28.242, my emphasis)[19]

The "synonyms" for Aristotle's terminus "plot" are "récit" and "déposition."

Dubos does not provide us with a fully developed "modern" reflection on historiography. He does not, for example, question the interpretive bias of the historian, and the eventual discrepancy between "facts" and "interpretation." Fundamental skepticism concerning the possibility of even distinguishing "facts" and "interpretation" is not present in his treatise. He simply accepts the historical record for what it is: our only source of knowledge about the past, which we can and should believe. Given this assumption, the task of the critic is to decide on the probability of literary works (or their elements, it does not much matter) based on the historical context of the period in which they were written or which they are intended to portray ("paint").[20]

In keeping with this task, the *Reflexions critiques* often more resembles an encyclopedia of early eighteenth-century historical knowledge and anthropological lore than a treatise on poetics. Imitation of nature seems to mean for Dubos imitation of history. As a result, Dubos refers to historical accuracy in paintings (e.g., characters should be drawn in surroundings appropriate to their period) as "la vrai-semblance *poëtique*" (cf. 1.30.255). Presumably this is merely a transfer of the term "decorum" from literature to a visual art, and indeed poetic probability—that is, the probability of the literary work—is called "la vrai-semblance historique."

Dubos and Breitinger

The presence of the *Reflexions critiques* in the *Critische Dichtkunst* is far more pervasive than has previously been recognized. Occasionally Breitinger will acknowledge that a passage comes from "der scharf-sinnige Herr Dübos." At other times he introduces his borrowing with "man hat angemercket, daß . . . ," while on still other occasions he simply uses what Dubos wrote as if it were his own. Whole pages may be excised, or Breitinger may insert an isolated sentence.[21] More important than how much Breitinger might have taken from Dubos, however, is the question of what he did with what he took.

The sixth chapter of the *Critische Dichtkunst*, "Von dem Wunderbaren und dem Wahrscheinlichen," has two main divisions. The first part is a theoretical reflection; the second contains commentaries on literary examples drawn from both ancient and modern poets. This first section is what most concerns us here. It is written partially in Breitinger's words, but approximately thirty percent of the text is adapted from the chapter on poetic probability by Dubos that we have just examined.

Breitinger's definition of the probable appears to be his own interpretation of or variation on the definition given by Dubos. He shares with Dubos the notion of probability as historical possibility, that is, as determined by what we know to be true or to have been true under certain circumstances. "Ich verstehe durch das Wahrscheinliche in der Poesie alles, was nicht von einem andern widerwärtigen Begriff, oder für wahr angenommenen Satze ausgeschlossen wird, was nach unsren Begriffen eingerichtet zu seyn, mit unsrer Erkenntniß und dem Wesen der Dinge und dem Laufe der Natur übereinzukommen, scheinet; hiemit alles, was in gewissen Umständen und unter gewissen Bedingungen nach dem Urtheil der Verständigen möglich ist, und keinen Widerspruch in sich hat" (1:134).

Breitinger differs from Dubos by generalizing the field of objects available for representation. Thus while Dubos was interested primarily in historical circumstances, Breitinger gives "Wesen der Dinge" and "Lauf der Natur" as poetic objects; whereas Dubos was concerned with "ce que les Historiens racontent," Breitinger says we should align ourselves with "dem Urtheil der Verständigen." A cursory reading of Breitinger's definition might suggest that he is reverting to exactly that category of probability that Dubos had just rejected: "la vrai-semblance métaphysique." But this is not what Breitinger means at all: "Man muß also das Wahre des Verstandes und das Wahre der Einbildung wohl unterscheiden; es kan dem Verstand etwas falsch zu seyn düncken, das die Einbildung für wahr annimmt: Hingegen kan der Verstand etwas für wahr erkennen, welches der Phantasie als ungläublich vorkömmt" (1:138). Breitinger is commenting here on the same problem in Aristotle—the "impossible probable"—that had moved Dubos to distinguish between metaphysical and historical probability.[22] But Breitinger changes one highly significant term. The sentence just quoted continues: ". . . und darum ist gewiß, daß das Falsche bisweilen wahrscheinlicher ist, als das Wahre. Das Wahre des Verstandes gehöret für die Weltweisheit, hingegen eignet der Poet sich das Wahre der Einbildung zu" (1:139). The substitution Breitinger makes is the exchange of "la vrai-semblance historique" for "das Wahre der Einbildung."

In context, this seems not so crucial. Breitinger had, on his previous page, provided a list of the standards used by the imagination in making its determinations about the true, the false, and the probable. He calls these standards the "Grundsätze des Wahnes" ("Wahn" here in its older meaning of "Meinung," "Glaube"), of which there are five: historical witness; sense impressions; tales generally accepted by the common people ("dem großen Haufen") over several generations; exaggerations or understatements (i.e., ones that are acceptable); and events that have happened before and can therefore [!] happen again (1:138). The list appears to be a simple categorization of Dubos's criteria for poetic probability. But Breitinger is radicalizing Dubos's concept of historical knowledge still further by applying it not just to poetic probability, but to a general psychological phenomenon, that is, the development and absorption of knowledge over time. Here we must compare briefly Breitinger's purpose with that of Neoclassicism proper.

The sharp distinction between the mind and the heart, expressed in Breitinger's terms "Verstandeswahrheit" and "das Wahre der Einbildung," runs throughout Neoclassicism. Its clearest formulation is perhaps Pascal's famous analysis in the *Pensées* of "l'esprit de géométrie" and "l'esprit de finesse."[23] Dubos refers to the split in the sentence quoted in the opening paragraph of this chapter and repeated so often in Breitinger commentaries because it is thought that this was one of Breitinger's few exact borrowings.

For Rapin, poetry was able to approach the workings of the heart in a way superior to philosophy, even though this approach proved to be based on little more than a quasi-mystical identification by the recipient with the poet's meaning. Thus his attitude toward "la coeur de l'homme" remained rather primitive, as is evident not only from his "mysticism" and his reliance on ancient depictions of "de grands sentimens," but also from his inability to explain the attraction of the poetic wondrous in any terms other than the perverse curiosity of the socially inferior: "Tout ce qui paroist incroyable est d'un grand ragoust à la curiosité du peuple. Car le peuple . . . n'a que du mépris pour ce qui luy paroist commun et ordinaire: il n'aime que ce qui est prodigieux. Mais les sages ne peuvent rien souffrir d'incroyable" (38–39). Breitinger makes an observation containing deceptively similar diction but expressing a quite different intent: "Die Verwunderung und die Leichtgläubigkeit sind Töchter der Unwissenheit. Daher ließt der rohe und unwissende Pöbel gemeiniglich die abentheurlichsten Erzehlungen von Hexen, Zauberern, weisen Frauen, Gespenstern, und die Romanen von den irrenden Rittern, mit dem größten Ergetzen, welches nicht geschehen könnte, wenn dieselben ihm ungläublich und unwahrscheinlich vorkämen" (1:140). Breitinger's nearly Socratic view at this point in explaining the appeal of the wondrous is inherited from Dubos: people are receptive to "lies" because they think, based on their experience (class, education, etc.), that they are true.

Dubos himself tells us in his opening chapter that he wants to explain the paradox of the pleasure we take in artistic or theatrical representations of sadness and horror, and our fascination in viewing pictures of things that would be otherwise repugnant. In addition to this broad psychological investigation ("rendre compte à chacun de son approbation & de ses degoûts," 1.1.3), Dubos also sets himself the task of explaining ("en Philosophe," 1.1.4) why paintings and poetic works have such an effect on us. The two issues are of course not isolated in his account, and his argument goes something like this: human beings need and want to be constantly stimulated. They would rather place themselves in actual danger than be forced to live without those experiences that excite the "movements" of the heart. Because they have discovered, however, that the arts can provide the desired stimulation without the dangers and consequences presented by the sometimes horrible experiences of life, they allow themselves to become engaged by artistic representations, knowing that they thereby fulfill their needs without having to take the risks of real experience. The remainder of Dubos's treatise appears to be an amplification of this explanation. His views on poetic probability *qua* historical possibility are presented in the context of the question: what kinds of representations are most likely to be believed, hence most likely to *move the heart*? It is easy to see the connection of this issue to his psychological argument. Because art is intended as a kind of replacement for the stimulus of "real life," the closer it is to historical reality (without being this reality—because it must remain representation to remain harmless), the better it will fulfill its intended function.[24]

Dubos's argument is based on an assumption about human nature, namely, that the movements of the heart are essential to existence. Breitinger accepts this assumption, but he transforms it, and the nature of this transformation indicates that he actually has considerable differences with Dubos despite his massive borrowings. A comparison of specific textual passages is necessary to indicate what Breitinger did with what "der scharfsinnige Herr Dübos" offered him.

The third chapter of the *Critische Dichtkunst*, "Von der Nachahmung der Natur," is pieced together from portions of the opening twelve (approximately) chapters of the first volume of the *Reflexions critiques* in which Dubos sets forth his thinking on the topic of imitation. As might be expected from his interest in the pleasurable sensations aroused by art, Dubos quotes (1.3.28) the often quoted passage from chapter 4 of the *Poetics* in which Aristotle explains the pleasure we take in viewing likenesses of objects from reality. Dubos does not include, however, Aristotle's explanation of why this should be the case, but only those opening lines in which Aristotle states the phenomenon (roughly: looking at likenesses of things in themselves painful to see causes us pleasure). Dubos then provides his own commentary: "Le plaisir qu'on sent à voir les imitations que les Peintres & les Poëts sçavent faire des objets qui auroient excité en nous des passions dont la réalité nous auroit été à charge, est un plaisir pur. Il n'est pas suivi des inconveniens dont les émotions serieuses qui auroient été causées par l'objet même, seroient accompagnées" (1.3.28). Breitinger quotes (1:69) the same limited version of Aristotle, and paraphrases Dubos by saying that "die strengen Leidenschaften" are made "erträglich, ja angenehm." Dubos then launches into a series of examples, half of which Breitinger omits. Breitinger picks up the text again at Dubos's mention of the death of Phaedra ("Une mort telle que la mort de Phédre . . . ," 1.3.29, and "Eine Art Todes, wie der Phedra war . . . ," 1:69), and continues translating this lengthy example to the end ("l'affliction n'est, pour ainsi dire, que sur la superficie de notre coeur . . . etc.," 1.3.29, and "Die Betrübniß liget so zu sagen nur an dem Rande unsers Hertzens . . . etc.," 1:70). But whereas Dubos then wants to go on with what is little more than a restatement of points already covered ("Nous écoutons donc avec plaisir les hommes les plus malheureux . . . ," 1.3.30), Breitinger interrupts Dubos in order to raise another issue in his own text: "Fraget man nun, woher und auf welche Weise dieses Ergetzen entstehe, welche die geschickte Nachahmung der Kunst durch ihre eigenthümliche Kraft zuwege bringet, so ist die Haupt-Ursache davon diejenige, welche Aristoteles im vierten Cap. seiner Poetik angiebt, weil man in einer geschickten und glücklichen Nachahmung . . . allezeit etwas neues innen wird" (1:70–71).[25] Breitinger then quotes in full the passage from 1.11.23–25 of the *Rhetoric* where Aristotle mentions art works in connection with the learning process that occurs when likenesses are examined.[26]

It would be too simple to claim that Breitinger favors "didactic" art and Dubos "entertaining" art, for Breitinger inserts Dubos's major statements about pleasure and artistic effect into the *Critische Dichtkunst*. Moreover, Breitinger's notion of the learning process cannot really be described in terms of a simple "sugar-coated pill" didacticism, nor in terms of the $\dot{\alpha}\pi\alpha\theta\iota\alpha$ ideal of Renaissance Stoicism. In introducing the passage from the *Rhetoric*, Breitinger says that likenesses of objects arouse a thought process in us ("dem Geist Anlaß zu Ueberlegungen und Betrachtungen giebt," 1:71), a process that is the centerpiece of his poetic theory. In order to appreciate fully his differences with Dubos on this issue, we must look at one more crucial "theft" from the *Reflexions critiques*, and Breitinger's treatment of it.

The poetics of Dubos are based on "historical probability" and the possibility of vicarious experience through art. I have already pointed out the complementarity of these positions. A corollary to them that Dubos mentions in different formulations throughout the *Reflexions critiques* is that the imitation of an object will have a weaker effect on us than that object itself would have had. Breitinger uses one of these passages in his own argument in his chapter on imitation: "Ich weiß zwar wohl, daß sich zwischen dem Eindruck, welchen die Natur durch die Gegenwart ihrer Urbilder auf das Gemüthe würcket, und demjenigen Eindruck, welchen auch die geschickteste Nachahmung der Kunst verursachet, allezeit welcher Unterschied befindet, aber dieses nicht in Ansehung der Art des Eindruckes, sondern in Ansehung seiner Kraft" (1:64).[27] The idea appears to combine Plotinian notions with Renaissance Neoplatonist aesthetics: the procession "outward" from the One into the absolute multiplicity of base matter is also a field of force growing ever weaker as it emanates out of the ultimate source of power, (as this source "overflows" from pure potentiality into intellection, soul, body, and, eventually, into matter). Each "level" or "degree" of emanation is a weaker form or "copy" of the previous degree. The work of art, as a material "copy" of the original object, is more removed from "reality" (the ultimate Reality being the source of power, the One) than the object is, and will exert on our minds less force ("elle est moins fort"—Dubos) than the object itself would have.[28]

Now, Dubos had predicated his entire theory of vicarious emotion on precisely this point, and Breitinger follows him in this—a certain part of the way. Continuing where the previously quoted passage ended, he says, again translating Dubos: "denn da die Gegenstände der Natur eine wahre Würcklichkeit haben, so muß ihre Würckung auch strenger, ernsthafter, und dauerhafter seyn, als die Würckung des nachgeahmten Bildes" (1:64).[29] This is a quasi-metaphysical reason (i.e., based on the structure of nature); then comes (Dubos's) psychological application of the principle to art: "und da ihre Absicht ist, durch diese nachgeahmten Rührungen zu belustigen, so ist nothwendig, daß ihre Eindrücke in einem geringeren Grade streng und dauerhaft seyn . . . indem alles Widrige und Unangenehme in den Gemüthes-Bewegungen von der Heftigkeit und Dauer derselben entstehet" (1:65). That is, the positive benefits of vicarious experience would be impossible if the effects of art were as strong as or stronger than those of reality. Breitinger then "interrupts" Dubos and presents his own interpretation of the discrepancy between the effect of the imitation and that of the object imitated:

> Unter den Mahlern ist denn derjenige der geschickteste Meister, der so lebhafte und entzükende Schildreyen verfertigt, daß die Zuseher sich eine Weile bereden, sie sehen das Urbild selbst ge-

genwärtig vor Augen. . . . Und unter den poetischen Mahlern verdienet ebenfalls derjenige den ersten Platz, der uns durch seine lebhaften und sinnlichen Vorstellungen so angenehm einnehmen und berücken kan, daß wir eine Zeitlang vergessen, wo wir sind, und ihm mit unserer Einbildungs-Kraft willig an den Ort folgen, wohin er uns durch die Kraft seiner Vorstellungen versetzen will.

(1:65)

The passage apparently merely amplifies Dubos's point that those imitations are the most successful that have a strong effect, that move (in Dubos's sense: stir up passions in) the recipient. But the passage conflicts with Dubos's belief in the superiority of painting over poetry.[30] Breitinger is leading in another direction altogether. "Die Nachahmung hat in der That mehr Kraft, die Aufmercksamkeit der Leute zu unterstützen, als die Natur selbst. . . . Die Copie ziehet uns stärcker an sich, als das Original" (1:72).

This is a reversal of "his" original position (copied from Dubos) that imitations exert *less* force on the recipient than the object imitated. The very few pages between that original position and its reversal contain the two quotations from Aristotle and Breitinger's comments on them, which have already been discussed. Breitinger apparently wants to modify the position of Dubos into a more "Aristotelian" one (a problem taken up shortly), and it is highly significant that his reversal follows directly after his citation of those central passages from Aristotle on imitation and learning that Dubos omitted from his own discourse.[31] Moreover, Breitinger appears to be actually responding to Dubos inasmuch as his reversal is yet another "stolen" direct translation—but of a position Dubos had rhetorically set up to refute.[32]

One need not, however, rely on this particular section of the *Critische Dichtkunst* to document Breitinger's departure from Dubos. It is more evident in Breitinger's first chapter, "Vergleichung der Mahler-Kunst und der Dicht-Kunst," in which he immediately sets out his own differences with the French critic from whom he took so much. Dubos was right, Breitinger says (1:15–16), to show in chapter 40 of his first volume that painting has a more immediate effect on the recipient because it works on the eye. But poetry is superior to painting precisely because it works more "slowly" than painting, and therefore produces images that are infinitely more complex: "So ist in der Poesie alles das Ergetzen, welches die andern Sinnen nur einzeln gewähren können, zusammen vereinet. Der Poet mahlet nicht für das Auge allein, sondern auch für die übrigen Sinnen" (1:19). Hence, whereas Dubos is interested in the various implications of art as spectacle, Breitinger is interested in literature as a method of generating knowledge, although not simply using the "sugar-coated pill"—which could not produce knowledge anyway but only transfer it from poet to recipient.

The generation of knowledge is linked in Breitinger's account to the stronger effect on the mind of the imitation of an object than the object itself. This emerges in what must be one of the longest sentences of the entire *Critische Dichtkunst*:

> Denn indem dieser künstliche Mahler mit einem jeden Worte, als mit einem neuen Pinsel-Zuge, sein Gemählde in der Phantasie des Lesers vollführet, und immer einen Begriff an den andern hinzusezet, so läßt er demselben keine Freyheit, mit flüchtigem und ungewissem Gemüths-Auge müssig herumzuschweifen, oder sich in der Vermischung des Mannigfaltigen zu verirren; sondern er bindet seine Aufmercksamkeit auf das Absonderliche, dessen künstliche Verknüpfung er ihm der Ordnung nach vorweiset, auch zuweilen kurtze, aber nützliche Unterrichte[33] miteinfliessen läßt, wodurch nothwendig Licht und Klarheit in dem Begriff entstehen muß, und auf diese Weise bleibet er allezeit meister, den Eindruck, den jeder Zug seiner Schilderey verursachen soll, auf denjenigen Grad zu erhöhen, und auf die Weise zu mässigen, wie es seiner Haupt-Absicht vorträglich seyn kan.

(1:22–23)

In this long passage the poet is said to transform the manifold and disparate elements of perceived reality into a unique whole: "das Absonderliche." This is fundamentally different from Rapin's "purification" of experience by the work, or from Dacier's depiction of "la belle Nature." For where the neoclassic process of idealization meant the exclusion of some perceptions, Breitinger means the organization of perception.[34] The poet provides, and the recipient participates in, the ordering of the elements of reality impinging on the senses at any given time, thereby creating/receiving a more carefully focused perspective ("Haupt-Absicht"/"Bindung der Aufmercksamkeit") than reality itself provides.[35] Thus whereas Dubos argues for vivid seeing (aroused by the painting or poem) as a means of simple stimulation, Breitinger argues for vivid seeing as a means of structuring experience.

This would appear to be an eminently Aristotelian undertaking. But Aristotle was not really interested in whether we saw the imitation of an object "more vividly" than we would see the object itself. He does not discuss the relative strength of the effect on the viewer of the imitation versus that of the object imitated. In short, he does not quantify the relationship between the imitation and the object because the imitation was for him not *of the object*: it referred to a *class* of objects. Breitinger's passage might, however, be interpreted in another, actually more obvious, Aristotelian sense: the poem as a representation of order, corresponding to Aristotle's concept of plot. But here again, a crucial difference remains. The order presented by Breitinger is not one of plot, with causally connected episodes, but the order of *things* viewed in nature. This is his neoclassic preoccupation.

A more likely candidate than Aristotle as a possible philosophic source for this passage would be Pascal, whose "esprit de finesse" seems remarkably well represented here. The dilemma posed by the mass of particulars of experience in which one becomes so easily lost ("sich verirren") is resolved by the artist with the intentional representation ("Haupt-Absicht"), which would allow the recipient via the poetic representation to come to terms with the multiplicity. As Pascal observes about the "esprit de finesse," or, we might say, about the artistic mind and the manifold perceptions it confronts: "Les principes sont dans l'usage commun et devant les yeux de tout le monde. On n'a que faire de tourner la tête, ni de se faire violence; il n'est question que d'avoir bonne vue, mais il faut l'avoir bonne; car les principes sont si déliés et en si grand nombre, qu'il est presque impossible qu'il n'en échappe."[36] Pascal's "bonne vue" would correspond to the artist's insight and subsequent representation, the "Haupt-Absicht." An important point in Pascal's description of the artistic-intuitive mind is the effortlessness ("ni de se faire violence") and immediacy with which it can, indeed must, grasp the particulars before it. Pascal elaborates this aspect of immediacy as his reflection progresses: "On les voit à peine, on les sent plutôt qu'on ne les voit; on a des peines infinies à les faire sentir à ceux qui ne les sentent pas d'eux-mêmes: ce sont choses tellement délicates et si nombreuses, qu'il faut un sens bien délicat et bien net pour les sentir. . . . Il faut tout d'un coup voir la chose d'un seul regard, et non pas par progrès de raisonnement, au moins jusqu'à un certain degré" (9–10). If we may transfer or apply this description to artistic production and reception, the significant points here are, first, that the intuitive insight, or merging of the particulars, is felt, not seen or visualized; and, second, that the insight occurs in an instant: "pas par progrès de raisonnement." In effect, Pascal is offering here the "classic" statement of neoclassic pessimism. It is indeed considerably more interesting than, say, Rapin's statements on poetic insight, but it captures none-theless the same belief in the essential inscrutability of experience—even for the intuitive mind itself, which grasps the particulars, to be sure, but which cannot articulate their connection.

There is, therefore, an important point of disagreement between Pascal and Breitinger, resembling Breitinger's disagreement with Dubos. It is the insistence on the intellective nature of the aesthetic insight as expressed by the words: "immer einen Begriff an den andern hinzusezet," "Verknüpfung," "Ordnung," "Licht," "Klarheit"—Cartesian termini in part, but also Leibnizian.[37] In order to understand in its entirety the creative process suggested by Breitinger, we may recur to the process of intellective integration elaborated by Leibniz, carried forth by Wolff, and described in the previous chapter in terms of *Erfindung*. There the process was explained as the poet's production of possible worlds. Now the model can be applied to Breitinger's notion of poetic reception. This in turn may clarify the nature and implications of the identity that exists for Breitinger between production and reception.

Breitinger's most important statements on poetic reception occur in the chapter "Von dem Wunderbaren und dem Wahrscheinlichen." On the basis of what he says there, and elsewhere in the *Critische Dichtkunst*, we may diagram the process of reception as an extension of the Leibnizian-Wolffian model of intellective integration (Figure 6). Breitinger's definition of these terms displays a high degree of correlation to the Leibnizian model. Starting at the bottom, "das Falsche" is that which is perceived as a contradiction to the present perceptual order: "Zudem ist das Falsche, und in gewissen Absichten Unmögliche keiner Nachahmung fähig, es ist ein Zero, ein Nichts, wovon der Verstand nichts begreiffen kan; und die Natur kan nichts widersprechendes hervorbringen" (1:63). The false corresponds to those possibles that are not (and may never be) compossible. It does not admit of representation, that is, it will never move from simple "petites perceptions" to perception. Because Breitinger is talking about a metaphysical process (i.e., about the process inherent in nature), the inability of the recipient to assimilate "das Falsche" is due not to its attempted but in fact highly improbable presentation in some poetic works, but to the nature of "das Falsche" itself. "Das Falsche" can be assimilated neither by the poet, nor by the recipient, for identical reasons. Attempted representations of it, such as in overly fantastical works, do not count as poesis; they show the improbable, which is impossible, because it lies beyond the "threshold" of compossibility and intelligibility (cf. 1:135–36).

The wondrous is defined in opposite terms from those used to de-

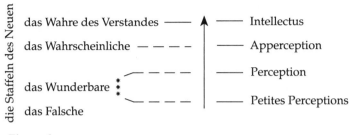

Figure 6.

fine the probable. But it is important to note that Breitinger makes the probable and the wondrous relative opposites and not absolute opposites. That is, they are the end points of a series of "Staffeln" that has "verschiedene Grade" (1:129 and 140). The wondrous is "die äusserste Staffel" (1:130) of a continuum of probability that Breitinger calls "die Staffeln [des Neuen]" (1:129). The importance of this scale is twofold. First, the wondrous in Breitinger's conception (contrary to the "Romantic" interpretation to which his work has been subjected) is not the fantastic image that "conflicts" with "reality." Breitinger does not view literature as that which aims for *Verfremdungseffekt*, to use the modern term. Second, the claim of the wondrous to probability is not a function of the degree to which it copies what we already have seen or already know. It is a new insight that is compatible with existing conceptions but does not simply reproduce them.[38]

Breitinger's full definition of the wondrous connects his poetics with Leibniz's system perhaps more clearly than any of his other definitions:

> Ich begreiffe demnach unter dem Nahmen des Wunderbaren alles, was von einem andern widerwärtigen Bildniß oder vor wahr angenommenen Satze ausgeschlossen wird; was uns, dem ersten Ancheine nach, unsren gewöhnlichen Begriffen von dem Wesen der Dinge, von den Kräften, Gesetzen und dem Laufe der Natur, und allen vormals erkannten Wahrheiten in dem Licht zu stehen, und dieselben zu bestreiten düncket. Folglich hat das Wunderbare für den Verstand immer einen Schein der Falschheit; weil es mit den angenommenen Sätzen desselben in einem offenbaren Widerspruch zu stehen scheinet.
>
> (1:130–31)

The most striking aspect of this definition is Breitinger's reliance on terms suggesting the split between appearance and reality. In Leibnizian language, Breitinger is saying that some things appear to be nonassimilative but can in fact be absorbed into the system. Our first reaction, however, is to reject them. Rejection of perception in Leibniz's system does not mean, however, that the mind "sees something" and "runs away from it." Rejection means that "petites perceptions" never "rise" to that level of activity where they represent themselves in perception. They are not compossible and remain unrecognized. Following this, the wondrous in Breitinger's system comprises not those things we reject, but those things we may have never noticed but then eventually assimilate. The wondrous appears or occurs at exactly that indefinable and constantly shifting point (represented by the asterisks) where "petites perceptions" become perception, become conscious. In his own terminology: it is where "das Falsche" becomes part of "das Wahrscheinliche." And *this* is why Breitinger says "Die Copie ziehet uns stärcker·an sich als das Original," because he is talking about the power of poetry to imitate something that we might not otherwise have seen or recognized. In this process, set in motion by the perception of the wondrous (in the work or in nature), that which "might be" is that which is coming to be.

The aesthetic insight is a rational (though not strictly *a priori*) process of intellective integration that Breitinger describes, as we have already seen, in terms of a "Vergleichungs-Prozeß." This comparison of new perception with previous perception is "Gemüthes-Beschäftigung" (1:72 and 74), "Ueberlegung in den Gedancken" (1:74), "Vergleichung mit unsren Meinungen, Erfahrungen, und angenommenen Sätzen" (1:134).[39] Breitinger conceives of poetic process as occurring in poets, in recipients, and in nature, whereby nature must be understood as history. He accounts for flux and growth in the historical system in two ways. On the one hand, there are infinite kinds of possible poetic recipients, and this for three reasons. First, at any given time, a variety of degrees of knowledge will be represented among all members of humanity: "[Es kan] einigen etwas in der Natur als fremd, seltzam, neu und wunderbar vorkommen . . . was andern gantz bekannt und etwas gewöhnliches ist . . . und das ungleiche Urtheil, welches von dem Neuen gefället wird . . . entstehet . . . von der ungleichen Fähigkeit und dem daher rührenden verschiedenen Maasse der Erkänntniß" (1:123–24). Second, individuals learn over time and, hence, change their own perception of what is wondrous and probable. The passage continues: "welches Ursache ist, daß noch unerfahrne Kinder alle Sachen ohne Unterschied mit einer dummen Bewunderung angaffen, weil ihnen alles fremd, neu und seltzam vorkommen muß" (1:124). Third, new historical individuals will be constantly entering the system, which changes its configuration: "Was

nun insbesondere die nach Zeit und Ort so verschiedenen Gewohn-
heiten, Sitten, Gebräuche, und Meinungen gantzer Völker anbelan-
get, so muß man freylich gestehen, daß das poetische Schöne in
dieser Absicht am wenigsten an eine besondere Zeit oder Ort kan
gebunden und festgehalten werden, alldieweil diese Sachen durch
ihre stete Veränderung den Begriff von dem Schönen, und den Preiß
des verwundersamen Neuen in diesem Stücke zugleich mitverän-
dern" (1:126). All of these passages may be applied to the poet as
well: poets have a variety of levels of knowledge; poets acquire
knowledge over time; and poets live in a variety of places and pe-
riods: "die besondern Absichten eines verständigen Scribenten [kön-
nen] unendlich verschieden seyn" (1:429). Because this sentence oc-
curs in Breitinger's discussion of the poet's organization of particulars
into the individual poetic work, one might add to the three sources
of variety already listed the additional one of changing perception or
apperception at any given moment in time, in the smallest historical
fragment possible. This would hold for the recipient as well. And
because an infinite variety of perceptions and impressions will be pre-
sented to an infinite variety of creators and recipients, there will
never be a fully articulatable set of aesthetic standards. Breitinger
thus anticipates, using the neoclassic diction available to him, the po-
sition of Friedrich Schlegel: "Darum ist es auch unmöglich, daß der
gute Geschmack durch Regeln, die ein vollständiges Systema der
Kunst ausmachen, gelehret und vorgetragen werde" (1:430).[40]

The constant flux in the system is its primary virtue, for it makes
possible the "poetic" process of nature, the process of *Bildung*. The
purpose of the system is the continual creation of form, of *Bild*, which
could not occur if the individual mind were imprisoned in the con-
templation of an achieved perfection. The production of form, the
poetic process, operates according to historically determined "Grund-
sätze des Wahnes." The etymological correspondence between "wäh-
nen," "einbilden," and "phantasieren" is still alive in Breitinger's dic-
tion, so that he can elsewhere speak of the "Grundsätze des Wahnes"
as the "Logik der Phantasie."[41] The production of form, the merging
of diffuse, numerous, unnoticed particulars of experience into a per-
ception, is an act of focusing executed in the aesthetic insight. Such
an insight is not, in Breitinger's view, "owned" by the poet and
"given" to the recipient. Because it is a process occurring in nature,
both the poet and the recipient have an equal "investment" in it.

The difference between Breitinger and previous neoclassic concep-
tions on this point may be illustrated by comparing Boileau's advice
to the poet with that given by Edward Young in 1759. When Boileau

says: "Pour me tirer des pleurs, il faut que vous pleuriez" (350), he is advocating the use of an ancient rhetorical device to help poets convey their meaning to their readers by encouraging poets to place themselves in the recipient's position. When Young writes: "Tread in [Homer's] steps to the sole fountain of immortality; drink where he drank, at the true Helicon, that is, at the breast of nature: imitate; but imitate not the composition, but the man,"[42] he is assuming that the developing poet, who is the recipient of Homer's works, can assume Homer's position vis-à-vis nature and participate in (or identify with) Homer's insights. Young's statement, however, does not reverse the neoclassic concept; it radicalizes it. Rather than merely acquiescing in the poet's meaning, recipients themselves step into the role of poet.

But the relationship between poets and recipients in the process of aesthetic insight remains a didactic one, for poets help readers to focus their multiple, scattered, unconscious perceptions: "Dieser künstliche Mahler . . . läßt [dem Leser] keine Freyheit, mit flüchtigem und ungewissem Gemüths-Auge müssig herumzuschweifen, oder sich in der Vermischung des Mannigfaltigen zu verirren" (1:22). The passage has already been quoted, but I introduce it again because of its extraordinary importance for Breitinger's argument. It tells us what the recipient "gets" from the poet. The poet does in fact provide the reader with a lesson, but it is strictly a formal one. That is, poets do not convey the "contents" of their aesthetic insight to the recipient, who would passively accept it (be "moved" by it). Instead, poets inform recipients by providing them with a lesson in the organization of experience itself.[43] Breitinger thus expresses a notion of *Bildung* that would receive ever greater elaboration in the course of the eighteenth century. The "lesson" to be learned from poesis changes thereby from the simple transference of a moral message from poet to reader, into the encouragement of the recipient to participate in an intellective creative process involving the formation of self-consciousness as an aspect of historical experience.

4. Perspectivism after Breitinger

In the poetic creation of a new configuration of perception, poets or their works act as a catalyst for a process of comparison of images of nature with existing knowledge that assumes the mutual participation of poet and reader alike, both of whom share, as members of the same culture, a similar set of criteria of probability. This simultaneous participation of poets and their audience in the revision of their perspective on nature has not been generally understood. Breitinger's discussions of the wondrous, for example, have been interpreted only in terms of the effect of the wondrous on the audience. The wondrous has been approached purely as content, as the poet's vision that forces itself on the reader, whereas Breitinger's own discussion of this term must be viewed in the context of the psychological process that he calls "Vergleichung der Begriffe." Both the reader and the poet are confronted with wondrous material, that is, it is constellated, at that point where it can be integrated. Moreover, this point is constantly shifting because it is a historically and culturally determined perspective.

The influence of Breitinger's book, although at first substantial, did not hold in the years following its publication for at least two reasons. First, the book was intended as a corrective to Gottsched's poetics, as its title indicates. The terms of the debate between Gottsched and the Swiss were soon confined, however, to an argument over the nature and value of the wondrous, which Gottsched and Bodmer appear to have agreed was the most important point of contention between them. Yet Breitinger's actual criticism of Gottsched in the *Critische Dichtkunst*—and this has, I believe, never been noticed—was not aimed at Gottsched's rejection of the wondrous but at his failure to conceive of language and literature in historical terms. Because Breitinger's reputation was determined primarily in the wake of the more flamboyant Bodmer, his argument for poesis as intellective activity was overlooked, while he himself took few steps to explicate it further.

Second, Gottsched's critique of Breitinger's notion of "Farben" was carried forth by Lessing, whose brilliant essay style convinced a generation of developing art theoreticians that Breitinger's concept of "poetische Mahlerey" amounted to a defense of Baroque "mahlende Poesie." The irony of Lessing's criticism in *Laokoon* is that his own notion of "prägnanter Augenblick" could be compared with Breitinger's concept of mimesis as intellective integration.[1] Lessing's criticism is important because it shows us how Breitinger's perspectivism was misunderstood by one of the most thorough, learned, and influential philologists of the mid-eighteenth century.

Lessing adopts from Dubos the proposition that the eye perceives spatially and the ear perceives temporally. That is, the "images" of a poem are presented in language, which is a temporal sequence of words. Poems thus strike the mind in a series of perceptions, whereas the eye can "take in" the spatial image in an instant, in one perceptual act. Lessing then argues that the clear perception of a thing in space demands that we be able to relate immediately all of its parts as a whole. The perception of the poetic object runs the risk of its unity being lost because the mind is not as likely to remember sequences of impressions as it is to retain a multiplicity presented in an instant. For the poem to have a vivid effect on the reader, therefore, it must imitate the effect of visual impressions: its unity must be instantly perceivable, in a temporal flash, so to speak.

In criticizing Dubos, Breitinger had for his part already made the psychologically astute observation that the mere visual confrontation with a scene provides no guarantee that one will remember it in detail.[2] What counts for Breitinger is the organization of perceptions such that the mind can accept and retain them. This is accomplished not simply by making objects visible but by making them intelligible. The ability of the artist to organize perceptions is not dependent on what could be visualized in a single picture (or moment). Breitinger praises Haller's "Alpen" (1:23–27) because it presents a natural sight in terms of the significance of the objects, the qualities of things as they appear (rather than their simple appearance to the eye), so that our impression of them "makes sense" to us.

"Poetische Mahlerey" is a way of presenting an *image* of nature rather than a *copy*. But Lessing takes Breitinger to task on precisely this point, claiming that Haller's famous description of the "Enzian," which Breitinger praises, is not naturalistic enough.[3] "Es mag seyn, daß alle poetische Gemählde eine vorläufige Bekanntschaft mit ihren Gegenständen erfordern," Lessing remarks sarcastically, but Haller's poetic description simply cannot compete ("wetteifern") with the imitation of a Huysum, for example. Lessing takes Haller's description to be a naturalistic representation that misses its mark because it has been embellished to the point of obscurity. He assumes that Breitinger's notion of vividness, which is illustrated with this Haller passage in the *Critische Dichtkunst*, aimed for extreme verisimilitude, even though Breitinger had defended nothing of the sort. He then criticizes Breitinger for having erred in praising Haller's "Alpen" for its verisimilar quality.

In other words, Lessing continues Gottsched's critique of embellishment and the "painting" of qualities that contribute to a complex total effect, although for entirely different reasons than Gottsched's. "Wie steht es um den Begriff des Ganzen?" he asks, insisting that the visual unity and immediacy of the description is lost. It is interesting that Haller defended himself against this charge, in an unsigned review of the *Laokoon* in 1766 in the *Göttingischen gelehrten Anzeigen*, and that his words reproduce the argument in the *Critische Dichtkunst* exactly: "Ein Dichter . . . kan die Eigenschaften ausdrucken, die inwendig liegen, die durch die übrige Sinne erkannt, oder durch Versuche entdeckt werden, und dieses ist dem Mahler verboten."[4] Haller's point had been a central criticism of Dubos in the first chapter of the *Critische Dichtkunst*: "Der Poet mahlet nicht für das Auge allein, sondern auch für die übrigen Sinnen" (1:19). Equally interesting is Haller's failure to acknowledge that he took this argument from Breitinger. The result of this in terms of Lessing's criticism of Breitinger is that Haller deflected criticism from himself (whether or not successfully is not at issue here), but Haller did not defend Breitinger, the real target of Lessing's attack.

One of Breitinger's principal admirers seems to have been Herder, who perhaps more than any other critic of the mid-eighteenth century appreciated the thrust of Breitinger's ideas. To be sure, Herder's references to Breitinger are not extensive, nor does he question Lessing's treatment of him in his own attack on the *Laokoon*. But as a student of Leibniz's thought he commends "den wahrhaftig Philosophischen Breitinger," the author of the "lehrreiche *Critische Dichtkunst*,"[5] for abandoning normative poetics in favor of a historical approach to the individual literary work. And he explicitly associates this new approach with Breitinger's notion of language. This praise appears not to have been registered in most critical circles.[6]

A treatise that appeared almost simultaneously with but probably independently of Breitinger's work was Johann Martin Chladenius's *Einleitung zur richtigen Auslegung vernünfftiger Reden und Schrifften*, published just two years after the *Critische Dichtkunst*, in 1742.[7] Chladenius was apparently well acquainted with many of the same classical sources that Breitinger cites, and he frequently mentions his admiration for Leibniz. It is therefore not surprising that his text bears some striking affinities to Breitinger's with regard to two significant—and interrelated—problems: first, perspectivism, which Chladenius explains in terms of his notion of "Sehe-Punckt," and second, the concept of metaphor.

Both authors remark that Leibniz is a philosopher with a special interest in language. Breitinger had integrated Leibniz's *Unvorgreifliche Gedanken* into his own reflections in his second volume. Chladenius for his part mentions repeatedly Leibniz's proclivity for the use of metephor.[8] For the modern reader, the poetic aspect of Leibniz's discourse is manifest. But Chladenius, writing in the age of Gottsched, was praising a *philosopher* for his use of a device often thought responsible for distortions, "darkness," or unnecessary and distracting ornamentation in scholarly prose. Chladenius does refer us at one point to "des Herrn Bülfingers und des Herrn Cantzens gelehrte Abhandlungen," in which Leibniz's doctrines, "welche in metaphorischer Gestalt vorgetragen waren," are rendered "begreiflich" (§ 569). Nevertheless, he says, our inability to understand Leibniz's metaphors is not the fault of the philosopher but rather of his readers, who have not yet sufficiently penetrated the meaning of Leibniz's system and hence the language in which it is expressed (cf. §§ 564–67).[9] Here Chladenius emphasizes, as Breitinger had, the importance of context in understanding the sense of a metaphor.

Whereas Gottsched would castigate authors for their metaphors, Chladenius views "darkness" as an opportunity: "Wenn man ein Buch verstehen lernet, so entstehen immer mehr und mehr Gedancken in uns, die wir vorhin, da wir es lasen, noch nicht gehabt haben. (§ 161.) Wenn nun dieses darum geschiehet, weil wir Stellen, die wir vorher gar nicht verstanden, nunmehro verstehen, (§ 163.) so wird uns eine dunckele Stelle deutlich, und in etwas fruchtbar, (§ 164.) . . . Mithin bestehet unser Verstehenlernen darinne, daß uns gewisse dunckele Stellen deutlich, und unfruchtbare Stellen fruchtbar werden" (§ 166). Chladenius is willing to tolerate metaphor in scholarly texts because, like Breitinger and unlike Gottsched, he views metaphor in terms of the formation of concepts: "Wenn wir ein Wort in verblümten Verstande brauchen, so entstehet allemal ein neuer allgemeiner Begriff in unsern Verstande" (§ 94). Thus, "die verblümten Reden haben noch einen andern Nutzen, als daß sie unsere Einbildungs-Krafft belustigen. Man kan nemlich allgemeine Begriffe daraus herleiten, die, wenn sie deutlich erklärt werden, die Wissenschafften erweitern helffen" (§ 96).

Breitinger has a nearly identical formulation with reference to metaphors in his *Gleichnis-Abhandlung*: "in einer Schrift [sind] die Gleichniß-Bilder vor andern hoch zu schätzen, welche nicht alleine den Geist erfreuen, sondern auch die Wissens-Begierde befriedigen;

welche einen Gedancken mit Schönheit ausschmücken, und zugleich den Verstand mit neuen Begriffen und Wahrheiten bereichern" (135). Both Chladenius and Breitinger may seem here to be chanting the "sugar-coated pill" formula of traditional ("Horatian") didacticism, but such an impression—resulting from an idiom that was rapidly becoming antiquated even as they used it—is deceptive. For the point of their statements is not that metaphors make moral truths *palatable*, but rather that certain kinds of metaphor make new ideas *possible*. Here again we see the shift in the eighteenth century from crude didacticism to a concept of *Bildung* as a new formation of consciousness through poetic language.

The "allgemeine Begriffe" to which Chladenius refers arise when a verbal expression is made more specific by the presence of a metaphor that has been derived through the process of abstraction. (We have already encountered a similar apparent paradox in Breitinger's discussion of vividness.) Chladenius gives as an example the use of the word "fliegen": "Wenn uns . . . eine geschwinde Bewegung vorgestellet wird, so kan uns davor, nach der Regel der Einbildungs-Krafft, das fliegen einfallen; und daher geschiehet es, daß wir von einer geschwind lauffenden, oder reitenden Person zu sagen pflegen, sie fliege" (§ 91). In this case, the image of a person moving rapidly is clarified by comparing it with the movement of a bird—not, however, with respect to the actual motion of the wings, but only with respect to its speed. Speed is therefore the quality that has been "abgesondert (abstrahirt)" (§ 94), transformed into a generic notion ("Geschlecht," § 94), and then applied to both "Arten (Species)" (§ 94), namely, bird and person.[10] Such expressions provide "Nachdruck" to ordinary words or statements by amplifying the "Umstände" that accompany the represented object (cf. § 114). The explication of these "Umstände" results in an increase in knowledge because the reader will learn to view an ordinary phenomenon (such as running) within a different context (that of rapid flight).

But the interpretation of metaphoric passages is fraught with problems for Chladenius because of the "gantz verschiedene und widrige Würckungen" (§ 125) that identical words appear to exert on different minds. Even when readers are fully informed about the literal meaning of the words, one must expect that metaphors will receive "verschiedene Aufnahme" (§ 125) from them. This difference he ascribes not to an inherent ambiguity of language itself, but to the effects of individual perspective: "Man [kan] nicht sagen, daß zwey Personen eine Sache aus einerley Sehe-Puncte sich vorstellen, indem sich in den Umständen ihres Leibes, ihrer Seele und ihrer gantzen Person allemal unzehliche Verschiedenheiten finden werden, daraus auch eine grosse Mannigfaltigkeit in denen Vorstellungen erfolgen muß" (§ 310). It is important to remember here that Chladenius, unlike modern historiographers, uses the concept of "Sehe-Punckt" to describe our understanding of things—not of texts.[11]

Disputes over textual meaning, such as over the significance of a metaphor, arise for Chladenius not simply because words, phrases, or texts spontaneously evoke different responses, but because readers have different standpoints that are closer to or further away from that of the author whose account of "die Sache" is under scrutiny (cf. §§ 310–14). "Correct" interpretation of the historical text follows when the reader or "Ausleger" succeeds in bringing his own perspective on history into harmony with the perspective of the author. This is achieved by examining the context of the author's work in order to understand his "Absicht" (cf. §§ 355–65).[12] The process is not unlike Breitinger's notion of literary interpretation, where the reader learns to occupy the poet's position vis-à-vis nature by attempting to traverse the historical distance between himself and the poetic work.

A considerable portion of Chladenius's treatise is an elaboration of how linguistic, historical, cultural, and psychological factors result in the various "Umstände" that have been precipitated into the historical text. Differences in "Sehe-Punckt" among different authors are determined not only by physical position (Chladenius's example here is that of three different observers of a battle), but also by the "verschiedene Verbindung" we have to things as well as our "vorhergehende Art zu gedencken, zu suchen, vermöge welcher dieser auf das, der andere auf jenes Achtung zu geben sich angewöhnt hat" (§ 308). Chladenius goes on to state in this same paragraph that "eine Rebellion wird anders von einem treuen Unterthanen, anders von einem Rebellen, anders von einem Ausländer, anders von einem Hofmann, anders von einem Bürger oder Bauer angesehen." Here he comes close to a notion of individual standpoint in the modern sense of "attitude" or interest based on social and psychological experience. More significant for our purposes here, however, is that he also comes close to Breitinger's notion of the "Grundsätze des Wahns," according to which judgments of probability about the literary work are made. But whereas Breitinger wanted to explain how we view a poem as a probable representation of nature, Chladenius wants to show how the truth of historical narratives can be established.

This difference in aims is, however, not the result of different methods but of different objects. Probability of the literary work was determined in Breitinger's poetics by a process of "Vergleichung der

Begriffe," whereby apparently contradictory representations were integrated into an existing configuration of perception. But Breitinger conceived of nature as a dynamically evolving system; our representations or understanding of it will therefore require constant readjustment. The object of the historical narrative, by contrast, is not conceived by Chladenius as a dynamic entity, but rather as a closed system of past events that is subject to a "wahren Verstand" (§§ 648–49). Historians may produce conflicting, even contradictory, accounts (§ 313), but it is possible through correct interpretation to reconcile them with each other: "Wenn zwey Geschicht-Schreiber einander widersprechen, ohngeachtet sie sich die Sache recht, aber aus verschiedenen Sehe-Punckten vorgestellt und vorgetragen haben, (§ 312.) so wird der Leser gemeiniglich glauben, die Verfasser wären einander so zuwider, daß der eine nothwendig recht, und der andere unrecht haben müsse. Gleichwol kan dieser Widerspruch nur scheinbar seyn, (§ 313.) und daher rühren, daß der Leser den einen, oder den andern Geschicht-Schreiber, oder beyde nicht vollkommen verstehet. Ein Ausleger soll demnach hier das widersprechende vereinigen" (§ 329).

Given such concern with dispelling any ambiguity in the historical record, it is curious that Chladenius would defend the use of metaphor in historical writing. Even though its analysis enhances our understanding of the historical context that it captures, it also creates "dunckele Stellen" in a text that result in misapprehensions. Yet for Chladenius the source of ambiguity in historical writing is our lack of knowledge of historical context rather than the metaphor itself. It is precisely Chladenius's commitment to historical truth that arouses his interest in metaphor. Besides adding precision and clarity to the historical document (if we assume, of course, that it has been "correctly" understood), metaphor also provides, potentially, insight into "die Sachen" that would be impossible to convey without it.

Both of these criteria are present in Chladenius's definition of what constitutes a "richtige Metaphor," that is, a correctly used metaphor. Metaphors are preferable to ordinary words in those cases where "der Metaphorische Ausdruck die Sache umständlich [i.e., in greater specificity] und durch ein Wort darstellet, welches durch ein [eigentliches] Wort *nicht geschehen könte*" (§ 121, my emphasis). "Die Noth," Chladenius continues, "welche uns antreibt, ein Wort in verblümten Verstande zu gebrauchen, bestehet in nichts anders, als in der Begierde sich so vollständig auszudrucken, als nur möglich ist, und also das nachdrücklichste Wort zu gebrauchen" (§ 122). Metaphor, in the hands of the historian, is a useful—and necessary—tool in the development of "neue Begriffe" that are in turn the source of new historical knowledge for the reader.

Chladenius's concept of metaphor is in fact the crack in the wall of his otherwise closed system of history, just as Breitinger's concept of the historicity of metaphor was the precondition for his move away from normative poetics. For here Chladenius provides a very early formulation of the historicity of historical understanding itself. This is clear from what he has to say about linguistic change. The meanings of ordinary words, he argues, change only when "die Sache" that they represent changes (cf. § 85), or when our attitude toward "die Sache" changes. Chladenius gives as an example the word "Tyrann" (§ 86), which he says originally had a neutral meaning but came to denote something negative as a result of certain changes in the behavior of those who carried this title. Conversely, when there are no changes in the "Sache" over time, the meaning of "eigentliche Wörter" remains constant. Here his examples are the words "Ordnung," "Nothwendigkeit," and "Aehnlichkeit" (§§ 88–90), terms whose definition the modern reader obviously finds highly subject to change.

Metaphors, by contrast, do not remain constant but dissolve into ordinary meanings simply because our *understanding* of the historical context of the words has changed over time: "Wenn nun kein eigentlich Wort vorhanden ist, wodurch die Eigenschafft der Sache könte ausgedrückt werden, oder der verblümte Ausdruck scheinet die Sache besser und eigentlicher [!] auszudrücken, so werden sich die Leute nach und nach an dieselbe Redens-Art gewöhnen. . . . Die Jugend, welche den Ausdruck beständig von andern hört, auch wohl eher, als ihr die eigentliche Bedeutung des Wortes recht bekannt worden, fängt an die verblümte Bedeutung gleich bey dem Worte zu gedencken, ohne sich der Sache, die es eigentlich bedeutet hat, zu erinnern" (§ 97).

The formulation could also have come from Breitinger, and its significance is the same for Chladenius: the reanimation of the original historical context in which the metaphoric sense of the word was generated provides new historical knowledge because it allows us to witness the original attitude or "Sehe-Punckt" of the historian[13] (or poet) toward the events (nature) he observed. This is the goal, at least, of interpretation. Its achievement would remain problematic for Chladenius because readers of history, bound as they are to their own "Sehe-Punckt," can never develop an absolute knowledge of the context of the past.[14] Subsequent developments in historicism would of course include an ever more radical questioning of the very possibility of the reader's identification with the standpoint occupied by the historical witness as the notion of an ultrapersonal perspective gave way to the notion of a strictly individual one.[15]

Peter Szondi, in his influential and enlightening *Einführung in die literarische Hermeneutik* that appeared posthumously in 1975, says that Chladenius made a momentous revision of an ancient rhetorical tenet. Whereas Cicero, Quintilian, and others had merely noted that metaphors sometimes arise when ordinary words are found to be inadequate,[16] Chladenius uses this explanation as the very foundation of his concept of metaphor. In fact, Szondi argues, it is metaphor and not "Sehe-Punckt" that is the focus of Chladenius's interest.[17] Here Szondi juxtaposes Chladenius with Gottsched, who had written: "Cicero lehrt im dritten Buche vom Redner im 38. Capitel ausdrücklich, daß die uneigentlichen Bedeutungen der Wörter zwar zu allererst aus Mangel und Dürftigkeit der Sprachen aufgekommen; hernach aber auch zur Anmuth und Zierde gebraucht worden."[18] Gottsched's critique of metaphor, Szondi rightly observes, is based on the belief that a metaphor is simply redundant: "Die Metaphore ist eine verblümte Redensart, wo man anstatt eines Wortes, das sich in eigentlichem Verstande zu der Sache schicket, ein anderes nimmt, welches eine gewisse Aehnlichkeit damit hat, und also ein kurzes Gleichniß in sich schließt." Gottsched thinks metaphors are ornamental because he views them as pleonasms. In allowing, however, Gottsched's position to stand for the entire "Poetik der Aufklärung" (91), Szondi forgets Breitinger, whose concept of metaphor, as we have already seen, is a remarkable anticipation of that of Chladenius. Szondi credits Chladenius with a stunning original insight, but Chladenius was merely one of at least two and probably several aesthetic thinkers who were indebted to both the rhetorical tradition and to Leibnizian ideas.

Szondi may have been led astray in his estimation by Chladenius himself: "Die Gelehrten, welche ehedem die Rede-Kunst in Regeln und Grund-Sätzen vorgetragen, haben zwar gemeiniglich auch von dem verblümten Verstande der Wörter gehandelt; aber doch nicht so, daß sie den Ursprung derselben aus der *Natur unserer Gedancken* deutlich hergeleitet hätten; daher auch schwer seyn wird, aus ihren Lehren von der Schönheit oder Unart einer verblümten Rede, ein gegründetes Urtheil zu fällen. . . . Wir müssen also von dieser Materie hier selbst so viel anführen, als zu Abhandlung der Regeln der Auslegung nöthig seyn wird" (§ 93, my emphasis). If Chladenius is honestly giving his impression here, it appears that he had seen neither the *Critische Dichtkunst* nor the *Gleichnis-Abhandlung*.

Additional evidence for this speculation appears in the "Vorrede" to his book. There Chladenius says he is working on a *pendant* to the *Einleitung* that will deal with the interpretation of literature. The present treatise will confine itself to historical and didactic writing. Poetic texts, however, deserve special consideration: "Denn wie hierinne eine besondere Art zu gedencken herrschet, so daß sie eine besondere Vernunfft-Lehre in sich zu halten scheinen, also ist auch ihre Auslegung gantz anders eingerichtet, als bey gantz dogmatischen und blossen historischen Büchern." Once again, Szondi credits Chladenius with an "außerordentlich kühnen Gedanken" (35) in the context of the early eighteenth century. But he apparently misses the fact that Breitinger, in the opening pages of his *Gleichnis-Abhandlung*, had already suggested just such a "spezifisch dichterische Logik" (Szondi, 35) in the form of his "Logik der Einbildungs-Kraft" or "Logik der Phantasie," which he makes responsible for the production of metaphor according to the principle of probability.[19]

Szondi believes (35) that Chladenius abandoned his plan for the study of literary hermeneutics because, as a historian, he lost interest in it. Such reasoning glosses over the crucial fact that in this period the "Art zu gedencken" of historians and poets was increasingly being described in similar terms. More likely is Chladenius's fear, at the threshold of the Kantian epistemological shift, that historians might lose sight of "the facts," might confuse "sinnreiche Geschichte" with "Poetische Geschichte" (§ 342). The former he understands as the historical account availing itself of metaphors; the latter is the quasi-historical narrative made more entertaining with imaginative embellishments "vor deren Wahrheit er [the historian] nicht stehen kan" (§ 342). (In a famous review of Herder's *Ideen*, Kant would later accuse his student of ignoring precisely this distinction.) Chladenius went on to publish, in 1748, his *Vernünfftige Gedanken vom Wahrscheinlichen, und dessen gefährlichen Mißbrauche*, which suggests his antipathy to "poetic" modes of historical apprehension—despite his interest in the aesthetic categories of metaphor and context.[20]

While Chladenius and Breitinger most likely availed themselves of common sources, the question of influence is less ambiguous in the case of the Swiss historian Jacob Wegelin, who was closely associated with Breitinger and Bodmer in Zurich before going to Berlin in 1765. There he promptly became a member of the Berlin Academy.[21] Although Wegelin published his major works after the appearance of the *Nouveaux essais* in 1765,[22] his notions of history and historiography are in some respects more understandable in the context of Breitinger's poetics than in strictly Leibnizian terms.

In his *Briefe über den Werth der Geschichte*, published in Berlin in 1783, Wegelin addresses three questions: Why is history important? What is its epistemological status? How can it achieve its greatest impact? Wegelin posits the study of history as an antidote to what he views in nearly pre-Schillerian fashion as the primary danger of modernity, namely, the tyranny of "Gewohnheit," "Gleichförmigkeit," and the formation of character "nach dem gesellschaftlichen Stempel."[23] In order to correct the "schlaffere Beschaffenheit des Geistes" (7) that results from such tyranny, we need, he says, to develop the native capacity of our minds to absorb a variety of different stimuli. This "zauberische Kraft unsers Witzes" (7), the imagination, occupies us with "tausend ersinnlichen Vorstellungen" (7) that are drawn from our social milieu ("von den Gegenständen des gesellschaftlichen Lebens [entlehnt]," 8).

Historians who merely allow "der todte Buchstabe" (5) to speak for them leave their readers "kalt und unempfindlich" (5) and thereby miss their mark. The historian's proper goal is the poetic reanimation of the past because "die lebendige Vorstellung seiner Originale belebt alsdann den Geist" (5), a process that has a profoundly ethical function: "Dieser mächtige Eindruck ist gewiß nicht ein Spiel des Geistes, sondern man verbindet damit das wahre Gefühl der menschlichen Würde" (5). History is capable of filling the soul "mit dem nachdenklichsten und tiefsten Schauer" (5); indeed this sublime effect proceeds out of "weit stärkern Empfindungen, als jemals durch die Kunst der Schaubühne hervorgebracht worden sind" (5).

The perceived proximity of history and poesis that Wegelin, like Breitinger, inherits from the French reception of Aristotle, causes him to return again and again to the issue of the boundary between the two disciplines. The problem is so vexing for him that in the final letter of his treatise he actually overturns one of his opening assertions: "Das Erhabene, das Umständliche, und das die Affecten heftig Erregende liegt ausser den Grenzen der Geschichte, und gehört nicht zu den Eigenschaften des Geschichtschreibers, dessen Absicht eigentlich nicht seyn soll, Erstaunen zu erwecken, oder zu ergötzen, und das Gemüth in die stärkste Bewegung zu setzen" (340–41). This apparent contradiction is symptomatic of Wegelin's desire, like Chladenius's before him, to appropriate the methods of poetic representation for historiography without blurring the epistemological distinction between history and poesis. Thus, in words so laden with historical usage as to border on cliché, Wegelin states that for poets, "nicht das Wahre, sondern das Wahrscheinliche . . . ist der Gegenstand seiner Bemühungen" (341–42). History, by contrast, would be empty and useless were it not based on "wirkliche und deutlich erkannte Thatsachen" (22). Historians must be concerned with "Wahrhaftigkeit" (341), whereas poets can base their work "auf der poetischen Möglichkeit" (342). Excluded from the historian's field of representation are "die abgezogenen Begriffe" (40), such as are found in the mathematical sciences, because Wegelin believes these "theoretische Wahrheiten" (41) have little relevance in the realm of attitudes, behavior, and events that constitute the historian's proper object. Here we recognize a distinction, already drawn by Breitinger and others, that is ultimately rooted in Leibniz's separation of the *vérités nécessaires* from the *vérités de fait*. Whereas the poet expresses virtual or potential truth, the historian investigates the actualized truths of fact.

Although Wegelin would like to think that history and poesis have different objects, the distinction he draws here does not demonstrate that assertion. For just as the French and Breitinger had done before him, Wegelin includes in his definition of "das Mögliche" the material of history itself. The most powerful "Romanzen," tragedies, and epics represent great historical figures and cast them in an embellished historical context (cf. 341–43). Such a notion of poesis as the fictionalized reworking of the historical record (as opposed to the purely fictive or "fantastic") had been circulating, as we saw in the previous chapter, at least since the Renaissance. What is "new" in Wegelin's work—but certainly not peculiar to it—is the degree to which he allows history to resemble poesis. This is nowhere more evident than in what he has to say about probability and possibility.

While the poet is confronted with the multiplicity of nature, the historian must somehow be able to capture "diese unbegrenzte Sammlung alles desjenigen, was die Menschen Gutes und Böses, Edles und Unedles, Natürliches und Künstliches, gedacht und gethan haben" (1). Wegelin believes that "die menschliche Betriebsamkeit [hat] so wenig einige [eigene?] Grenzen, als die Vorstellungskraft von dem Möglichen und Wahrscheinlichen" (101). In view of this wide range of possible human actions, the historian must decide which accounts of historical events are believable. Quite unlike Chladenius, Wegelin uses the category of probability to evaluate the legitimacy of the historical record. Human actions are not merely reflections of "ein allgemeiner Lauf der Dinge" (83), but also and primarily manifestations of "ein besonderer gesellschaftlicher Gang der Angelegenheiten einer Nation, welcher . . . das öffentliche Urtheil von dem Guten und Wahren bildet" (83). Historians are therefore not looking for general truths of human existence; instead their object is the *attitude* of specific historical groups toward "das Wahre."

In evaluating the historical record, the historian must decide to what degree it captures the "herrschenden Meinungen des Zeitalters und der Gesellschaft" (12). "Es kann"—Wegelin is echoing Breitinger—"eine Sache in folgenden Zeiten ungereimt scheinen, weil sie mit dem Zusammenhange der Umstände nicht mehr paßt, aber sie ist anfänglich nie so beschaffen gewesen. Daher wir niemals irgend einem Volke, in uneingeschränktem Sinne, Thorheit und Unschicklichkeit zuschreiben dürfen, weil diese Begriffe, wenn wir sie auf so verschiedene Gegenstände anwenden, nicht nach unsern eigenen, vorgefaßten Urtheilen, sondern nach den verschiedenen Nationalumständen, und abwechselnden Verhältnissen, beurtheilt werden müssen" (52–53).

Sometimes the attitudes or events we encounter in the historical record conflict so strongly with what we know about the "ordentlichen Lauf der Dinge" that they appear "wunderbar" (54). Yet such an impression is based on the "eingeschränktern Fähigkeit des Lesers und Erzählers" (54), their joint failure to imagine how widely things may vary from their own expectations. The wondrous actions of the past will cease to be seen as "ausserordentlich" (54) as soon as the reader is provided with information about the "Nationalumstände" (53), in the context of which the extraordinary event will appear as probable.

Wegelin concedes, however, that there have also been truly extraordinary events in history, that is, events that were viewed as wondrous in their own time. Any historical age can occasionally produce "das Originelle" (195), an utterly new idea, attitude, or activity that appears as a "Widerspruch" (195) to what is generally thought to lie in the realm of "Möglichkeit" (196) for a specific set of "Localumstände" (196). Here the wondrous effect derives from the failure of the historically represented community itself to imagine a new state of affairs. But original thinkers have had a remedy for this shortcoming: "Statt daß sie ihre Begriffe weit über den Gesichtskreis des Volks erheben wollten, bestrebten sie sich mit größtem Fleisse, sich nach der Sinnesart eines jeden zu bequemen" (197). Original notions can be made accessible to a community when they are brought into "eine gewisse Verbindung und Vergleichung" (197) with the "besondern sinnlichen Vorstellungen" (197) with which a community is already familiar. New historical projects—we might even say historical change per se—occurs for Wegelin when original minds attend to the integration of their ideas into the existing configuration of experience.

Such a concept of historical evolution within individual cultures is more than a little reminiscent of Breitinger's notion of how poesis captures the ceaseless transformations in our apprehension of nature.

History and poesis are established here as analogous processes. The new and the possible is made probable, and the probable is then actualized. History for Wegelin is a "stuffenweise geschehende Entwickelung unserer Fähigkeiten" (24), just as the individual "Charakter eines Volks" is the "stuffenweise geschehene Ausbildung und Entwickelung seiner ursprünglichen Anlagen" (13). Every culture or "Nation" (13) has a characteristic "Art zu handeln" (13) that is in turn linked to the "Entstehungsart eines . . . Volks" (13). The determinacy of "Volkscharacter" (13) means that only certain kinds of actions will be generated within certain cultures (cf. 13). Individual actions—that is, actions of individuals as well as the web of action within individual periods—can only be grasped within the larger context of national character. "Um einen solchen Charakter würdig zu fassen, ist es nöthig, eine anschauende Erkenntnis aller Triebfedern öffentlicher Handlungen zu haben, und zu diesem Ende alle Thaten eben diesselben Volks auf einmal zu übersehen" (13–14).

The extraordinary ideas and actions of original minds are therefore not arbitrary but ultimately understandable when one has acquired a sufficiently broad perspective on any given culture or period. Like Breitinger, Wegelin is trying to reconcile the "skiagraphic" view of the whole with the "skenographic" attention to vividness that provides the illusion of presence ("anschauende Erkenntnis") at the historical scene, which in turn forms the basis of historical understanding. If we examine now Wegelin's use of the metaphors of painting and perspective, it is possible to see how he establishes the writing of history as an analogue to the process of history itself.

The explication and elaboration of "Nationalumstände" and "abwechselnden Verhältnisse" produce what Wegelin calls the "Colorit der Geschichte" (12–13). It is based on "die *Kunst*, den Charakter ganzer Nationen, und die charakteristischen Züge der merkwürdigsten Personen eines Volks, der historischen Wahrheit gemäs, richtig und wirksam zu *zeichnen*" (13, my emphasis). Wegelin distinguishes this kind of historical writing from the "Jahrbücher der Mönche" that were compiled out of "ihre Unwissenheit in der Kunst, das Zeitalter, worin sie lebten, zu charakterisiren, und die wenigen Züge des vorhanden Grosen und Edlen in einem *wohlgezeichneten* National*bilde* zu vereinigen" (16, my emphasis). The historian may not simply amass or collect a multitude of particulars from the past. We need to see not merely the actuality of events, but the *significance* of their actuality. The purpose of poetic effect in historical writing is nonetheless not the arousal of "staunende Bewunderung" (29), which is little more than a temporary "Betäubung des Geistes" (29). Historical materials, however fantastic, remain "blose Gegenstände der Neugierde" and are quickly forgotten when it cannot be shown how they relate ("zusammenhängen") to the "Natur und den Grundtrieben der Seelen" (26). The historian should seek to provide vivid representations that depict ("darstellen") characters and events as "malerisch, und gleichsam gegenwärtig" (340). Placing events and behavior in such a "historisches Licht" (28) allows them to be apprehended as "wichtig und interessant" (28). Wegelin is taking full advantage of the metaphors already developed in the aesthetic disciplines. History needs to be presented from a certain "Gesichtspunct" (38) if it is to affect us. The historian should create a "Gemälde" (4, 14, 16, etc.) that makes psychological sense to the reader because of its "vorzügliche Anordnung aller Theile" (14). The "Geschichtsforscher" interested in the vivid reconstruction of what has been lost may have to deal with "Fragmenten der Geschichte wie ein geschickter Maler und Bildhauer, der ein halb verloschenes Gemälde und eine verstümmelte Bildsäule, einigen Original-Zügen zufolge, ausbessert, und in einen vollständigeren Zustand setzt" (4).

But such filling out of the historical record is far from arbitrary on the historian's part. Wegelin shares the position that Breitinger had staked out in his poetics against the attitude toward history of the *modernes*. The past, he argues, is not to be painted in such a way as only to make it more palatable to modern readers, that is to say, more entertaining. The disjunction between past and present should not and cannot be destroyed. We occupy, he says, a "Dunstkugel" in space whose atmosphere prevents us from viewing "die himmlischen Körper . . . auf derjenigen Stelle . . . wo sie sich wirklich befinden" (12). Their position can only be apprehended through the distortions of "Strahlenbrechung." Similarly, the "praktische und moralische Urtheile der Seele," preserved in the historical record, deviate from "dem Ausdrucke der Wahrheit" (12). Understanding the difference between past and present is essential for modern ethical consciousness because it allows us to put our own attitudes and actions in a historical context. "Wie könnten wir uns auch irgend einen erträglichen Begriff von der menschlichen Freyheit, und der Sittlichkeit unserer Handlungen machen, wenn uns nicht die allgemeinen und besondern Handlungsarten der Menschen mittelst der Geschichte bekannt wären?" (24). The very source of "Fanaticismus" (33), an extreme form of enthusiasm, lies precisely in the inability to view one's own actions and thoughts against a larger historical picture: "der Schwärmer sieht eine Begebenheit . . . nicht in dem Zusammenhange aller mitwirkenden Ursachen, Verhältnisse und Absichten an, sondern er reißt davon ein einzelnes Stück ab, und giebt demselben eine weit ausgebreitetere Würde, als der Zusammenhange des Ganzen wirklich erlaubt" (33).

At this point we can return to Wegelin's dilemma regarding the priority of poetic effect or "truth" in historical writing. Because history is not only composed of events but also of culturally and temporally specific attitudes, our historical understanding must have an emotional component if we are to appreciate the significance of the past. "Im historischen Sinne ist nicht so wohl die Frage von der Wahrheit überhaupt, und allgemein betrachtet, als von der Wirkung, welche eine jede wahrhafte Begebenheit auf die regen Kräfte der Seele macht" (26). The arousal of the "Kräfte der Seele" (26), a Leibnizian term, is most easily achieved by imagining ourselves as participants in the original historical setting. Thus Wegelin finds that "die wirksamste Geschichte wäre also diejenige, welche sich am wenigsten in der Ausführlichkeit und Erzählungsart von den Romanzen unterschiede" (27). This genre has been most effective in penetrating "die besondersten, innern und äusern Angelegenheiten seiner Personen" (27) so that readers feel they are present ("anschauend," 27) at the scene.

Such illusionistic presence is the condition of possibility for historical understanding itself. Wegelin distinguishes between the ability to imagine how previous ages and cultures experienced the world and the arbitrary construction of fantasy images divorced from probable historical knowledge. The exercise by writers and readers alike of the historical imagination, stimulated by the painterly and perspectivist skill of the historian, contributes to the development of our consciousness as members of a distinct period and culture. In other words, the experience of history is, in Wegelin's conception, itself an aspect of cultural-historical evolution. Nowhere does Wegelin identify perspectivism and the act of "contextualizing" as characteristic of modernity. But his adaptation of the metaphor of painting indicates the degree to which he views history as an interpreting rather than as a reporting activity. If a Hans Georg Gadamer can ignore the significance of historical "painting" in his comprehensive work on the development of modern hermeneutics,[24] we may assume that the process by which history moved closer to poesis in the eighteenth century has not been given sufficient attention.

Scholars of the German literary tradition have most recently tended to argue, following the example set by Hans Peter Herrmann in 1970, that Breitinger's poetics cannot be viewed as an "anticipation" of Romanticism. Allowing Breitinger this role, it has rightly been shown, was the approach of an ideologically motivated and now completely untenable *Genieästhetik* that was fixated on an incorrectly understood concept of *das Wunderbare*. But perhaps Breitinger's connection to Romanticism, or rather, the significance of ideas developed by Breitinger and others, should be sought elsewhere than in a narrowly defined field of German literary history. The perspectivist notion of interpretation that he and others put forth appears to have had considerable impact on the emergence of German historicism, which itself existed in a state of dynamic interaction (*Wechselwirkung*) with Romantic poetics. The work of Novalis and Friedrich Schlegel, to name only two, is unthinkable apart from contemporary theories of history and historiography. "Ein Geschichtschreiber [müßte] notwendig ein Dichter sein," the Graf von Hohenzollern remarks in *Heinrich von Ofterdingen*, "denn nur die Dichter mögen sich auf jene Kunst, Begebenheiten schicklich zu verknüpfen, verstehen."[25] Breitinger's poetics did not "influence" Romantic authors. Nevertheless, some of the ideas he articulated eventually found their way back to the poets—via the historians.

Notes

Introduction

1. The secondary literature on this topic is of course enormous. Presentations that I found especially useful are Allan Megill, "Aesthetic Theory and Historical Consciousness"; Hinrich C. Seeba, "'Der wahre Standort'"; and by the same author, "Lessings Geschichtsbild." For a concise review of contemporary notions of historical perspectivism, see Rudolf Vierhaus, "Wie erzählt man Geschichte?"

2. Herder uses "Gemälde" in a number of places throughout his oeuvre to designate the vivid historical account. In *Auch eine Philosophie*, for example, he writes: "Gehe hin, mein Leser, und fühle noch jetzt hinter Jahrtausenden die so lang erhaltne reine Morgenländische Natur, belebe sie dir aus der Geschichte der ältesten Zeiten . . . welch ein Gemälde, wenn ichs dir liefern könnte, wie es war! . . . Niemand in der Welt fühlt die Schwäche des allgemeinen Charakterisirens mehr als ich. Man mahlet ein ganzes Volk, Zeitalter, Erdstrich—wen hat man gemahlt? . . . Das ganze lebendige Gemälde von Lebensart, Gewohnheiten, Bedürfnissen . . . müßte dazu kommen"; see *Werke*, 5:486–87 and 501–2, and cf. 4:389–90. Although a good deal has been written on Herder's concept of "Bild," his use of the word "Gemälde" as a *topos* of the rhetorical tradition under investigation in this study has not, to my knowledge, been noticed. The issue deserves, however, a separate monograph and can only be alluded to here. Demandt, *Metaphern für Geschichte*, 373, comments on Herder's use of the term, but is apparently unaware of its rhetorical context. Thus he understands "Gemälde" as history itself, the "thing" to be represented, rather than as the historian's construction.

3. Claudio Guillen, "Metaphor of Perspective," 317, notes that "perspective" remained a *terminus technicus* of the fine arts, while "point of view" became the popular term used in other disciplines. The German equivalents are "Sehe-Punkt" or "Gesichts-Punkt."

4. Cf. Möller, *Rhetorische Überlieferung*; Schmidt, *Sinnlichkeit und Verstand*; Wetterer, *Publikumsbezug und Wahrheitsanspruch*; Schlegel, *Zur Wirkungsästhetik der Poetik Bodmers und Breitingers*. The most sophisticated attempt thus far to interpret Breitinger in terms of Wolffian categories is by Wellbery, *Lessing's "Laocoon*," a book that is discussed later in this Introduction.

5. Cf. Dacier, *Poëtique*, 110–11; Breitinger, *Dichtkunst*, 2:106–7; Braitmaier, *Geschichte der Poetischen Theorie*, 208.

6. Pascal, *Pensées*, 17.

7. Wolfgang Preisendanz, "Mimesis und Poiesis," 539. Although Preisendanz alludes briefly (538, 539) to the fact that Aristotle's *Poetics* was "umge-

deutet" in the Renaissance, he does not appear to have grasped the complexity or extent of the revisions.

8. See my review of this work in *German Quarterly* 61 (1988): 304–5.

9. Chapter 2 of my study contains additional comments on his argument.

10. Crüger, J. C. *Gottsched und die Schweizer*, p. LXII.

11. Goethe, *Werke*, 9:262.

12. Cf. "Und doch zeigt sich gerade hier wieder Breitinger's begriffliche Schwäche. Er ist . . . nicht imstande, seine eigene Grundkonzeption gegen die ablenkende Fülle überkommener Gesichtspunkte und den Druck bereits fest geformter Gedanken durchzusetzen," Herrmann, *Naturnachahmung*, 262; "Wieder hatte er den Schlüssel für sein Problem buchstäblich in der Hand. . . . Aber der Gedanke kommt nicht ins Offene. . . . Einmal mehr hat die Wahrheitsfrage dem alten rhetorischen Wirkungsgesichtspunkt weichen müssen," 263–64.

13. Ibid., 195–98.

14. Wellbery, *Lessing's "Laocoon,"* registers his agreement with Herrmann's evaluation of Breitinger on p. 260, n. 61. Further citations of Wellbery's study are in the text in parentheses.

15. Windfuhr, *Barocke Bildlichkeit*, 457 and 461.

16. Wellbery, from whom one would most expect this attention, has only three citations from the second volume, and all of them are taken from the ninth chapter, "Von dem mahlerischen Ausdruck."

17. For my distinctions between the semiotic and hermeneutic approaches, I draw in part on Wellbery's own lucid presentation (44–48) of what he calls these different "theory types." Unlike Wellbery, however, I do not view these interpretative models as mutually exclusive and I do not confine them to particular historical strata.

18. Knodt, "*Negative Philosophie*," 11, takes the extreme step of accusing Wellbery of subscribing to a Romantic teleology—contrary to his own assertions—because his paradigms, she argues, merely replicate with different terminology traditional categories of periodization and traditional notions of "epistemologische Transformation" in the eighteenth century.

19. Bosse, in his seminal article "'Dichter kann man nicht bilden,'" rightly disputes (122) the common belief that the autonomy of the reader is strictly a "Besonderheit der romantischen Kunstphilosophie." As evidence he cites (in n. 173) a passage published in 1799 by the "unromantischen Kantianer" J. A. Bergk: "Jedes Buch, das wir lesen, muß in uns die Kräfte in Thätigkeit sezzen, die dazu gehören, eine gute Composition zu machen. Der Dichter muß unsere Einbildungskraft und unsern Verstand, der Philosoph unsere Vernunft beschäftigen, um in uns selbst die Operationen in Gang zu bringen, die zur Hervorbringung von irgend etwas nöthig sind, und uns dadurch selbst zum Gegenstand der Reflexion zu machen. Die Erscheinungen, die der Dichter malt, der Philosoph erklärt, müssen in unserm Gemüthe hervorgerufen werden, wenn wir uns durch Lesen zur Selbstthätigkeit und zur Freiheit empor schwingen wollen." Bosse points out that the notion of "Selbsttätigkeit" during the act of reading is rooted in Herder's

and Humboldt's concept of the "Arbeit des Geistes" found in their writings on language. But Bergk's observation is equally significant, as we shall see, as a restatement of the process Breitinger calls "Gemüthes-Beschäftigung."

Chapter 1

1. Breitinger, *Critische Dichtkunst*, 2:9. Regarding Breitinger's comparison of sounds and colors, cf. Dryden, "A Parallel of Poetry and Painting," 147: "Expression, and all that belongs to words, is that in a poem which colouring is in a picture"; also, Richardson, *The Theory of Painting*, 5: "The Pleasure that Painting, as a Dumb Art, gives us, is like what we have from Musick; its beautiful Forms, Colours and Harmony, are to the Eye what Sounds, and the Harmony of that kind are to the Ear." The comparison is as old as the *ut pictura* simile itself, and occurs, for example, in Plato's *Cratylus*, 431B–D.

2. In my treatment of the problem of knowledge and representation I am indebted to Trimpi, *Muses of One Mind*, esp. part 2. Trimpi's analysis of what he refers to as "the ancient dilemma of knowledge and representation" has supplied me with my own terms of analysis in this chapter. For a preliminary statement of the dilemma, see his text 83–106.

3. The works in question are Cordemoy's *Discours Physique de la Parole* of 1677 and Wallis's *Treatise on Speech* of 1653. Breitinger's attention may have been drawn to Wallis by Christian Wolff, *Vernünfftige Gedancken von Gott, der Welt und der Seele des Menschen*, who mentions (§ 324) Leibniz's correspondence with Wallis regarding the "Verbindungs-Kunst der Zeichen." (Wolff's work is cited henceforth as *Metaphysik*.) I am grateful to Thomas P. Saine for allowing me to use his copy of the first edition.

4. For the immediate historical context of this debate, see Aarsleff, "An Outline of Language-Origins Theory since the Renaissance," in *From Locke to Saussure*, 278–92; for a description of the nature-convention debate as it derived from antiquity, see Kayser's excellent article, "Böhmes Natursprachenlehre."

5. Cf. Cordemoy, *Discours*, 34–35: "Cette extréme difference qu'il y a entre ces signes & nos pensées, en nous marquant celle qui est entre nostre Corps & nostre Ame, nous donne en mesme temps à connoistre tout le secret de leur union . . . si l'on conçoit que les hommes puissennt par institution ioindre certains mouvemens à certaines pensées, on ne doit pas avoir de peine à concevoir que l'Autheur de la Nature en formant un homme, unifie si bien quelques pensées de son Ame à quelques mouvemens de son Corps" (34–35). (Linguistic signs as "mouvemens de son Corps" are conceived of by Cordemoy as movements of the breath that strike the ear and eventually the brain.) I use the word "skepticism" with reference to Cordemoy because he appears to repeat Cratylus's skeptical arguments and his solutions; see esp. *Cratylus*, 438C.

6. Breitinger quotes from *Orator*, 55, and Quintilian, 8.5. (I have not been able to determine what edition of Quintilian Breitinger used; the passage in

question may be found at 8.3.16, Loeb edition.) Breitinger's linking of euphony with the historical development of language is, however, an Epicurean notion, see Kayser, "Böhmes Natursprachenlehre," 529, and cf. my n. 8.

7. Cf. 2:19: "Dieses machet neben anderm, daß das Urtheil über die Härtigkeit oder Fliessendheit einer Sprache so ungleich herauskommt, indem eine jede Nation hierinn ihrem eigenen Geschmacke trauet, den sie in ihrem Gehöre und in ihrem Munde hat."

8. Although Kayser explains the Epicurean argument for the existence of various languages, adopted by Breitinger, as an ancient refutation of the conventionalist position, Breitinger seems to allign himself more with convention theories. In another passage on the arbitrary nature of signs (2:200–202), he quotes Horace's *Ars poetica*, lines 60–71: "As forests change their leaves with each year's decline, and the earliest drop off: so with words . . . all mortal things shall perish," quoted from the Loeb edition, pp. 455–57. (All further quotations from this work are from this edition, cited with line numbers in the text.) Brink, in his Horace commentary, 151, observes that in context Horace's point is simply "that language is as prone to change as other creations of man." Moreover, Breitinger's three laudatory references to John Locke's *An Essay concerning Humane Understanding*, about which I will have more to say, are all from Locke's third book, "On Words," where a completely unambiguous defense of the conventionality of language is presented.

9. Breitinger's suggestion (2:59–60) for the remedy of this problem is identical to Leibniz's: "ein sprachkündiger Mann" should compile a dictionary of the excellent vocabularies of Opitz, Fleming, and others; cf. § 33 of "Unvorgreifliche Gedanken, betreffend die Ausübung und Verbesserung der teutschen Sprache," which Breitinger knew and admired, in Leibniz, *Hauptschriften*, 2:519–55, where he calls for a German "Sprachbrauch," "Sprachschatz," and "Sprachquell."

10. The same praise is given Opitz by Leibniz in his "Unvorgreifliche Gedanken," §§ 63–65.

11. 2:311. The reference is to "Unvorgreifliche Gedancken," § 61.

12. Häntzschel, "Die Ausbildung der deutschen Literatursprache des 18. Jahrhunderts durch Übersetzungen: Homer-Verdeutschungen als produktive Kraft," in Kimpel, *Mehrsprachigkeit*, mentions (117–18) in passing Breitinger's and Gottsched's differing approaches to translation, but he underestimates the similarities between Breitinger and Herder in this regard.

13. The passage may be a paraphrase of Locke: "It is not enough for the perfection of Language, that Sounds can be made signs of Ideas, unless those signs can be so made use of, as to comprehend several particular Things: For the multiplication of Words would have perplexed their Use, had every particular thing need of a distinct name to be signified by"; see *Essay*, 3.1.3.

14. Cf. 2:308: " . . . deswegen er auch behauptet, daß alle Wörter, mit welchen die abgezogenen Begriffe von uncörperlichen Dingen ausgedrückt werden, figürlich seyn . . . "

15. Breitinger's text at 1:15 is a translation of Dubos's words, "La vûë a plus d'empire sur l'ame que les autres sens . . . ," from Dubos, *Reflexions critiques*, 1.40.393. (Further citations of Dubos in the text and notes will give volume, chapter, and page number.) Breitinger also reproduces Dubos's citation of Horace's *Ars poetica*, 180–81, on the primacy of sight over the other senses. Brink, in his edition of Horace, 245–46, finds that this passage has less to do with a "philosophical doctrine of vision" than with the issue of vivid style and (rhetorical) psychagogia. Dubos may be indebted to da Vinci, who argues for the primacy of sight in his treatise on painting; cf. my chapter 3, n. 30.

16. The problems inherent in this statement and its relation to the problem of language were anticipated by Plato; cf. *Cratylus*, 432A–C. Dubos exhibits here the neoclassic confusion between image and copy, which Breitinger is trying to avoid; cf. Trimpi, *Muses of One Mind*, 106–8, where this passage from the *Cratylus* is discussed.

17. "Les mots doivent d'abord réveiller les idées dont ils ne sont que des signes arbitraires. Il faut ensuite que ces idées s'arrangent dans l'imagination, & qu'elles y forment ces tableaux qui nous touchent & ces peintures qui nous interessent" (1.40.394).

18. While the notion of poetic or rhetorical effect through proper organization of particulars had been elaborated by Plato and Aristotle, Breitinger says, at 1:422–24, that he has been supported in these thoughts by Longinus, and quotes from chapter 10 of Περὶ ὕψους at length. There Longinus praises the sublimity of a poem by Sappho as deriving from the "skill with which she selects and combines the most striking and intense of those symptoms" (i.e., of the passion of love); quoted from the Loeb edition of Longinus, *On the Sublime*, 10.1. (All further quotations from this work are from this edition.)

19. Wellbery, *Lessing's "Laocoon,"* analyzes the Enlightenment's desire to transform arbitrary signs into natural signs, but mentions only in passing Breitinger's discourse on metaphor in this context (195). Breitinger is interested in constructing some sort of mimetic relationship between words and things, although not of the naive or mystical sort, where words are equated with things. In this, however, he differs from Locke, who attempted to resolve the problem by saying that words have no connection to things at all, but that we *assume* they do for purposes of communication: "But though Words, as they are used by Men, can properly and immediately signifie nothing but the Ideas, that are in their Minds; yet they in their Thoughts, give them a secret reference to two other Things. First, They suppose their Words to be Marks of the Ideas in the Minds also of other Men, with whom they communicate. . . . Secondly, Because Men would not be thought to talk barely of their own Imaginations, but of Things as really they are; therefore they often suppose their Words to stand also for the Reality of Things" (*Essay*, 3.2.4–5). These distinctions are related to Locke's discussion of "phantastical" and false ideas in his second book, the former deriving from man's power to "make an Idea neither answering the reality of Things, nor

agreeing to the Ideas commonly signified by other Peoples Words" (*Essay*, 2.31.25). This in turn will form the basis for Addison's concept of the imagination, which "makes new Worlds of its own"; see the *Spectator*, no. 419, 3:573. Why Breitinger did not follow this particular path of reasoning is discussed in detail in chapter 2.

20. *Gleichnis-Abhandlung*, 135.

21. These criteria are taken from Breitinger's chapter on style, "Von der Schreibart insgemein." Although he refers the reader (2:306) to Aristotle, *Poetics*, 22.3, regarding the use of the "eigentliches Wort" (Aristotle's "ordinary word") and the figurative expression, his guidelines for the use of metaphor do not seem to be particularly Aristotelian. Whereas the third consideration bears some resemblance to Aristotle's judgment in *Rhetoric*, 3.2.12 (quoted from the Loeb edition), that "metaphors must not be far-fetched," the first two considerations appear to derive from Cicero, *De Oratore*, 3.38.155: "Metaphor . . . sprang from necessity due to the pressure of poverty. . . . when something that can scarcely be conveyed by the proper term is expressed metaphorically, the meaning we desire to convey is made clear." (My attention was drawn to this passage in *De Oratore* by E. M. Cope in his commentary on *The Rhetoric* [London, 1877], 377.) Breitinger is of course indebted to a massive rhetorical tradition, and the actual source of his ideas may not be ultimately traceable. His theories of language, at least, appear to be more Stoic than Aristotelian, as this passage demonstrates; and cf. n. 6.

22. Gottsched, *Versuch einer Critischen Dichtkunst*, vol. 6, no. 1, of *Werke*, 24. (All further quotations of Gottsched's work are from this volume of this edition and are cited in the text by page number only.) I shall return to the problem of metaphor in chapter 4.

23. The interpretation of Horace's comparison in terms of parallel construction was first carried out by Trimpi, "Meaning," 1–34, where an exhaustive philological justification of the importance of the parallel construction is presented. This study has since been augmented by two additional articles, cited in nn. 25 and 27.

24. Horace's reference to Homer actually occurs at line 359, just before the *ut pictura* passage. What he says there, at lines 347–60, is that in long works, such as those by Homer, an occasional imperfection should not be allowed to ruin our appreciation of the entire work. This anticipates his subsequent point that not all poetic compositions should be judged according to the standards appropriate to (what he probably meant as) epideictic forms.

25. For a complete discussion of these terms, see Trimpi, "The Metaphorical Uses."

26. See Trimpi, "Meaning," 7–11.

27. Cf. Trimpi, "Horace's 'Ut Pictura Poesis': The Argument for Stylistic Decorum," esp. 33.

28. *Critias*, 107B–D. See also Trimpi, *Muses of One Mind*, 99–101, for a discussion of this passage as a description of the "ancient dilemma of knowledge and representation" and as it relates to Horace's simile.

29. These two statements are grounded in Stoic conceptions of a coincidence between human *ratio* and cosmic order, but Longinus represents the liberal tradition in this regard: coincidence is "sympathy," or participation in natural order, rather than, as in more conservative notions, identity of the human and cosmic. An interesting philological exposition of this ancient (ultimately Pythagorean) concept is Spitzer's *Classical and Christian Ideas of World Harmony*.

30. Cf. also *Ars poetica*, 32–36: "There is a craftsman who in bronze will mould nails and imitate waving locks, but is unhappy in the total result, because he cannot represent a whole figure." That is, he excels at insignificant detail and cannot succeed with the larger sculpture of which these details would only be embellishment.

31. Gottsched's diction requires comment: "Vers" confuses line with poem; cf. Adelung, *Grammatisch-kritisches Wörterbuch*, 4. Theil, Sp. 1111–12, where "Vers" is said to mean "die Zeile eines Gedichtes." The example given is the phrase "ein Vers aus dem Horaz." Adelung also notes that "da Vers, so wie Reim, nur die äußere Form eines Gedichtes ausdrückt, so wird es auch in der edlern Schreibart und von vorzüglichen Gedichten nicht gern mehr für das Gedicht selbst gebraucht," *except* in popular usage: "im gemeinen Leben." Horace has of course *poesis* and not *versus*. With this inaccurate translation, Gottsched betrays either his lack of sophistication with basic literary terms or his desire to reproduce the popular term. The use of "schön" in the line "das sind die schönen Werke der Poeten" is probably sarcastic, inasmuch as he then states that these "Schönheiten" are completely ephemeral.

32. Gottsched is merely adhering to traditional views of Horace inherited from the Renaissance. Trimpi, "Meaning," 1, explains that he began his inquiry into the Horatian lines by attempting "to understand the liberties which the Renaissance had taken with Horace's phrase—since some norm had to be established before departures from it could be measured . . . [but] the normative meaning had never been departed from because, from the earliest commentaries on, it had never been understood." Weinberg, *Literary Criticism*, 1:72, notes that "the *Ars poetica* did not come to the Renaissance as a naked text" and discusses, 72–79, the determining role of ancient commentaries in the Renaissance neoclassic use of the Horation simile.

33. See Spingarn's discussion of the term in the introduction to his *Critical Essays*, 29–31. Gottsched's definition is based on Christian Wolff's *Metaphysik*, § 858: "Wer scharfsinnig ist / der kan sich deutlich vorstellen / auch was in den Dingen verborgen ist und von andern übersehen wird (§ 850). Wenn nun die Einbildungs-Krafft andere Dinge hervor bringet, die er vor diesem erkand / welche mit den gegenwärtigen etwas gemein haben (§ 238); so erkennet er durch dasjenige / was sie mit einander gemein haben / ihre Aenlichkeit (§ 18). Derowegen da die Leichtigkeit die Aenlichkeit wahrzunehmen / der Witz ist (§ 366); so ist klar / daß Witz aus einer Scharfsinnigkeit und guten Einbildungs-Krafft und Gedächtnis entstehet (§ 248)." (The numbers in parentheses are Wolff's references to definitions from previous para-

graphs.) Similar definitions of "Witz" are found in Breitinger: "Der Witz ist ein Vermögen des Geistes, die sinnlichen Vorstellungen mit einander zu vergleichen, und die Uebereinstimmungen in demjenigen, worinn sie von einander unterschieden werden, leicht wahrzunehmen. . . . Der Witz hat daran genug, daß er sich die Dinge nach ihrer Aehnlichkeit vorstellet, in so ferne sie ähnlich oder verschieden sind" (2:104); and Locke, 2.11.2: "For Wit [lies] most in the assemblage of Ideas, and [puts] those together with quickness and variety, wherein can be found any resemblance or congruity." The differences between Breitinger and Gottsched regarding wit are best addressed not by scrutiny of a single passage or definition, but by reviewing their poetic conceptions as a whole. The problem is taken up again in chapter 2.

34. *The Poetics*, Fyfe's translation, Loeb edition, 22.17. (All quotations from Aristotle's works, unless otherwise noted, are from the Loeb editions, and will be cited in the text by section number.)

35. Gaede, "Gottscheds Nachahmungstheorie," argues that Gottsched is the first critic in the German context to realize fully, by arguing for the work as a copy of the harmonious order of the universe, what he (Gaede) views as Aristotle's equation of a logical "Verknüpfungsprinzip" with the "Seinsprinzip" (111–12)—in other words, the equation of mind and nature. Gaede refers his reader to 1051b of Aristotle's *Metaphysics*, where, however, one may find the observation that "It is not because we are right in thinking that you are white that you are white; it is because you are white that we are right in saying so." It is not clear to me how Gaede arrives at the equivalence of ontological and logical categories in Aristotle ("Seinsprinzip" and "Verknüpfungsprinzip") when clearly Aristotle means that being and truth stand in *relation* to each other. In Gottsched's (typically neoclassic) attempt to make them identical lies precisely the difference between him and Aristotle.

36. Concerning the Sophistic conflation of human law and natural law, see Heinimann, *Nomos und Physis*.

37. Pope's term is from the "Essay on Criticism," in *Works*, 1:260, line 174. Pope and Breitinger may have been influenced by Le Bossu's comments on Horace's simile in his widely read treatise on the epic: "Pictures have their Shadows, their Distances, and their Point of Sight, without which they lose all their Grace and Regularity. The Images that adorn the Arch of a very high Cupola, are very large where they are, and to those who view them pretty near, represent only Members that are monstrous in their Projections. A Man would render himself ridiculous, if he seriously found fault with those mishapen Postures, which Men of Understanding greatly admire. . . . 'Tis just so with the Works of the Poets" (*Bossu's Treatise*, 6.8.263–64). Trimpi, "The Metaphorical Uses," 407–9, gives the ancient sources of this "second distortion," esp. in Vitruvius, who is a probable influence on this passage from Le Bossu.

38. The phrase "nackte Blösse" refers to Gottsched's definition of "Mahlerey." In the first chapter of the *Critische Dichtkunst*, "Vergleichung der

Mahler-Kunst und der Dicht-Kunst," Breitinger says, 1:12–13, that "in dem erstern Versuch," that is, in Gottsched's *Versuch einer Critischen Dichtkunst* of 1730, poetic painting was interpreted "in dem engen Verstand," which means, Breitinger says, that objects are only depicted in terms of "Klarheit." Indeed Gottsched, 195–96, admits the term "poetische Mahlerey" only for naturalistic description, which is for him "die geringste Art [der Nachahmung]." Gottsched does not appear to have recognized that the extreme verisimilitude he defended was but another kind of strict naturalism.

39. Finsler, *Homer in der Neuzeit*, 395–405, provides to my knowledge the only analysis of Breitinger's use of French and English sources in his study of Homer.

40. Cf. 1:11–12. The evaluation and absorption of the critical issues of antiquity played a constitutive role in Europe as a whole during those centuries in which a vernacular literary language was being developed: Italy in the late fourteenth, fifteenth, and early sixteenth centuries, England in the sixteenth century, and France and Germany as already noted. It is astounding that Blackall made no reference at all to this European phenomenon in which Germany eventually participated.

41. Horace, *Epistles*, 2.1.34–38. Jauß, "Ästhetische Normen," offers the best explanation to date of competing concepts of perfection among both the *anciens* and the *modernes*.

42. A similar temporalization of the Horatian simile may be found in Le Bossu, in the passage cited in n. 37, which continues, 264: "We may likewise fall into these false Criticisms for want of Learning and a deep reach. We would fain have Homer and Virgil form the Customs and Manners of their Personages according to the modern Mode. We think their ways of speaking fantastical, because they would be ridiculous, if turn'd Verbatim into our Language." The "fantastical" speech corresponds to the "monstrous" figures painted in the cupola, which, when seen from too much proximity (or in the case of speech, according to modern criteria alone) appear distorted. The passage anticipates Breitinger's own thoughts on translation, as set forth in the first section of this chapter.

43. La Motte, *Discours sur Homere*, 1.

44. The question of distortion by the reader was treated most fundamentally by Plato in his comparison of painting (i.e., not the skiagraphic image) to written discourse (versus oral discourse) in *Phaedrus*; see esp. 275D–E (although this passage must be read in context with the entire dialogue, which concerns the problem of written and oral expression).

45. Breitinger's criticism of La Motte is to be found mainly at 1:435–504, where he probably intended to attack Gottsched instead of La Motte.

46. Pope's words (7:12): "We ought to have a certain Knowledge of the principal Character and distinguishing Excellence of each: It is in that we are to consider him, and in proportion to his Degree in that we are to admire him. No Author or Man ever excell'd all the World in more than one Faculty, and as Homer has done this in Invention, Virgil has in Judgment. . . . Homer was the greater Genius, Virgil the better Artist." This judgment of

the two poets was a *topos* even in antiquity; cf. Quintilian, 10.1.46–47 and 10.1.85–86. Breitinger could have gotten his ideas there, of course, but his phrasing of them is Pope's.

47. Pope, 7:8: "Homer makes us Hearers, and Virgil leaves us Readers."

48. Pope, 7:9: "An excellent modern Writer allows, that if Virgil has not so many Thoughts that are low and vulgar, he has not so many that are sublime and noble." Breitinger wants to use Pope's formulation, but he is also copying Pope's allusion to yet another critic. Pope may have had in mind here the *Spectator*, no. 279; see the editor's interpolation in the passage cited.

49. See Shankman, *Pope's "Iliad,"* esp. 74–100 and 165–70, for a fine argument regarding Pope's use of Aristotelian and Horatian categories.

50. The distinction between "Haufen" and those who are "gelehrt" is not actually present in Horace's *ut pictura* context. Breitinger was perhaps familiar with this Horatian distinction from *Epistles*, 2.1.182–84, where Horace regrets that a sense of the value of agonistic discourse, the discourse that appeals to the ear instead of to the eye, has been lost in society as a whole (the translation in the Loeb edition has "rabble") as well as among educated listeners. Horace was a favorite of seventeenth- and eighteenth-century neoclassic thinkers, and it is not unlikely that Breitinger would have read his works with an eye to their interrelationship.

51. According to Shankman, *Pope's "Iliad,"* 79, this indeed was Pope's identical dilemma when translating Homer for an audience that could not have the same relationship to agonistic discourse as Homers's original listeners: "For while in the 'skiagraphic' style of spoken oratory—to which Aristotle compares the style of Homer—high finish is superfluous and uncalled for, the utmost literary polish is indeed *required* in written compositions—such as Pope's *Iliad*—because here the reader is given the opportunity to scrutinize the text at leisure" (emphasis in original).

52. Cf. 2:403–4: "Seine [the poet's] Erzehlung muß als ein sichtbares Gemählde die Sachen nicht bloß erzehlen, sondern zeigen, und das Gemüthe in eben diejenige Bewegung setzen, als die würckliche Gegenwart und das Anschauen der Dinge erweken würde. Dazu ist die gemeine und gewohnte Art zu reden viel zu schwach: Sein gantzer Ausdruck muß darum gantz neu und wunderbar, d. i. viel sinnlicher, prächtiger, und nachdrücklicher seyn. Und darum erstreket sich seine Freyheit in Anwendung der figürlichen Redensarten, so wohl was ihre Zahl, als die Neuheit der Bilder und die Verwegenheit der Translationen oder Verwendungen anbelanget, ohne Vergleichung weiter als des Redners seine."

53. Breitinger offers at this point one of the longest actual quotations in his entire *Critische Dichtkunst*, extending from 1:473–76, and continued at 1:494–95. The passages from Pope are at 7:7–8.

54. Quintilian, 6.2.27–35.

55. See Kustas, *Byzantine Rhetoric*, 172–75.

56. See Bretzigheimer, *Johann Elias Schlegels poetische Theorie*, 33–43, for an

excellent overview of this conflation of terms in the Renaissance. She over-
looks, however, Breitinger's confusion.

57. "Zudem müssen auch die Tadler dieses Poeten selbst gestehen, daß er
auch in theologischen Sachen mitten in der diken Finsterniß, die ihn umge-
ben hatte, zuweilen die Wahrheit erblicket" (1:162). Breitinger is quoting,
without saying so, a passage to which he then refers his reader, Mme Da-
cier's quotation of La Motte in *Des Causes de la Corruption du Goust*, 112–13:
"'Au milieu de cette nuit épaisse du Paganisme,' dit il, 'il n'a pas laissé d'en-
trevoir quelquefois le vray,'" and agreeing with her statement (104) that
Homer's works display "la conformité de plusieurs de ses idées avec beau-
coup de veritez de nos Livres Saints." See also Kapitza's discussion of "Das
Offenbarungsargument" in his excellent study *Ein bürgerlicher Krieg in der ge-
lehrten Welt*, 367–73, and cf. 431–32.

58. I am following here Shankman's conclusion that "Pope wishes to
make sense of Homer as a poet" (*Pope's "Iliad,"* 3), as well as Pope's own
remark in his *Iliad* preface, 7:5, that he wants to explain "the great and pe-
culiar Characteristick which distinguishes him from all other Authors."

59. Breitinger refers his reader in a note to Horace's *Ars poetica*, line 73,
and to "Quintilian, Lib. X.c.I." The passage Breitinger has in mind is ob-
viously 10.1.46–47 in which Homer is described as an "Ocean" and the
source of "inspiration for every department of eloquence"; and cf. Strabo's
Geography, 1.1.2, a locus to which Breitinger also refers in his *Gleichnis-
Abhandlung*, 284.

60. See Friedl, *Homer-Interpretation*, for a brief historical review of the
problem as it developed out of antiquity, and Simonsuuri, *Homer's Original
Genius*, for a discussion of the eighteenth-century use of ancient images of
Homer.

61. The meticulous collection and discussion of texts carried out by
Bleicher, *Homer in der deutschen Literatur*, neglect the Neoplatonic reception
of Homer altogether.

62. Walzel, *Prometheussymbol*, 24–30; Blumenberg, "Nachahmung der
Natur."

63. All quotations are from the incompletely paginated prefaces of the
original editions named in the text. An evaluation of the Swiss contribution
to textual criticism is provided by Henne, "Eine frühe kritische Edition
neuerer Literatur."

64. In one of his discussions of the development of German as a literary
language, Herder criticizes Triller's edition according to standards conso-
nant with Breitinger's: "Auch mit Opitzens Sprache sollten wir vertrauter
werden, und ein Glossarium über ihn aus dem wahren Geist unserer
Sprache, würde uns die stattlichen Veränderungen und Verbesserungen ei-
nigermaßen verleiden, die Triller mit ungeweihten Händen sich erfrechet
hat, ihm unterzuschieben" (Herder, *Werke*, 2:43). Herder also notes else-
where (1:149; 1:156; 2:28–29) that Breitinger was among the first critics in
Germany to engage in theoretical reflections on language.

Chapter 2

1. Breitinger, *Gleichnis-Abhandlung*, 200, and cf. 201–3. Breitinger is discussing a passage that can be found on p. 328 in vol. 6, no. 2, of Gottsched's *Dichtkunst*.

2. The definition at 1:57 also has "das Vermögen seiner [the poet's] Kunst [erstrecket sich] eben so weit, als die Kräfte der Natur selbst"; the poet should therefore study well "was in ihren Kräften annoch verborgen lieget." The reference to nature's unrealized potentialities ("Kräfte der Natur") expressed in the art work comes from Renaissance Neoplatonism; cf. Albrecht Dürer, "Lehre von menschlicher Proportion": "Dann warhafftig steckt die kunst inn der natur, wer sie herauss kan reyssenn, der hat sie" (3:295) and "ein fleissiger erbetter mag [die Natur] zw grund ersuchen vnd . . . vill wunders finden, das hÿrin begraben leit" (3:239). The excellent study by Möller, *Rhetorische Überlieferung*, esp. 44–82 and 137–39, suggests that the places in Breitinger's text marked by Neoplatonist vocabulary were lifted from Muratori. Regarding the Breitinger passage quoted in this note, see Möller, 74.

3. Herrmann, *Naturnachahmung*, 251–52. My remarks on his argument primarily concern his pages 234–38 and 249–64.

4. Although Herrmann was correct to point out the superficial analogy that had been drawn between Leibniz and Breitinger, his attempt to dismiss the Neoplatonic context of Breitinger's possible worlds in favor of a strictly Wolffian source was not universally accepted; see most recently Bretzigheimer, *Johann Elias Schlegels poetische Theorie*, 17–23, and Möller, *Rhetorische Überlieferung*, in places too numerous to cite. Herrmann's interpretation has been carried forward by John Neubauer, *Symbolismus und symbolische Logik*, 109–12, and Wetterer, *Publikumsbezug*, 211–14.

5. *Freiheit und Form*, 105–18.

6. Cf. *Monadologie*, § 33; *Essais de Théodicée*, § 37. Both works appear in Gerhardt, *Die philosophischen Schriften*, vol. 6. (Subsequent quotations from or references to these works will be based on this volume of this edition. Citations give paragraphs rather than pages.) Leibniz provides an additional discussion of truths of fact and truths of necessity in his *Nouveaux essais sur l'entendement humain*, 4.2.1. (All citations of this work, abbreviated henceforth as *Essais*, will be from vol. 6, no. 6, of *Gottfried Wilhelm Leibniz: Sämtliche Schriften und Briefe*, ed. Deutsche Akademie der Wissenschaften [Berlin: Akademie Verlag, 1962]. The *Essais* are divided into "Livre," "Chapitre," and paragraphs, all of which will be given by number, as I have done in this note.)

7. Windelband, *Lehrbuch*, 342, identifies Leibniz's truths of fact with *a posteriori* knowledge and truths of necessity with *a priori* knowledge. Schepers, in Ritter, *Historisches Wörterbuch*, s.v. "A priori/a posteriori," 466, points out that for Leibniz only the divine intellect is capable of pure *a priori* knowledge. Humans remain dependent on experience for their access to the nec-

essary truths, although Leibniz is by no means completely consistent on this point, in passages cited by Schepers.

8. *Théodicée*, § 37.

9. *Principes de la Nature et de la Grâce*, § 11, ed. Gerhardt, vol. 6, henceforth cited as *Principes*. Cassirer, *Leibniz' System*, 534, notes (approvingly) that Leibniz's "scharfe, dualistische Trennung" between the laws of physics and the laws of mathematics was criticized by Bertrand Russell in his work on Leibniz.

10. *Théodicée*, "Discours preliminaire," § 3.

11. Lovejoy, *Great Chain of Being*, based his discussion (in his chapter 5) of Leibniz's use of the principle of plenitude on the thesis that it was Leibniz's intention for all possibles to be actualized according to universal necessity. His thesis has been challenged by J. Hintikka, "Leibniz on Plenitude."

12. That God is not forced to grant real existence to all of the necessary truths is the basis of Leibniz's critique of Spinoza's determinism; cf. *Théodicée*, § 173.

13. Ibid., § 116.

14. Cassirer, *Freiheit und Form*, 109, is quoting from 1:56–57, and has modernized Breitinger's orthography.

15. *Monadologie*, § 46. This aspect of Leibniz's thought was not lost on the theologian Breitinger. He says at 1:135 that God is not capable of bringing about the impossible, which is defined as the contradictory. Breitinger would have found this restated in Christian Wolff's *Metaphysik*, § 1022.

16. See Möller, *Rhetorische Überlieferung*, 137, for the Muratori passage copied by Breitinger that refers to the necessary truths.

17. 1:138–39; Muratori's corresponding terms (Möller, *Rhetorische Überlieferung*, 73) are "Vero secondo l'Intelletto" and "Vero secondo la Fantasia." Muratori qualifies the former term as "Vero necessario, o evidente, o moralmente certo," while the latter term is "Vero possibile, probabile, e credibile." In the former category Muratori includes not only knowledge provided by the exact sciences, but also by history—"factual truths," as it were. These qualifications appear to be reflected in Breitinger's text at 1:60–61, where he discusses "zwo Gattungen des Wahren in der Natur" that he calls "das historische Wahre" and "das poetische Wahre." The distinction between historical and poetic truth in Muratori and Breitinger ultimately derives, however, from Aristotle's discussion of history and poesis, and does not correspond to Leibniz's distinction between *vérités de fait* and *vérités nécessaires*. (Failure to see this was indeed the source of Cassirer's mistake.) But Breitinger, *unlike Muratori*, does not conflate "das Wahre des Verstandes" with "das historische Wahre." Instead, he is distinguishing two kinds of *vérités de fait*, poesis and history, from the *vérités nécessaires* ("das Wahre des Verstandes"). The entire matter is taken up again systematically in chapter 3 of this study. Here the problem of terms demonstrates how tricky the question of sources can be. For while Breitinger may have borrowed words from Muratori (or Aristotle), he factored them into his reading of Leibniz and Wolff.

18. Cf. e.g. Preisendanz, "Nachahmungsprinzip in Deutschland," 79: "Für Breitinger selbst handelte es sich nur darum, das Wunderbare . . . innerhalb eines noch durchaus rationalistischen Horizonts legitimieren zu können," so that one should not attribute to him "die Vorstellung einer sehr weit gehenden Autonomie des poetischen Gebildes." Wetterer, *Publikumsbezug*, 222, concludes that "Breitinger [läßt] . . . keinen Zweifel daran, daß auch er [i.e., like Gottsched] nicht bereit ist, Poesie vom Anspruch auf Wahrheit und Vernünftigkeit gänzlich zu entbinden." During the last twenty years, critics have generally argued against finding stirrings of "Romantic genius" in Breitinger's work, as did, e.g., Böckmann, *Formgeschichte*, 573, who says that in Zurich "die Dichtung wird als selbstgenugsame Schöpfung der Phantasie anerkannt. Sie braucht nicht mehr am Maßstab der Verständigkeit gemessen zu werden," an interpretation that has virtually nothing to do with Breitinger's text but which occurred in various permutations throughout the nineteenth century and the first two-thirds of this century as part of the ideological program of *Germanistik*. A detailed description of the reception of Breitinger's work lies outside the bounds of this study.

19. I am following here Megill, "Aesthetic Theory and Historical Consciousness," esp. 39–40. Megill argues convincingly (versus the influential positions of Cassirer and Meinecke) that "historism" (not Rankean "historicism") developed out of late seventeenth-century aesthetics, which Megill characterizes as "the contextual mode of evaluation," a term consonant with Breitinger's enterprise as I attempt to describe it in this study. See Megill's opening remarks and notes for further clarification of the terms "historism" and "historicism." Cf. Kapitza's discussion "Die Vollendung am Anfang: Unterscheidung der Künste von den Wissenschaften," in *Ein bürgerlicher Krieg*, 378–89, which concerns the German context of this problem (without, however, much reference to Breitinger); also Simonsuuri, *Homer's Original Genius*, chap. 1 ("Ancients and moderns: the problem of cultural progress") and chap. 7 ("Vico's discovery of the true Homer").

20. Cf. Möller, *Rhetorische Überlieferung*, 23: "In dem Maße, wie ein Gegenstandsbereich vom Prozeß wissenschaftlicher Klärung erfaßt wird, wird das Geschmacksurteil vom Verstandesurteil ersetzt. Ein wesentlicher Grund für Gottscheds Versuch, die Poetik auf ein philosophisches Fundament zu stellen, besteht darin, diesen Prozeß der Verwissenschaftlichung auch auf dem Gebiet der freien Künste einzuführen. . . . Deshalb versucht er die Regeln der Poesie mit einer Genauigkeit zu bestimmen, die dem geometrischen Verfahren nahekommt." Möller does not pursue this issue with reference to the *querelle*, nor does he contrast it with Breitinger's enterprise. Gottsched's attempt at "Verwissenschaftlichung" must be understood, however, in the context described by Jauß, "Ästhetische Normen," 44–47, namely in terms of the conflict spawned by the *querelle* between "vollendete Perfektion" (exemplified by literature) and "unbegrenzte Perfektibilität" (the "telos" as it were of the physical sciences). Gottsched's poetics are "geometric" not because Gottsched puts literature on a par with the sciences (a thesis maintained by Borjans-Heuser, *Bürgerliche Produktivität*), but because for

him all poetic knowledge has been forever discovered and need only be de-
ductively *re*-produced.

21. Cf. *Dichtkunst*, 1:115–17; *Gleichnis-Abhandlung*, 286–93.

22. Breitinger did read Leibniz as well as Wolff. Certainly he knew, as a
literate person in the early eighteenth century, the *Théodicée*. He probably
read the *Monadologie*, published in German and Latin in 1720–21, and per-
haps also the *Principes*, which first appeared in 1718. He may have seen the
Meditationes de cogitione in the *Acta eruditorum* of 1684 because he wrote a
textbook on logic at the same time he was preparing his *Critische Dichtkunst*.
The only Leibniz text to which he makes specific reference (2:46 and 311)
is the *Unvorgreifliche Gedancken, betreffend die Ausübung und Verbesserung der
teutschen Sprache*. He did not know, of course, the *Nouveaux essais*. In this
and the following chapter, I use Leibniz's system as a *model* to explain Brei-
tinger's poetics, not as a source. His specific indebtedness to Wolff will be
discussed later in this chapter.

23. *Meditationes de cognitione*, in *Monadology and Other Philosophical Essays*,
trans. Paul Schrecker and Ann Martin Schrecker (Indianapolis: Bobbs-Mer-
rill, 1965), 6. (Further references to this work are based on this translation.)
The passage continues with Leibniz's distinction between what is thinkable
and what is possible expressed as the difference between nominal and real
definitions: "Hobbes, who pretended that all truths are arbitrary, because
they depend on nominal definitions . . . did not consider . . . that the re-
ality of a definition does not depend upon us and that not any notions
whatever can be combined together" (7). Cf. *Essais*, 3.3.15: "Ce qu'on sup-
pose possible est exprimé par la definition, mais cette definition n'est que
nominale quand elle n'exprime point en même temps la possibilité. . . . Il
ne depend donc pas de nous de joindre les idées comme bon nous semble, à
moins que cette combinaison ne soit justifiée ou par la raison qui la monstre
possible, ou par l'experience qui la monstre actuelle, et par consequent pos-
sible aussi."

24. *Meditationes*, 6–7; cf. also *Essais*, 3.10.7.

25. *Monadologie*, §§ 36–38 and 45. With the *a posteriori* proof, Leibniz an-
swers one of the two great questions of metaphysics (cf. *Principes*, 7), i.e.,
why something exists rather than nothing. It is curious, in view of his mathe-
matical insights, that he considered this question answerable, or even pos-
sible. For just as an infinite chain of contingent beings does not include
a first member that could be the cause of all subsequent contingents, so
Leibniz states that it is not possible to give the greatest number (cf. *Essais*,
2.17.1), that is, to specify the end of an infinite sequence. Yet sufficient rea-
son, even though it be said to stand outside the chain of contingents that it
actualizes, appears to do just that.

26. *Essais*, 4.10.7: "Et c'est déja quelque chose que par cette remarque
[i.e., the assertion of God's possibility] on prouve, que *supposé que Dieu soit
possible, il existe*, ce qui est le privilege de la seule Divinité" (emphasis in the
original). Beierwaltes, *Platonismus*, 118, notes that the identification of pos-
sibility and necessary existence in the divine mind is a fundamental Neoplo-

tinian concept: "Der Gegensatz von *Möglichem* zu *Wirklichem* ist sowohl in Schellings Absolutem als auch in Plotins absolutem Geist aufgehoben. Im Absoluten ist das Mögliche als ein zeithaft Noch-nicht-Wirkliches undenkbar, es destruiert dessen Unendlichkeit; der Geist ist als Denken seiner selbst denkendes Leben und dies heißt: reine Wirklichkeit" (emphasis in the original); cf. also 51: "Die Frage nach dem Verhältnis von Sein und Denken ist seit Parmenides eine Grundfrage der Philosophie und der philosophischen Theologie. Plotin hat zuerst dieses Verhältnis als Identität und damit als Wesenskonstituens des absoluten Geistes gedacht."

27. *Théodicée*, §§ 7 and 53.

28. *Principes*, § 10; cf. *Monadologie*, § 54, and *Théodicée*, § 201.

29. Politella, *Platonism, Aristotelianism, and Cabalism*, 33, points out that Leibniz "speaks of a 'fall' into matter, or sin, only when he argues with theologians; the real life of the Monad does not, as the Plotinian or Cabalistic spark of life, diminish in its glory as it descends into the inferior worlds of creation." Thus the goal of existence in Leibniz's conception was not the reabsorption into the Godhead, or Plotinian One, but rather the *continual* approximation to the divine; cf. 24–27. That the existents should strive to be like the divine even though they do not lose their value through actualization is based on a conscious "ambiguity" (26–27) that allows Leibniz to maintain the dignity of the individual existent as well as of the divine unity out of which it arose.

30. Leibniz wants to show, in contrast to Descartes, that God is not a completely arbitrary being who freely dictates necessity and, in contrast to Spinoza, that the world is not absolutely determined, thus making human choices irrelevant.

31. *Théodicée*, § 173.

32. Ibid., § 7.

33. Ibid., § 37.

34. Lovejoy, *Great Chain of Being*, 172.

35. A concise overview of Leibniz's critique of Descartes is provided by Windelband, *Lehrbuch*, 360–65.

36. Cf. Cassirer, *Leibniz' System*, 514–20.

37. *De ipsa natura*, trans. Schrecker, 102.

38. *Monadologie*, § 61.

39. For all of the terms in this paragraph, see *De ipsa natura*, esp. 104 and 106–8.

40. Cf. *Monadologie*, § 57, and *Principes*, § 2: "C'est comme dans un centre ou point, tout simple qu'il est, se trouvent une infinité d'angles formés par les lignes qui y concourent."

41. *De ipsa natura*, 97.

42. *Monadologie*, § 14.

43. Ibid., § 7.

44. *Principes*, § 4; *Monadologie*, §§ 11–15.

45. *Monadologie*, § 60.

46. Ibid., §§ 42 and 49. The Neoplotinian undercurrent in Leibniz's sys-

tem is evident in his identification of Mind with the unifying of a multi-
plicity represented in matter; cf. my n. 26, and Beierwaltes, *Platonismus*, 24,
for an additional historical clarification of this issue.

47. The example illustrates the difficulty of the relationship in Leibniz's
thought between the *a priori* and the *a posteriori*. Although Leibniz does not
mention it, the astronomer must rely on mathematics to develop his knowl-
edge, cf. n. 7. Near the end of the *Essais* (at 4.17.23), Leibniz suggests that *a
priori* knowledge is embedded in experience: "le comment [d'un] fait," such
as the rising of the sun, reveals "la raison *a priori* de cette verité." In the
opening argument of the *Essais*, he had offered the proposition that the
senses provide the "occasion" for our becoming conscious of innate (*a
priori?*) knowledge (1.1.1). Cf. 1.1.11 for an even more emphatic statement:
"Les idées intellectuelles et les veritez qui en dependent sont distinctes, et
ni les unes ni les autres n'ont point leur origine des sens; *quoiqu'il soit vrai
que nous n'y penserions jamais sans les sens*" (my emphasis). Why, however,
one being should develop *a priori* knowledge and another not (or not to the
same degree) is not explainable by the effects of the outer world, but only by
the individuality of each being: "Toutes les pensées et actions de notre ame
viennent de son propre fonds" (1.1.1), which appears to be Leibniz's point
in *Monadologie*, §§ 26–29.

48. Cf. Windelband, *Lehrbuch*, 362–63.

49. *Principes*, § 4.

50. *Meditationes*, 10; *Essais*, 2.2.1.

51. *Monadologie*, § 30.

52. Ibid., §§ 14 and 23. In the *Monadologie*, the distinction between "pe-
tites perceptions" and "perception" is not clear. Both terms are used to de-
scribe the death state; cf. § 21.

53. Ibid., §§ 60–61; cf. *Essais*, 2.21.5.

54. *Principes*, § 3.

55. Cf. Lovejoy, *Great Chain of Being*, 332: "A qualitative continuum, at all
events, is a contradiction in terms. Wherever, in any series, there appears a
new *quale*, a different *kind* of thing, and not merely a different magnitude
and degree of something common to the whole series, there is *eo ipso* a
breach of continuity" (emphasis in the original). Lovejoy points out here the
difficulty of divorcing degrees of force in the monads from the category of
quantity, as Leibniz attempts to do.

56. *Essais*, 2.1.15 and 2.21.47.

57. *Monadologie*, § 15.

58. *Théodicée*, § 360; *Monadologie*, § 22; and cf. the preface to the *Essais*,
(Akademie ed., p. 55): "en consequence de ces petites perceptions le pres-
ent est plein de l'avenir, et chargé du passé. . . . Ces perceptions insensibles
marquent encore et constituent le même individu, qui est caracterisé par les
traces, qu'elles conservent des estats précedens de cet individu, en faisant
la connexion avec son estat present"; also cf. 2.1.12, where Leibniz argues
against Locke's definition of the individual as a conscious entity: "Ce n'est
donc pas le souvenir qui fait justement le même homme. . . . Car il faut sa-

voir que chaque ame garde toutes les impressions precedentes [i.e., whether or not one is aware of them] . . . l'avenir dans chaque substance a une parfaite liaison avec le passé, c'est ce qui fait l'identité de l'individu."

59. *Principes*, § 3; *Monadologie*, § 79.

60. Cf. e.g. *Monadologie*, § 14; *Principes*, § 4; and the preface to the *Essais*.

61. *Monadologie*, § 23: "Une perception ne sauroit venir naturellement que d'une autre perception, comme un mouvement ne peut venir naturellement que d'un mouvement"; *Essais*, 2.1.9: "Un estat sans pensée dans l'ame, et un repos absolu dans le corps me paroissant également contraires à la nature, et sans example dans le monde"; *Théodicée*, § 403: "Toute perception presente tend à une perception nouvelle, comme tout mouvement qu'elle represente rend à un autre mouvement."

62. The monads, or simple substances, come into being only at the creation, and are not created or destroyed naturally (*Monadologie*, §§ 1–6). Composite substances, including bodies, are likewise not subject to creation and annihilation but only to gradual alteration (§§ 72–73).

63. Ibid., § 58.

64. *Essais*, 2.1.15 and 2.21.39.

65. *Théodicée*, § 201.

66. Because increasing intelligibility equals greater integrative activity: "Toute action est un acheminement au plaisir, et toute passion un acheminement à la douleur" (*Essais*, 2.21.72).

67. Ibid., 2.21.37: "L'amas de ces petits succés continuels de la nature qui se met de plus en plus à son aise, en tendant au bien et jouissant de son image, ou diminuant le sentiment de la douleur, est déja un plaisir considerable et vaut souvent mieux que la jouissance même du bien; *et bien loin qu'on doive regarder cette inquietude comme une chose imcompatible avec la felicité*, je trouve que l'inquietude est essentielle à la felicité des creatures, la quelle ne consiste jamais dans une parfaite possession qui les rendroit insensibles et comme stupides, mais dans un progrés continuel et non interrompu à des plus grands biens" (emphasis in the original).

68. See, e.g., Aristotle's distinction between demonstration and dialectic in the *Topica*, 1.1. The problem of unattainable certainty is discussed in my chapter 1 with reference to the σκιαγραφία and Aristotle's conception of rhetorical style.

69. Breitinger could also have gotten this idea from Wolff, who carries forward Leibniz's notion of perfectibility with reference to the arts and sciences ("die Kunst") in his *Vernünfftige Gedancken von der Menschen Thun und Lassen*, § 366: "Wir finden auch, daß der Mensch geschickt ist theils durch die Kräffte seiner Seelen, theils durch die Kräffte des Leibes ein Ding ausser ihm zur Würcklichkeit zu bringen, was ohne ihn seine Würcklichkeit nicht erreichen würde. . . . Z. E. Durch die Geschicklichkeit eines Poetens kommet ein Gedichte zu seiner Würcklichkeit, welches ohne ihn sonst nimmermehr dieselbe würde erreichet haben." Beetz, *Rhetorische Logik*, 8–9, discusses the complicated linguistic context of "Kunst" at the turn of the eighteenth century.

70. For Muratori's indebtedness to Plotinus, Neoplatonism, and Leibniz (with whom Muratori corresponded for several years), see von Stein, *Ästhetik*, esp. 309–17.
71. This passage merges Liebnizian-Wolffian categories with the Aristotelian problem of history and poesis set forth in the *Poetics*. The problem is discussed in chapter 3.
72. The entire passage from Breitinger just quoted was lifted from Dubos, cf. my chapter 3, n. 21. Addison's "influence" here can be at best only indirect.
73. Breitinger says (1:267) he is disagreeing here with Muratori's position. His reasons for this, given in the following paragraphs, are based (I believe) on his reading of Wolff.
74. *Monadologie*, §§ 56 and 60: "Cette representation [i.e., each monad] n'est que confuse dans le detail de tout l'univers et ne peut être distincte que dans une petite partie des choses . . . autrement chaque Monade seroit une Divinité."
75. The italicized sentences in § 171 are not in the first edition. They were added for the second edition in 1722. See the list of variants provided by Charles A. Corr in the Olms reprint of the *Metaphysik* in *Christian Wolff: Gesammelte Werke*, 1. Abt., Deutsche Schriften, 2:724.
76. Wolff, *Metaphysik*, §§ 404, 409–12.
77. I summarize here Wolff's remarks in *Metaphysik*, §§ 242–46 and 362–67. "Erfindung" or *inventio* is, of course, a *terminus technicus* of the rhetorical tradition, which I leave out of consideration at this time in order to focus on Breitinger's use of the Wolffian notion. In my following remarks I have been aided by the editor's "Einführung" and "Anmerkungen" to Christian Wolff, *Vernünfftige Gedanken von den Kräften des menschlichen Verstandes*, cited henceforth as the *Logik*, and also (to a lesser degree) by Dieter Kimpel, "Programm der literarischen Bildung," in Schneiders, ed., *Christian Wolff 1679–1754*, 203–36.
78. Cf. Baeumler, *Irrationalitätsproblem*, 149: "Es is also kein Unterschied zwischen Geist, Witz und Phantasie; nur der (allerdings nicht unbedeutende), daß die Definition des Witzes eine bestimmte *Methode* des Schaffens angab, während der Phantasiebegriff bei der Bestimmung der willkürlichen schöpferischen Verbindung überhaupt stehen blieb" (emphasis in original). With due respect to the author of what is perhaps the best book ever written on early eighteenth-century German poetics, Baeumler seems to have missed the fact that Wolff ascribes an arbitrary function to both "Einbildung" *and* "Witz." Moreover, the second "Manier" of the imagination, explained in my text, functions according to a rational method of creation, so that Baeumler's statement regarding Wolff's "Phantasiebegriff" is completely untenable.
79. *Logik*, 140.
80. The discrepancy between Leibniz and Wolff on this point may ultimately derive from Wolff's differences with Leibniz concerning the monad. Wolff had criticized Leibniz for his panpsychism, the notion that all monads

represent (*vorstellen*) the entire universe (cf. *Metaphysik*, §§ 598–99 and 742–53). While Leibniz had assumed the universe to be a plenum, in keeping with Cartesian physics, Wolff followed the Newtonian conception of the universe that included vacuums. Hence Wolff seems to posit a far lesser degree of *interconnection* between the monads, or "Geister" as he prefers to call them, than Leibniz had, which would in turn produce an unresolvable ontological disjunction between the divinely created "best possible" world and the humanly conceived possible worlds of the "Romainen." (Breitinger, following Muratori, tends more toward Leibniz in this matter than to Wolff.) Wolff's departure from Leibniz based on his adherence to Newtonian physics is analyzed by Saine, *Kopernikanische Revolution*, 48–53, 150–57, and 174–78.

81. Breitinger may also have in mind here (with "Lüge") Locke's discussion of false ideas at 2.31.21–26.

82. Cf. *Dichtkunst*, 1:74–75. The passage quoted in my text refers to poetic reception but also to production. The question of the identity between poet and recipient is discussed in my chapter 3. Here I am suggesting that poet and recipient are involved in a parallel process of apperception.

83. Both Baeumler, *Irrationalitätsproblem*, 142, and Möller, *Rhetorische Überlieferung*, 74–75, give the passages from Muratori that Breitinger apparently used as models for his statements on the wondrous.

Chapter 3

1. Bender's observation is found on page 158* of the "Nachwort" in volume 2 of the *Critische Dichtkunst*. He interprets the passage as an anticipation of "Empfindsamkeit," but he does not mention the more important point that it also expressed a neoclassic commonplace.

2. The three authors I have chosen for my exposition were all widely read in their own time, hence were considered "authorities" of sorts, and therefore may be described as "typical." They are René Rapin, an *ancien*, Bernard de Fontenelle, a *moderne*, and Dubos, who wrote after the *querelle* had subsided but whose work nonetheless addresses the major points of the earlier neoclassic literary feud. Reference is also made to Boileau.

3. Although "verisimilitude" is a better translation of *vraisemblance*, I use "probability" throughout the text because the critics under discussion thought they were using, or "improving," the Aristotelian concept: Bray, *Doctrine classique*, 115–16, notes that French Neoclassicism, as opposed to the Italian, would attempt to move from "la parole du maître" to reason as the basis of poetic rules. I am indebted in the following pages to Bray's discussion of *vraisemblance*, esp. 191–239.

4. Fontenelle's position is discussed later. Bray, *Doctrine classique*, 225–26, notes that Corneille was less interested in *le vrai* per se, than in exploiting the historical record for obscure and marvelous events. The position of the *modernes* is shared by Dennis, "The Advancement and Reformation of Mod-

ern Poetry," in *Works*, 1:237: "'Tis plain, [the Ancient Grecian Poets] had no clear and distinct Idea, of one Supreme and Infinite Being: For either the Knowledge of the True God must be drawn from Reason, or Revelation. From Revelation they could not draw it, because their own Revelation was not true. . . . and the Exercise of Reason was too little known among them" (by which presumably is meant post-Cartesian scientific method). Nevertheless, "the Gentleman who writ the History of Oracles [Fontenelle], treats [pagan Religion] as a Fiction, and a Fiction so palpable, as not to be worth the answering. But, perhaps, that Gentleman had not consider'd this Matter enough" (1:235). Dennis constructs the rest of his argument on the value of religion, be it "true" (i.e., Christian) or "false" (pagan), for poetic production and reception.

5. *L'Art poétique*, chant 3, verses 47–48, p. 339. (Subsequent citations are in the text by page number.)

6. Rapin, *Réflexions*, 39. (Further references are given in the text.)

7. Cf. Bray, *Doctrine classique*, 218: "Sur le précepte de la convenance, Scaliger esquisse une sorte de réalisme historique: il faut que les personnages soient en harmonie avec les temps et les lieux où on les représente comme ayant vécu."

8. Cf. Chapelain's comment: "Tout écrivain qui invente une fable, dont les actions humaines font le sujet, ne doit représenter ses personnages, ni les faire agir que conformément aux moeurs et à la créance de son siècle," quoted by Bray, *Doctrine classique*, 225.

9. For a concise discussion of Plotinus's use of Aristotelian terms and its effect on art theory, cf. Panofsky, *Idea*, esp. chaps. 1 and 2. Additional discussion of Plotinian notions follows at later points in my text.

10. Dacier, *Poëtique*, 433. (Further citations of this work are by page number only in the text.)

11. Rapin's distortion of Aristotle may stem from a misunderstanding in the early reception of the *Poetics*; cf. Weinberg, *Literary Criticism*, 1:388–89, commenting on "the first of the 'great commentaries' [on the *Poetics*]," that of Robortello: "The imitation is not only of human actions and passions (as in Aristotle) but of all kinds of objects as well." That is, the poetic work is not seen as an interpretation of events, as plot, but as a mirroring of "things" in reality (however this last term may be defined). A constant theme of Weinberg's study is the conflation of Aristotle's *Poetics* with Horace's *Ars poetica*, which was itself thought to recommend exact "painting" of "reality" or "truth"—again, terms that have varying definitions.

12. Rapin's notion of the artistic experience as the perception of a generality based on identification appears to owe a lot to Plotinus's essay on Beauty, *Enneads*, 1.6.1 (which may have entered the neoclassic context via Renaissance Neoplatonism). Thus, beauty "in bodily forms . . . is something that the soul . . . fuses with." But the beauty of base objects is a lesser form of the divine beauty that it is our purpose to know, through identification: "For the eye must be adapted to what is to be seen, have some likeness to it, if it would give itself to contemplation. No eye that has not become like

unto the sun will ever look upon the sun. . . . Let each one therefore become godlike and beautiful who would contemplate the divine and beautiful" (quotation from pp. 35 and 43).

13. The entire passage in question is the following: "La grande règle de traiter les moeurs, est de les copier sur la nature, et sur tout, de bien étudier le coeur de l'homme, pour en sçavoir distinguer tous les mouvemens. C'est ce qu'on ne sçait point: le coeur humain est un abysme d'une profondeur, où la sonde ne peut aller, c'est un mystère impénétrable aux plus éclairez: on s'y méprend toujours, quelque habile qu'on soit. Mais au moins il faut tâcher de parler des moeurs conformément à l'opinion publique" (43–44).

14. *Oeuvres*, 3:22. (Further quotations of Fontenelle are cited by page number in the text).

15. Fontenelle appears to be paraphrasing *Poetics*, 1451b15 ff., at this point: "What is possible is plausible; now what has not happened we are not yet sure is possible, but what has happened seems clearly possible; for (we say) it would not have happened if it were impossible" (trans. G. Else, *Aristotle's Poetics: The Argument*, 315). In his commentary, Else classes this as a "vulgar error" (317) in logic. The significant thing here is Fontenelle's restriction of the possible, and then the probable, to that which has already happened and/or which we have already seen. But "things as they were or are" is only one of the three possible sources of the probable in Aristotle's account.

16. Fontenelle may have in mind here Corneille's distinction between "le vraisemblable ordinaire" and "le vraisemblable extraordinaire": "L'ordinaire est une action qui arrive plus souvent ou du moins aussi souvent que sa contraire, l'extraordinaire est une action qui arrive, à la vérité, moins souvent que sa contraire"; see Pierre Corneille, "Discours de la Tragédie," in *Oeuvres*, 839.

17. A parallel case of Fontenelle's neoclassic reversion may be found in his influential *Digressions sur les anciens et les modernes* of 1688. There he appears to argue against the unjustified authority granted to classical antiquity by the *anciens* in favor of the equal capacity of all ages to have important insights. But this argument eventually reveals itself to be a mere rhetorical device for dethroning the *anciens* in order to assert the superiority of the modern period. Fontenelle thus fails to discredit the neoclassic position, but instead uses it, in inverted form, for his own ends; cf. Jauß, "Ästhetische Normen," 32–33: "Auch das Denken der fortschrittsgläubigen *Modernes* bewegt sich noch im klassischen Zirkel der Vollkommenheit, nur daß der 'Punkt der Vollendung' jetzt aus einer unwiederbringlichen Vergangenheit in eine zu erstrebende Zukunft verlegt ist . . . die Norm einer einst erfüllten, im gegenwärtigen Zeitalter erreichten oder erst in Zukunft erreichbaren Perfektion gehört . . . zu den erst noch selbstverständlichen Voraussetzungen und Gemeinsamkeiten der Ausgangspunkte . . . der *Querelle*."

18. Breitinger refers to this passage at 1:496 as part of his continuing attack on Fontenelle's best friend, La Motte, but Breitinger's criticism is also aimed at Gottsched, who "stole" nearly all of La Motte's faultfinding in Homer for his own *Versuch einer kritischen Dichtkunst*. The debate over poetic

probability between Dubos and La Motte is carried out not only in the same terms but with the very same words twenty years later in the German context.

19. The opening sentence, "Je sçais bien que le faux est quelquefois plus vrai-semblable que le vrai," is the neoclassic paraphrase of Aristotle's preference for the "impossible probable" over the "possible improbable." The substitution of terms comes about when the probable is identified with the true (cf. Fontenelle's "une petite portion du vrai") and then reduced to the historical. Thus the sentence reads, in agreement with the sense of the rest of the passage, "I know that that which has not happened [cannot happen —i.e., is "impossible" or "false"] may seem more probable [believable] than that which has actually happened. However, . . . " Dubos's real difficulties here are indicated by his need to create two kinds of probability: "métaphysique" and "historique." For Aristotle's qualified admission of the impossible probable, see Else's discussion of chapter 24.

20. In fairness to Dubos, it is probably expecting too much of him to present a critique of the problem of periodization when he had only just come up with the idea of "period" at all, namely in his reflection on the difference between "le siècle" and "l'âge" at 2.12.128–44. Krauss, *Studien zur Aufklärung*, 9, thinks that this distinction is "Ausdruck des sensualistischen, an Lockes *Essay concerning human understanding* orientierten Sprachbewußtseins." But might it not also (or even primarily) stem from Dubos's application of (Aristotelian) poetic probability to history itself, which would create the concept "historical context" or "l'âge"?

21. The following is a preliminary list of those borrowings from Dubos that Breitinger worked into his text as if they were his own words, with these exceptions: nos. 6 and 16 are introduced by "Man hat [gesagt]" without further identification; nos. 8 and 11 contain a "sagt Dubos" but no quotation marks or text citation; nos. 3, 7, and 17 are paraphrases but restate Dubos's words so closely that I have assigned them to this list. I do not give the many passages where Dubos's words are cited in quotation marks, accompanied by volume and chapter. The left side of the equation refers to Breitinger, the right side to Dubos: (1) 1:15 = 1.40.393–94; (2) 1:64 = 1.3.27; (3) 1:68 = 1.3.28; (4) 1:69–70 = 1.3.29–30; (5) 1:72 = 1.10.66–67; (6) 1:73–74 = 1.12.75; (7) 1:79 = 1.26.221; (8) 1:81–82 = 1.6.51; (9) 1:85 ("Alleine die Sachen") = 1.8.63; (10) 1:85 ("Die Unruh") = 1.1.11; (11) 1:86 ("Die verständigen") = 1.6.52–53; (12) 1:86 ("Eben daher") = 1.9.66; (13) 1:132–33 ("Auf einer Seiten . . . getrieben") = 1.28.238–39; (14) 1:133 ("In den Romanen . . . Eckel") = 1.28.239–40; (15) 1:143–44 ("Was nun erstlich") = 1.24.183–84; (16) 1:148 = 1.25.213; (17) 1:479–80 = 1.30.255–56. Some of these passages are discussed in my text.

22. Breitinger writes out (at 1:280–82) a lengthier version of the Dubos passage and identifies its author. The problem of the "impossible probable" exercised all neoclassic critics, and Breitinger's comments may be a generic response not tied to a specific context. The passage at 1:138–39 may also be a conflation of sentences by Dubos and Muratori; see my chapter 2, n. 17.

23. Pascal, *Pensées*, 9–10. The perception of the mind-heart split becomes

particularly acute in the *querelle*, in the form of the debate over the relative value and achievements of the natural sciences versus the arts. Spingarn, *Critical Essays*, notes in his introduction, 89, that Pascal (in his *Fragment du Traité du Vide*) was the first to point out the distinction between the arts and sciences. Cf. also Kristeller, "The Modern System of the Arts," in *Renaissance Thought*, 2:194, who argues that in the *querelle* "the ground is prepared for the first time for a clear distinction between the arts and the sciences, a distinction absent from ancient, medieval or Renaissance discussions of such subjects even though the same words were used." Both Kristeller and Spingarn, however, acknowledge the importance of Bacon's *Advancement of Learning* as an early formulation of the issue. The problem is extraordinarily complicated, because there seems to have been wide disagreement among all parties about the terms of the debate (e.g., Fontenelle locates "reason" in Cartesian categories, Dubos in Aristotelian logic).

24. Although Dubos was much more sympathetic to the arts than to the sciences, while Fontenelle was more interested in the sciences than in the arts, Dubos states his position in words highly reminiscent of Fontenelle; cf. Fontenelle's *Oeuvres*, 3:14: "Ce plaisir qu'on prend à pleurer est si bizarre, que je ne puis m'empêcher d'y faire réflexion. . . . Le coeur aime naturellement à être remué, ainsi les objets tristes lui conviennent, et même les objets douloureux, pourvu que quelque chose les adoucisse. . . . On pleure les malheurs d'un héros à qui l'on s'est affectionné, et dans le même moment l'on s'en console, parce qu'on sait que c'est une fiction." With proper qualifications, one may see here an anticipation of certain ideas of both Lessing and Schiller.

25. Else, in his edition of Aristotle's *Poetics*, 128, notes that the substitution of works of art for Aristotle's "likenesses" was made by Victorius, and Else himself goes so far as to suggest that Aristotle really meant something like "drawings, models, reproductions used for teaching . . . laboratory equipment." The point is that Aristotle meant for reproductions to convey knowledge about classes of objects; therefore they are pleasurable. Were they photographically accurate "paintings" of another object, no learning would occur.

26. Breitinger was probably referred to the parallel passage in the *Rhetoric* by Dacier, *Poëtique*, 37, who does not, however, quote it. Breitinger's incorrect citation reads: "in dem ersten B. seiner Rhetorick im zweyten Cap.," whereas Dacier has, correctly, "dans le Chapitre XI, du premier Livre de sa Rhetorique." Breitinger may have written the arabic numeral "11" in his manuscript, which his printer (or he himself) later mistook for a roman "II." Whatever the cause of the discrepancy, Breitinger apparently used Dacier's translation as his primary edition of the *Poetics* (even though his Greek was quite good), inasmuch as his German quotations of Aristotle are exact translations of Dacier's French; cf., e.g., *Dichtkunst*, 1:71 and Dacier's rendering of the same passage, p. 31.

27. Dubos has at 1.3.26 "comme l'impression que l'imitation fait n'est différente de l'impression que l'objet imité feroit, qu'en ce qu'elle est moins fort, elle doit exciter dans notre ame."

28. Cf. Plotinus, *Enneads*, 5.1.10 and 5.2.11. Although an impression, according to the sensation theories of e.g. Locke, is subject to degrees of strength based on the source of the perception (cf. Locke, 2.7.4–5), the passage from Dubos that Breitinger restates is more directly related to Dubos's ideas on the relative merits of painting versus poetry. At issue here is the strength of the perception ("Eindruck" or "impression") as a function of the degree of reality of its source. (Note that warm things do not have less "reality" for Locke than hot things, only a weaker effect on our sense of hotness.) Painting produces stronger impressions than poetry in Dubos's account precisely because its depictions are closer to being nature itself than those of poesis are. Dubos defends painting over poesis on the same grounds as da Vinci had, whose treatise on painting he does not cite but must have read while preparing his own eighteenth-century continuation of the "paragone"; cf. da Vinci, *Trattato della pittura*, 5: "Von der Einbildung zur Wirklichkeit ist gerade solch' ein Abstandsverhältnis, wie vom Schatten zum schattenwerfenden Körper, und dasselbe Verhältnis besteht zwischen der Poesie und Malerei."

29. Cf. Dubos, 1.3.26–27: Breitinger inverts the statement; Dubos says the impression made by the imitation, compared with that made by the object imitated, is "pas aussi profonde," "pas serieuse," and "elle s'efface bientôt."

30. Cf. 1.40, where Dubos not only argues in favor of the stronger effect of painting over poetry on the recipient, but also suggests (1.40.395) that plays owe their very effect to their visual reception, i.e., to their performance, or to spectacle (thus controverting *Poetics*, 6.28: "Spectacle, while highly effective, is yet quite foreign to the art and has nothing to do with poetry"; also cf. 14.1–2). I do not understand Kristeller's assertion, *Renaissance Thought*, 2:198, that Dubos "is not interested in the superiority of one art over the others, as so many previous authors had been."

31. As evidence of Dubos's intention, see 1.9.64: "L'esprit ne sçauroit jouïr deux fois du plaisir d'apprendre la même chose, comme le coeur peut jouïr deux fois du plaisir de sentir la même emotion. Le plaisir d'apprendre est consommé par le plaisir de sçavoir."

32. 1.10.66–67: "On pourroit objecter que les tableaux où nous ne voïons que l'imitation de differens objets qui ne nous auroient point attachez, si nous les avions vûs dans la nature, ne laissent pas de se faire regarder longtems. Nous donnons plus d'attention à des fruits & à des animaux représentez dans un tableau, que nous n'en donnerions à ces objets mêmes. La copie nous attache plus que l'orginal. Je répons que, lorsque . . . " (I have omitted Breitinger's sentence about "die Früchte und die Thiere" from my quotation of 1:72.) These differing attitudes with respect to poesis as purely emotive rather than intellective experience carry over further into their poetics. Dubos says at 1.28.239: "Il ne me paroît donc pas possible d'enseigner l'art de concilier le vrai-semblable & le merveilleux. Cet art n'est qu'à la portée de ceux qui sont nez Poëtes, & grands Poëtes." Breitinger says, on the contrary, that this "Verbinding des Wunderbaren und Wahrscheinlichen" that is "die vornehmste Schönheit der Poesie" (1:133) may be understood because Aris-

totle has given us the "Grundstein und das Band der Vereinigung" (1:137), which he then relates to his own "Grundsätze des Wahnes."

33. These are not the "useful lessons" of the Horatian tradition; the phrase means "useful bits of information."

34. The process of idealization and the process of organization of the multiple particulars seem to reflect a tension in the original Plotinian conception of the return, or "epistrophe"; cf. Armstrong, *Plotinus*, 38–39: "If [the soul] devotes itself selfishly to the interests of the particular body to which it is attached it becomes entrapped in the atomistic particularity of the material world. . . . But the mere fact of being in body does not imply imprisonment in body. That only comes if the soul surrenders to the body. . . . Matter then is responsible for the evil and imperfection of the material world: but that world is good and necessary." Idealization would stress the renunciation of the "base" particular; Breitinger (like Leibniz) stresses the preservation of the particular in the unique-universal. Breitinger does not mean, however, that the author should try to represent all particulars of a scene in a "naturalistic copy." Organization means that the artist must decide on an order of significance in what he sees.

35. At 1:171, Breitinger describes the "Einheit einer Fabel" with the words "wenn nemlich alle Züge und Linien derselben in einem gewissen Gesichtes-Punct mit einander übereintreffen." This recalls Leibniz's definition of the monad in *Principes*, § 2: "C'est comme dans un centre ou point, tout simple qu'il est, se trouvent une infinité d'angles formés par les lignes qui y concourent."

36. *Pensées*, 9. (A further quotation from Pascal is cited in the text by page number.)

37. Leibniz appears to describe the "esprit de finesse" in the preface to the *Essais* (53): "Ces impressions sont ou trop petites et en trop grand nombre, ou trop unies, en sorte qu'elles n'ont rien d'assez distinguant à part, mais jointes à d'autres, elles ne laissent pas de faire leur effect, et de se faire sentir au moins confusément dans l'assemblage." Given that the *Nouveaux Essais* were written as an attempt to explain the nature and function of the "petites perceptions," Leibniz seems to find the same inadequacy in the neoclassic model of the inscrutable mind as Breitinger later would. Most interesting is Leibniz's inclusion in this passage of the preface of an oblique reference to neoclassic aesthetics: "Ces petites perceptions sont donc de plus grande efficace qu'on ne pense. Ce sont elles, qui forment *ce je ne say quoy*, ces gouts, ces images des qualités des sens, claires dans l'assemblage, mais confuses dans les parties" (54–55; my emphasis).

38. Panofsky, *Idea*, chap. 4, n. 51, describes a new usage of the terms "eikastic" and "phantastic" imitation in the Renaissance in a way that bears on Breitinger's scale of probability. Whereas the original Platonic distinction (*Sophist*, 235D) was between objectively correct likenesses and semblances made to accommodate the perspective of the viewer, the terms later came to indicate the imitation of existing objects and nonexisting objects (e.g., chimera) respectively. Breitinger appears to be attempting, with his scale, a negotiation between these two types of representation, such that the imagina-

tion remains anchored in experience but also goes beyond it in the creative moment. Birmelin, "Philostrats Apollonios," discusses the Aristotelian concept of imagination (which she shows to be at work in Philostratus's *Life of Apollonius of Tyana*, 6.19), as the negotiation between the known and the unknown, whereby new knowledge is produced. Imagination in this account is not merely reproductive, as most modern accounts of Aristotle would have it, but in the first instance productive. It seems that one may therefore ascribe an Aristotelian intention to Breitinger at this point.

39. The word "Gemüth," in its broadest designation as an emotional-intellective faculty, is omnipresent in the *Critische Dichtkunst*, but the post-Idealist tradition transforms Breitinger's use of this term into "Gefühl," a significant distortion of the text. Breitinger himself uses "Gefühl" only twice in the first four chapters (for example) of the *Critische Dichtkunst*, where it means "the sense of touch" (1:16), and sense impression as opposed to "Verstand" (1:80). "Gemüth" appears fifty-four times.

40. This passage may have been lifted from Muratori; see Baeumler, *Irrationalitätsproblem*, 52, who quotes parallel phrasing in Italian but without reference to Breitinger.

41. Cf. *Gleichnis-Abhandlung*, 4–13, esp. 9. The important term here is *wähnen*, which, unlike the last two, has now fallen out of general usage. Adelung, *Grammatisch-kritisches Wörterbuch*, 4. Theil, Sp. 1342–43, gives the meaning "dafür halten, meinen, glauben, im weitesten Verstande; eine im Hochdeutschen veraltete Bedeutung, worin es aber in den ältern Oberdeutschen Schriften häufig vorkommt." Under the entry "Wahn" he gives the (antiquated) meaning "Eine jede Meinung, d. i. Urtheil nach bloß wahrscheinlichen Gründen. . . . Wahn [ist] noch so viel als Vermuthung." Adelung notes that this "allgemeine Bedeutung" is still present in Opitz. Breitinger may have found it there, or it may be alive in his Swiss (i.e., "Oberdeutsch") vocabulary; cf. his use of the term at 2:93. Meyer, "Restaurative Innovation," in Bürger, *Literarische Öffentlichkeit*, 39–82, argues contrary to the philological context of the term that Breitinger's use of "Wahn" means his poetics were conceived as an aid to theologians resisting the demise of religious fanaticism.

42. Young, "Conjectures on Original Composition," 341.

43. Some of the social-historical implications of this difference—which most decidedly need not always have had a liberating function—are described by Schulte-Sasse, "Das Konzept bürgerlicher Öffentlichkeit," in Bürger, *Literarische Öffentlichkeit*, 83–115, in terms of the transition from "Moral" to "Sitte" in the eighteenth century, whereby literature acts as the primary medium of socialization, a process in which poets play the role of a "vorausdenkende Elite" (95).

Chapter 4

1. Wellbery, *Lessing's "Laocoon,"* refers to Breitinger's "close proximity" (203) to Lessing, and notes (210) that "Lessing makes exactly the same ob-

servation [i.e., regarding distinct cognition and poetry] as Breitinger, but he interprets it in an entirely different way." Wellbery argues that Lessing's critique of Breitinger is based on "the changing perspective on poetic language that develops across the work of Baumgarten, Meier and Mendelssohn" (207). For a different approach to *Laokoon* that analyzes Lessing's contribution to the development of historical hermeneutics, see Seeba, "'Der wahre Standort,'" an article to which I am much indebted in the present chapter.

2. Cf. 1:22: "Fraget ihr jemand, der entweder in der Natur, oder in der künstlichen Vorstellung eines Gemähldes eine weitläuftige Durchsicht gesehen hat, was vor einen Begriff dieselbe in seinem Gehirn hinterlassen habe, wie flüchtig, dunkel und ungewiß wird seine Beschreibung herauskommen?"

3. Lessing, *Laokoon*, vol. 9 of *Schriften*. Quotations in my text come from 102–4.

4. Haller is quoted by Guthke, *Literarisches Leben*, 138–39. Guthke also cites (138) Haller's repetition of this phrase in an open letter to Gemmingen of 1772: "Die Poesie mahlt, was kein Pinsel mahlen kann: Eigenschaften andrer Sinne neben dem Gesichte."

5. Herder, *Werke*, 4:19 and 15:540; cf. also 18:128, 2:40–41, and my chapter 1, n. 64.

6. Bosse, "'Dichter kann man nicht bilden,'" points out (119) that Breitinger's *Critische Dichtkunst* was widely used as a "Schulpoetik" well into the 1770s, being recommended by Basedow and other "Reformpädagogen." Bosse interprets this as a conservative trend in the latter eighteenth century, during which the more modern works of Herder and Hamann were sidelined. If this be the case, Breitinger's obscurity should be defined as the infrequency with which he is cited by other theoreticians and should not suggest that his book was not read—which it apparently was.

7. A useful review of Chladenius's life and work is given by Reill, *German Enlightenment*, 105–12. Reill describes Chladenius as one of the originators of modern hermeneutic theory, a distinction that was challenged by Gadamer, *Wahrheit und Methode*, 171–72, in his revision of Dilthey's and Wach's approaches. To my knowledge, the works of Breitinger and Chladenius have never been critically compared. In this study I can only outline a few aspects of their conceptual commonality.

8. Chladenius, *Einleitung*, §§ 61, 309, 567, and 639. (Further citations of his work are in the text by paragraph number in parentheses.)

9. See also his unpaginated "Vorrede": "Denn so können z. E. Leser öffters nicht in einem Philosophischen Buche fortkommen, ob es ihnen gleich nicht an Erkänntniß der Sprache fehlet, auch das Buch gar nicht zweydeutig abgefasset ist, sondern bey behorig [*sic*] zubereiteten Lesern den allergewissesten Verstand hat. Eben solcher Anstoß findet sich öffters bey denen historischen Büchern, ohne daß der Verfasser, und die Einrichtung des Buches die geringste Schuld daran haben. . . . Daher, wenn der Leser dieselben [i.e., necessary] Begriffe nicht schon hat, so können die Worte nicht die Wirckung bey ihm thun, noch die Begriffe veranlassen, welche bey einem andern Leser, der gehörig unterrichtet ist, gewiß erfolgen werden."

10. Breitinger uses the identical example of "fliegen" to illustrate exactly the same point about abstraction in his *Gleichnis-Abhandlung,* 34–35, with the added observation that the metaphoric use of this term is based on an "Optischer Betrug." This is interesting given the origin of perspectivism in optics and the fine arts. Of course Chladenius need not have seen this passage in Breitinger. Their common classical source was probably the description of Poseidon's rapid stride and his "flying" horses in book 13 of the *Iliad,* which may have been turned into a neoclassic critical *topos* by Longinus's reference to it in his chapter 9.

11. Leventhal, "Semiotic Interpretation," 234, takes this aspect of Chladenius's exposition to mean that "the notion of *Sehepunkt* is always discussed in terms of the author, never in regard to the interpretational position of the reader." This statement is apparently contradicted by what Chladenius says, e.g., at § 324 regarding the interpretor's relation to the student of history: "Ein Ausleger muß also die Geschichte, die er auslegen will, aus beyden Sehe-Punckten sich vorstellen, theils wie sie derjenige sich vorstellt, dem sie unglaublich vorkommt, theils wie sie der Scribent sich vorgestellt hat." Leventhal's aim is to deny any perspectivity to the reader at all; cf. my n. 15.

12. Cf. Guillen, "Metaphor of Perspective," 317: "A point of view is not always individual, or subjective in an individual sense. It can also be ultra-personal. Dürer's perspective apparatus did not necessarily set up a personal field of vision: a number of people could occupy the same position. This distinction becomes operative [outside the fine arts] in the area of opinions or experiences collectively shared, such as politics, class prejudices, religion." Chladenius's and Breitinger's use of perspective betrays its status as a term in transition between its use in the fine arts and in the historical sciences. Chladenius notes (§ 309), however, that he takes the term from Leibniz (probably from *Monadologie,* § 57), who himself may have borrowed it from the artists.

13. I use "historian" here in Chladenius's conflated sense as one who has "Einsicht in die Geschichte" *either* "aus eigener Erfahrung" *or* "aus anderer Leute Zeugniß" (307), a definition that illustrates the emerging tendency to identify the position of authors and readers.

14. Cf. Reill, *German Enlightenment,* 110, for a discussion of this problem in Chladenius's later work, the *Allgemeine Geschichtswissenschaft* of 1752. In the *Einleitung,* Chladenius admits (§ 157) that "alle Bücher der Menschen, und ihre Reden, [werden] etwas unverständliches an sich haben."

15. Leventhal, "Semiotic Interpretation," 234, overlooks the possibility of an ultrapersonal or multipersonal perspective in the Enlightenment: "The task of the interpretor in Chladenius's theory is to see through the perspectivity of the author's presentation . . . in order to obtain a more global and rational representation of the ideas themselves." Relying on the theories of Foucault, Gadamer, and, most recently, Wellbery, Leventhal recognizes *only* the utterly individual perspective *or* its destruction in the "transparency of the sign." He does not consider that the attempt by Enlightenment readers to occupy the author's perspective might not be based exclusively on the urge to assume an impersonal, totalizing, standpoint—although this is cer-

tainly one of the strands of Enlightenment thought—but rather on the desire to identify with, i.e., act as, author. Cf. n. 19 of my Introduction.

16. See my chapter 1, n. 21, for the passage in question from *De Oratore*.

17. Szondi, *Einführung*, 36. I arrived at the same conclusion independently of Szondi through my study of Breitinger. Subsequent quotations from Szondi's work are in the text by page number in parentheses.

18. This and the following lines from Gottsched's *Versuch einer Critischen Dichtkunst* are quoted by Szondi, 91. Gottsched incorrectly identifies the work in question as Cicero's *Orator*.

19. Cf. *Gleichnis-Abhandlung*, 6–9.

20. Cf. Adelung, *Gelehrten-Lexico*, 2:302. Henn, "Sinnreiche Gedancken," esp. 252–55, provides an excellent discussion, with a slightly different focus than my own, of Chladenius's initial interest in poetic language and his subsequent essay on probability.

21. For Wegelin's biography, see Reill, *German Enlightenment*, 118–19. Wach, *Das Verstehen*, 3:42–52, says only in passing that Wegelin draws on Leibniz and other French sources for his theories. Wach's real interest lies in what he finds to be the striking similarities between Wegelin and Humboldt, while acknowledging that "direkte Beziehungen . . . sind mir allerdings nicht bekannt" (46). As an exponent of nineteenth-century German historiography, he wants to see Wegelin as a "Vorläufer" (43) of Classicism rather than as an heir to the German reception of the French *querelle*. Hence he fails to consider that Wegelin's attention may have been directed to French sources by the Swiss.

22. Reill, *German Enlightenment*, 119, emphasizes this, as well as Wegelin's acquaintance with Breitinger and friendship with Bodmer. But Bodmer was known to enjoy—and to advertise—his role of mentor to younger men, as the episodes with Klopstock and Wieland attest. That Breitinger's influence on Wegelin may have been as great as Bodmer's cannot be excluded.

23. Wegelin, *Briefe*, 7. Further citations are in the text in parentheses.

24. Gadamer, *Wahrheit und Methode*.

25. Novalis, *Schriften*, 1:259. My attention was drawn to this particular passage by Seeba, "Literatur und Geschichte," 206.

Bibliography

Primary Works

Addison, Joseph, and Richard Steele. *The Spectator*. Edited by Donald F. Bond. 3 vols. Oxford: Clarendon, 1965.

Adelung, J. C., ed. *Fortsetzung und Ergänzungen zu Christian Gottlieb Jöchers allgemeinem Gelehrten-Lexico*. 1787. Reprint. Hildesheim: Olms, 1960.

———. *Grammatisch-kritisches Wörterbuch der Hochdeutschen Mundart*. 4 vols. Leipzig: Breitkopf, 1793–1801.

Aristotle. *The Metaphysics*. Translated by Hugh Tredennick. Loeb Classical Library. Cambridge: Harvard University Press, 1947.

———. *The Poetics*. Translated and edited by Ingram Bywater. Oxford: Clarendon, 1909.

———. *La Poëtique d'Aristote Traduite en François avec des remarques*. Translated and edited by André Dacier. Paris: Barbin, 1692.

———. *Aristotle's Poetics: The Argument*. Translated and edited by Gerald F. Else. Cambridge: Harvard University Press, 1963.

———. *The Poetics*. Translated by W. Hamilton Fyfe. Loeb Classical Library. Cambridge: Harvard University Press, 1973.

———. Περὶ Ποιητικῆς. Translated and edited by A. Gudeman. Berlin: de Gruyter, 1934.

———. *Posterior Analytics. Topica*. Translated by Hugh Tredennick and E. S. Forster. Loeb Classical Library. Cambridge: Harvard University Press, 1976.

———. *The Rhetoric*. Introduction by E. M. Cope. Edited by E. M. Cope and J. E. Sandys. 4 vols. Cambridge: Cambridge University Press, 1877.

———. *The "Art" of Rhetoric*. Translated by John Henry Freese. Loeb Classical Library. Cambridge: Harvard University Press, 1975.

Bacon, Francis. *The Advancement of Learning*. Vol. 4, no. 1, of *The Works*. Edited by James Spedding, R. E. Ellis, and D. D. Heath. 14 vols. London: Longman, 1857–74.

Bodmer, Johann Jacob. *Critische Abhandlung von dem Wunderbaren in der Poesie*. 1740. Reprint. Stuttgart: Metzler, 1966.

———. *Critische Betrachtungen über die Poetischen Gemälde der Dichter*. 1741. Reprint. Frankfurt a.M.: Athenäum, 1971.

Boileau, Nicolas. *L'Art poétique* in vol. 2 of *Oeuvres complètes*, edited by A. Ch. Gidel, 281–399. Paris: Garnier, 1872.

Breitinger, Johann Jacob. *Critische Abhandlung Von der Natur den Absichten und dem Gebrauche der Gleichnisse*. 1740. Reprint. Stuttgart: Metzler, 1967.

———. *Critische Dichtkunst Worinnen die Poetische Mahlerey in Absicht auf die Erfindung Im Grunde untersuchet und mit Beyspielen aus den berühmtesten*

Alten und Neuern erläutert wird. 2 vols. 1740. Reprint. Stuttgart: Metzler, 1967.

Chladenius, Johann Martin. *Einleitung zur richtigen Auslegung vernünfftiger Reden und Schrifften.* 1742. Reprint. Düsseldorf: Stern, 1969.

Cicero. *De Oratore.* Translated by E. W. Sutton. Edited by E. W. Sutton and H. Rackham. Loeb Classical Library. Cambridge: Harvard University Press, 1976.

———. *Orator.* Translated by H. M. Hubbell. Loeb Classical Library. Cambridge: Harvard University Press, 1971.

Cordemoy, Gerauld de. *Discours Physique de la Parole.* 1677. Reprint. Stuttgart: Frommann, 1970.

Corneille, Pierre. *Oeuvres complètes.* Edited by A. Stegmann. Paris: Seuil,1963.

Dacier, Anne Lefèvre. *Des Causes de la Corruption de Goust.* 1714. Reprint. Geneva: Slatkine, 1970.

Da Vinci, Leonardo. *Trattato della pittura.* Translated and edited by H. Ludwig. 1882. Reprint. Osnabruck: Zeller, 1970.

Dennis, John. *The Critical Works.* Edited by E. N. Hooker. 2 vols. Baltimore: Johns Hopkins University Press, 1939.

Descartes, René. *Les passions de l'âme.* Edited by G. Rodis-Lewis. Paris: J. Vrin, 1955.

Dryden, John. "A Parallel of Poetry and Painting." In *Essays of John Dryden,* edited by W. P. Ker, 2:115–53. Oxford: Clarendon, 1900.

Dubos, Jean Baptiste. *Reflexions critiques sur la poësie et sur la peinture.* 3 vols. Paris: Mariette, 1733.

Dürer, Albrecht. "Lehre von menschlicher Proportion." In *Dürers Schriftlicher Nachlaß,* edited by H. Rupprich, 3:17–306. Berlin: Deutscher Verlag für Kunstwissenschaft, 1969.

Fontenelle, Bernard de. *Oeuvres complètes.* Edited by G.-B. Depping. 3 vols. 1818. Reprint. Geneva: Slatkine, 1968.

Goethe, Johann Wolfgang von. *Werke.* Edited by Erich Trunz. 9th ed. 14 vols. Munich: Beck, 1981.

Gottsched, Johann Christoph. *Ausgewählte Werke.* Edited by Joachim Birke, Brigitte Birke, and P. M. Mitchell. 12 vols. Berlin: de Gruyter, 1968–87.

Herder, Johann Gottfried von. *Sämtliche Werke.* Edited by Bernhard Suphan. 33 vols. Berlin: Weidmann, 1877–1913.

Horace. *Horace on Poetry: The "Ars Poetica."* Edited by C. O. Brink. Cambridge: Cambridge University Press, 1971.

———. *Satires, Epistles, Ars Poetica.* Translated by H. R. Fairclough. Loeb Classical Library. Cambridge: Harvard University Press, 1926.

La Motte, Antoine Houdar de. *Discours sur Homere. Oeuvres,* 2:1–137. Paris: Prauly, 1754.

Le Bossu, René. *Monsieur Bossu's Treatise of the Epick Poem.* Translated by W. J. London: Tho. Bennet, 1695.

Leibniz, Gottfried Wilhelm. *Hauptschriften zur Grundlegung der Philosophie.* Edited by Ernst Cassirer. 2 vols. 1906. Reprint. Hamburg: Meiner, 1966.

———. *Kleine Schriften zur Metaphysik.* Translated and edited by Hans Heinz Holz. Darmstadt: Wissenschaftliche Buchgesellschaft, 1965.

———. *Monadology and Other Philosophical Essays.* Translated by Paul Schrecker and Anne Martin Schrecker. Indianapolis: Bobbs-Merrill, 1965.

———. *Nouveaux essais sur l'entendement humain.* Vol. 6, no. 6, of *Sämtliche Schriften und Briefe.* Edited by the Deutsche Akademie der Wissenschaften. Berlin: Akademie Verlag, 1962.

———. *Die philosophischen Schriften.* Edited by C. J. Gerhardt. 7 vols. 1885. Reprint. Hildesheim: Olms, 1965.

Lessing, Gotthold Ephraim. *Laokoon: oder über die Grenzen der Mahlerey und Poesie.* Vol. 9 of *Sämtliche Schriften.* Edited by Karl Lachmann and Franz Muncker. Stuttgart: Göschen, 1886–1924.

Locke, John. *An Essay concerning Humane Understanding.* 1690. Reprint. Menston/Yorkshire: Scholar Press, 1970.

Pseudo-Longinus. *On the Sublime.* Translated by W. Hamilton Fyfe. Loeb Classical Library. Cambridge: Harvard University Press, 1973.

———. *On the Sublime.* Edited and with an introduction by D. A. Russell. Oxford: Clarendon, 1964.

Novalis. *Das Dichterische Werk.* Vol. 1 of *Schriften.* Edited by Paul Kluckhohn and Richard Samuel. Stuttgart: Kohlhammer, 1960.

Pascal, Blaise. *Pensées de Pascal.* Edited by Léon Brunschvicg. Paris: Cluny, 1934.

Plato. *The Collected Dialogues.* Edited by Edith Hamilton and Huntington Cairns. Princeton: Princeton University Press, 1969.

Plotinus. *The Essential Plotinus: Representative Treatises from the Enneads.* Edited and translated by E. O'Brien. 1964. Reprint. Indianapolis: Hackett, 1975.

Pope, Alexander. *The Twickenham Edition of the Works of Alexander Pope.* Edited by John Butt. 11 vols. London: Methuen, 1961–69.

Quintilian. *Institutio Oratoria.* Translated by H. E. Butler. Loeb Classical Library. Cambridge: Harvard University Press, 1969.

Rapin, René. *Les Réflexions sur la poétique de ce temps et sur les ouvrages des poètes anciens et modernes.* Edited by E. T. Dubois. Geneva: Droz, 1970.

Richardson, Jonathan. *An Essay on the Theory of Painting.* 1725. Reprint. Menston/Yorkshire: Scholar Press, 1971.

Strabo. *The Geography.* Translated by H. L. Jones. Loeb Classical Library. Cambridge: Harvard University Press, 1960.

Triller, Daniel Wilhelm. "Vorrede." In *Martin Opizen von Boberfeld Teutsche Gedichte in vier Bände abgetheilet.* Franckfurt am Mayn: Varrentrapp, 1746.

Wallis, John. *Grammar of the English Language with an introductory grammatico-physical Treatise on Speech.* 1653. Translated and edited by J. A. Kemp. London: Longmann, 1972.

Wegelin, Jacob. *Briefe über den Werth der Geschichte.* 1783. Reprint. Königstein: Scriptor, 1981.

Wolff, Christian. *Vernünfftige Gedancken von Gott, der Welt und der Seele des*

Menschen, Auch allen Dingen überhaupt. Halle: Rengerische Buchhandlung, 1720.

————. *Vernünfftige Gedancken von Gott, der Welt und der Seele des Menschen, Auch allen Dingen überhaupt.* Edited and with an introduction by Charles A. Corr. Vol. 1, no. 2, of *Gesammelte Werke.* Edited by H. W. Arndt. Hildesheim: Olms, 1983.

————. *Vernünfftige Gedancken von den Kräften des menschlichen Verstandes und ihrem richtigen Gebrauche in Erkenntnis der Wahrheit.* Edited by H. W. Arndt. Vol. 1, no. 1, of *Gesammelte Werke.* Edited by H. W. Arndt. Hildesheim: Olms, 1978.

————. *Vernünfftige Gedancken von der Menschen Thun und Lassen, zur Beförderung ihrer Glückseligkeit.* Introduction by H. W. Arndt. Vol. 1, no. 4, of *Gesammelte Werke.* Edited by H. W. Arndt. Hildesheim: Olms, 1976.

Young, Edward. "Conjectures on Original Composition." In *Critical Theory since Plato,* edited by Hazard Adams, 338–47. New York: Harcourt Brace Jovanovich, 1971.

Secondary Works

Aarsleff, Hans. *From Locke to Saussure: Essays in the Study of Language and Intellectual History.* Minneapolis: University of Minnesota Press, 1982.

Abrams, M. H. *The Mirror and the Lamp: Romantic Theory and the Critical Tradition.* 1953. Reprint. London: Oxford University Press, 1977.

Armstrong, A. H. *Plotinus.* London: George Allen, 1953.

Auerbach, Erich. "Passio als Leidenschaft." *PMLA* 56 (1941): 1179–96.

Bächtold, Jakob. *Geschichte der Deutschen Literatur in der Schweiz.* Frauenfeld: Huber, 1919.

Baeumler, Alfred. *Das Irrationalitätsproblem in der Ästhetik und Logik des 18. Jahrhunderts bis zur Kritik der Urteilskraft.* 1923. Reprint. Darmstadt: Wissenschaftliche Buchgesellschaft, 1981.

Beetz, Manfred. *Rhetorische Logik: Prämissen der deutschen Lyrik im Übergang vom 17. zum 18. Jahrhundert.* Tübingen: Niemeyer, 1980.

Beierwaltes, Werner. *Platonismus und Idealismus.* Frankfurt a.M.: Klostermann, 1972.

Bender, Wolfgang. *Johann Jacob Bodmer und Johann Jacob Breitinger.* Sammlung Metzler, no. 113. Stuttgart: Metzler, 1973.

————. "Johann Jacob Bodmer und Johann Miltons 'Verlohrenes Paradies.'" *Jahrbuch der deutschen Schillergesellschaft* 11 (1967): 225–67.

————. "Rhetorische Tradition und Ästhetik im 18. Jahrhundert: Baumgarten, Meier und Breitinger." *Zeitschrift für deutsche Philologie* 99 (1980): 481–506.

Betteridge, H. T. "Klopstock's Correspondence with Bodmer and Breitinger: Amendments and Additions." *Modern Language Review* 57 (1962): 357–72.

Bing, Susi. *Die Naturnachahmungstheorie bei Gottsched und den Schweizern und ihre Beziehungen zu der Dichtungstheorie der Zeit.* Würzburg: Trilitsch, 1934.

Birke, Joachim. *Christian Wolffs Metaphysik und die Zeitgenössische Literatur-und Musiktheorie: Gottsched, Scheibe, Mizler*. Berlin: de Gruyter, 1966.

—. "Gottscheds Neuorientierung der deutschen Poetik an der Philosophie Wolffs." *Zeitschrift für deutsche Philologie* 85 (1966): 560–75.

Birmelin, Ella. "Die kunsttheoretischen Gedanken in Philostrats Apollonios." *Philologus* 88, n.s. 42 (1933): 149–80; 392–414.

Blackall, Eric A. *The Emergence of German as a Literary Language*. Cambridge: Cambridge University Press, 1959.

Bleicher, Thomas. *Homer in der deutschen Literatur: Zur Rezeption der Antike und zur Poetologie der Neuzeit*. Stuttgart: Metzler, 1972.

Blumenberg, Hans. "'Nachahmung der Natur': Zur Vorgeschichte der Idee des schöpferischen Menschen." *Studium Generale* 10 (1957): 266–83.

—. *Der Prozeß der theoretischen Neugierde*. Frankfurt a.M.: Suhrkamp, 1966.

—. "Wirklichkeitsbegriff und Möglichkeit des Romans." In *Nachahmung und Illusion*, edited by H. R. Jauß, 9–27. Munich: Fink, 1969.

Böckmann, Paul. *Formgeschichte der deutschen Dichtung*. 2d ed. Hamburg: Campe, 1965.

Borjans-Heuser, Peter. *Bürgerliche Produktivität und Dichtungstheorie: Strukturmerkmale der poietischen Rationalität im Werk von Johann Christoph Gottsched*. Frankfurt a.M.: Lang, 1981.

Bosse, Heinrich. "'Dichter kann man nicht bilden': Zur Veränderung der Schulrhetorik nach 1770." *Jahrbuch der Internationalen Germanistik* 10 (1978): 80–125.

Braitmaier, Friedrich. *Geschichte der Poetischen Theorie und Kritik von den Diskursen der Maler bis auf Lessing*. Frauenfeld: Huber, 1888.

Brandes, Helga. *Die "Gesellschaft der Maler" und ihr literarischer Beitrag zur Aufklärung: Eine Untersuchung zur Publizistik des 18. Jahrhunderts*. Bremen: Schünemann, 1974.

Bray, René. *La Formation de la doctrine classique en France*. 1927. Reprint. Paris: Nizet, 1963.

Bredvold, Louis I. "The Tendency towards Platonism in Neoclassical Aesthetics." *Journal of English Literary History* 1 (1934): 91–119.

Bretzigheimer, Gerlinde. *Johann Elias Schlegels poetische Theorie im Rahmen der Tradition*. Munich: Fink, 1986.

Brown, F. Andrew. "Locke's 'Essay' and Bodmer and Breitinger." *Modern Language Quarterly* 10 (1949): 16–32.

—. "Locke's 'tabula rasa' and Gottsched." *Germanic Review* 24 (1949): 3–7.

Bruck, Jan, Eckhart Feldmeier, Hans Hiebel, and Karl Heinz Stahl. "Der Mimesisbegriff Gottscheds und der Schweizer: Kritische Überlegungen zu Hans Peter Herrmann, 'Naturnachahmung und Einbildungskraft.'" *Zeitschrift für deutsche Philologie* 90 (1971): 563–78.

Buch, Hans Christoph. *"Ut Pictura Poesis": Die Beschreibungsliteratur und ihre Kritiker von Lessing bis Lukács*. Munich: Hanser, 1972.

Bürger, Christa, Peter Bürger, and Jochen Schulte-Sasse, eds. *Aufklärung und literarische Öffentlichkeit*. Frankfurt a.M.: Suhrkamp, 1980.

Busch, Ernst. "Klopstocks Messias und die poetische Theorie von Bodmer und Breitinger." *Germanisch-Romanische Monatsschrift* 29 (1941): 92–106.

Cassirer, Ernst. *Freiheit und Form: Studien zur deutschen Geistesgeschichte.* Berlin: Bruno Cassirer, 1916.

———. *Leibniz' System in seinen wissenschaftlichen Grundlagen.* Marburg: Elwert, 1902.

———. *Die Philosophie der Aufklärung.* 2d ed. Tübingen: Mohr, 1932.

Crüger, Johannes. *Joh. Christoph Gottsched und die Schweizer Joh. J. Bodmer und Joh. J. Breitinger.* 1884. Reprint. Darmstadt: Wissenschaftliche Buchgesellschaft, 1965.

Danzel, Theodore Wilhelm. *Gottsched und seine Zeit: Auszüge aus seinem Briefwechsel.* Leipzig: Dyk, 1848.

Deku, Henry. "Possibile Logicum." *Philosophisches Jahrbuch der Görres-Gesellschaft* 64 (1956): 1–21.

Demandt, Alexander. *Metaphern für Geschichte: Sprachbilder und Gleichnisse im historisch-politischen Denken.* Munich: Beck, 1978.

Dilthey, Wilhelm. *Weltanschauung und Analyse des Menschen seit Renaissance und Reformation.* Vol. 2 of *Gesammelte Schriften.* Leipzig: Teubner, 1921.

Dockhorn, Klaus. *Macht und Wirkung der Rhetorik: Vier Aufsätze zur Ideengeschichte der Vormoderne.* Berlin: Gehlen, 1968.

Draper, John. "Aristotelian 'Mimesis' in Eighteenth-Century England." *PMLA* 36 (1921): 372–400.

Ellege, Scott. "The Background and Development in English Criticism of the Theories of Generality and Particularity." *PMLA* 62 (1947): 147–82.

Faust, August. *Der Möglichkeitsgedanke: Systemgeschichtliche Untersuchungen.* Heidelberg: Winter, 1931.

Feuerbach, Ludwig. *Geschichte der neuern Philosophie: Darstellung, Entwicklung und Kritik der Leibnizischen Philosophie.* Ansbach: Brügel, 1837.

Finsler, Georg. *Homer in der Neuzeit von Dante bis Goethe.* Leipzig: Teubner, 1912.

Flemming, Willi. *Der Wandel des deutschen Naturgefühls vom 15. bis zum 18. Jahrhundert.* Halle: Niemeyer, 1931.

Friedl, A. J. *Die Homer-Interpretation des Neuplatonikers Proklos.* Würzburg: Dittert, n.d.

Funke, Gerhard. *Der Möglichkeitsgedanke in Leibnizens System.* Bonn: Köllen, n.d.

Gadamer, Hans-Georg. *Wahrheit und Methode: Grundzüge einer philosophischen Hermeneutik.* 2d ed. Tübingen: Mohr, 1965.

Gaede, Friedrich. "Gottscheds Nachahmungstheorie und die Logik." *Deutsche Vierteljahrsschrift* 49 (1975, Sonderheft): 105–17.

Gose, Walter. "Ein theologischer Brief Breitingers." *Jahrbuch der deutschen Schillergesellschaft* 13 (1969): 1–12.

Guillen, Claudio. "On the Concept and Metaphor of Perspective." In *Literature as System: Essays toward the Theory of Literary History,* 283–371. Princeton: Princeton University Press, 1971.

Guthke, Karl S. *Literarisches Leben im achtzehnten Jahrhundert in Deutschland und in der Schweiz.* Bern: Francke, 1975.

Häntzschel, Günter. *Johann Heinrich Voß: Seine Homer-Übersetzung als sprachschöpferische Leistung.* Munich: Beck, 1977.

Heinimann, Felix. *Nomos und Physis: Herkunft und Bedeutung einer Antithese im griechischen Denken des 5. Jahrhunderts.* Basel: Reinhardt, 1945.

Henn, Claudia. "'Sinnreiche Gedancken': Zur Hermeneutik des Chladenius." *Archiv für Geschichte der Philosophie* 58 (1976): 240–64.

Henne, Helmut. "Eine frühe kritische Edition neuerer Literatur: Zur Opitz-Ausgabe Bodmers und Breitingers von 1745." *Zeitschrift für deutsche Philologie* 87 (1968): 180–96.

Herrmann, Hans Peter. *Naturnachahmung und Einbildungskraft: Zur Entwicklung der deutschen Poetik von 1670 bis 1740.* Bad Homburg: Gehlen, 1970.

Hettner, Hermann. *Geschichte der deutschen Literatur im achtzehnten Jahrhundert.* 6th ed. 4 vols. Braunschweig: Vieweg, 1913.

Hintikka, J. "Leibniz on Plenitude, Relations, and the 'Reign of Law.'" In *Reforging the Great Chain of Being: Studies of the History of Modal Theories,* edited by S. Knuuttila, 259–86. Boston: Reidel, 1980.

Hohner, Ulrich. *Zur Problematik der Naturnachahmung in der deutschen Ästhetik des 18. Jahrhunderts.* Erlangen: Palm & Enke, 1976.

Hüppauf, Bernd, ed. *Literaturgeschichte zwischen Revolution und Reaktion.* Frankfurt a.M.: Athenäum, 1972.

Jauß, H. R. "Ästhetische Normen und geschichtliche Reflexion in der 'Querelle des Anciens et des Modernes.'" Introduction to *Parallele des anciens et des modernes en ce qui regarde les arts et les sciences par M. Perrault de l'Académie Française,* edited by H. R. Jauß, 8–64. Munich: Eidos, 1964.

Kaiser, Gerhard. "'Denken' und 'Empfinden': Ein Beitrag zur Sprache und Poetik Klopstocks." *Deutsche Vierteljahrsschrift* 35 (1961): 321–43.

Kapitza, Peter K. *Ein bürgerlicher Krieg in der gelehrten Welt: Zur Geschichte des Anciens et des Modernes in Deutschland.* Munich: Fink, 1981.

Kayser, Wolfgang. "Böhmes Natursprachenlehre und ihre Grundlagen." *Euphorion* 31 (1930): 521–62.

Kimpel, Dieter, ed. *Mehrsprachigkeit in der deutschen Aufklärung.* Hamburg: Felix Meiner, 1985.

Knight, Dorothy. "Thomas Blackwell and J. J. Bodmer: The Establishment of a Literary Link between Homeric Greece and Medieval Germany." *German Life and Letters* n.s. 6 (1952–53): 249–58.

Knodt, Eva M. *"Negative Philosophie" und dialogische Kritik: Zur Struktur poetischer Theorie bei Lessing und Herder.* Tübingen: Niemeyer, 1988.

Kortum, Hans. *Charles Perrault und Nicolas Boileau: Der Antike-Streit im Zeitalter der klassischen französischen Literatur.* Berlin: Rütten & Loening, 1966.

Kowalik, Jill Anne. Review of *Johann Elias Schlegels poetische Theorie im Rahmen der Tradition,* by Gerlinde Bretzigheimer. *German Quarterly* 61 (1988): 304–5.

Krauss, Werner. *Studien zur deutschen und französischen Aufklärung.* Berlin: Rütten & Loening, 1963.

Kristeller, Paul Oskar. *Renaissance Thought.* 2 vols. New York: Harper & Row, 1961.

Kustas, George L. *Studies in Byzantine Rhetoric*. Thessalonica: Patriarchal Institute of Patristic Studies, 1973.

Lempicki, Sigmund von. *Geschichte der deutschen Literaturwissenschaft bis zum Ende des 18. Jahrhunderts*. 2d ed. Göttingen: Vandenhoeck & Rupprecht, 1968.

Leventhal, Robert S. "Semiotic Interpretation and Rhetoric in the German Enlightenment 1740–1760." *Deutsche Vierteljahrsschrift* 60 (1986): 223–48.

Lovejoy, Arthur O. *The Great Chain of Being: A Study of the History of an Idea*. Cambridge: Harvard University Press, 1936.

————. "'Nature' as Aesthetic Norm." In *Essays in the History of Ideas*, 69–77. Baltimore: Johns Hopkins University Press, 1948.

Mahnke, Dietrich. *Leibnizens Synthese von Universalmathematik und Individualmetaphysik*. 1925. Reprint. Stuttgart: Frommann, 1964.

Mansfeld, Franz. "Das literarische Barock im kunsttheoretischen Urteil Gottscheds und der Schweizer." Dissertation, University of Halle-Wittenberg, 1928.

Manso, J. K. F. *Übersicht der Geschichte der deutschen Poesie seit Bodmers und Breitingers kritischen Bemühungen*. Vol. 8, no. 1, of *Nachträge zu Sulzers allgemeiner Theorie der schönen Künste*. Leipzig: Dyk, 1806.

Martinson, Steven D. *On Imitation, Imagination, and Beauty: A Critical Reassessment of the Concept of the Literary Artist during the Early German "Aufklärung."* Bonn: Bouvier, 1977.

Megill, Allan. "Aesthetic Theory and Historical Consciousness in the Eighteenth Century." *History and Theory: Studies in the Philosophy of History* 17 (1978): 29–62.

Meinecke, Friedrich. *Die Entstehung des Historismus*. Edited by C. Hinrichs. 4th ed. Munich: Oldenbourg, 1965.

Meusel, J. G., ed. *Lexikon der vom Jahre 1750 bis 1800 verstorbenen teutschen Schriftsteller*. 1802. Reprint. Hildesheim: Olms, 1967.

Möller, Uwe. *Rhetorische Überlieferung und Dichtungstheorie im frühen 18. Jahrhundert: Studien zu Gottsched, Breitinger, und G. Fr. Meier*. Munich: Fink, 1983.

Monk, Samuel H. *The Sublime: A Study of Critical Theories in XVIII-Century England*. 1935. Reprint. Ann Arbor: University of Michigan Press, 1960.

Moore, Cecil A. "Did Leibniz Influence Pope's Essay?" *Journal of English and Germanic Philology* 16 (1917): 84–102.

Müller, Jan-Dirk. "J. J. Bodmer's Poetik und die Wiederentdeckung mittelhochdeutscher Epen." *Euphorion* 71 (1977): 336–52.

Neubauer, John. *Symbolismus und symbolische Logik: Die Idee der Ars Combinatoria in der Entwicklung der modernen Dichtung*. Munich: Fink, 1978.

Panofsky, Erwin. *Idea: A Concept in Art Theory*. Translated by J. S. Peake. New York: Harper & Row, 1968.

Pfeiffer, Rudolf. *History of Classical Scholarship*. Oxford: Clarendon, 1968.

Phelps, Leland. "Gottsched to Herder: The Changing Conception of Metaphor in Eighteenth-Century Germany." *Monatshefte* 44 (1952): 129–34.

Politella, Joseph. *Platonism, Aristotelianism, and Cabalism in the Philosophy of Leibniz*. Philadelphia: University of Pennsylvania Press, 1938.

Preisendanz, Wolfgang. "Die Auseinandersetzung mit dem Nachahmungsprinzip in Deutschland und die besondere Rolle der Romane Wielands ('Don Sylvio,' 'Agathon')." In *Nachahmung und Illusion*, edited by H. R. Jauß, 72–93. Munich: Fink, 1969.

———. "Mimesis and Poiesis in der deutschen Dichtungstheorie des 18. Jahrhunderts." In *Rezeption und Produktion zwischen 1570 und 1730*, edited by W. Rasch, H. Geulen, and K. Haberkamm, 537–52. Bern: Francke, 1972.

Reichmann, Eberhard. "Die Begründung der deutschen Aufklärungsästhetik aus dem Geist der Zahl." *Monatshefte* 59 (1967): 193–203.

Reill, Peter Hanns. *The German Enlightenment and the Rise of Historicism*. Berkeley: University of California Press, 1975.

Rieck, Werner. *Johann Christoph Gottsched: Eine kritische Würdigung seines Werkes*. Berlin: Akademie Verlag, 1972.

Ritter, Joachim, ed. *Historisches Wörterbuch der Philosophie*. Vol. 1, s.v. "Apperzeption" and "A priori/a posteriori." Basel: Schwabe, 1971.

Robertson, J. G. *Studies in the Genesis of Romantic Theory in the Eighteenth Century*. Cambridge: Cambridge University Press, 1923.

Saine, Thomas P. *Von der Kopernikanischen bis zur Französischen Revolution: Die Auseinandersetzung der deutschen Frühaufklärung mit der neuen Zeit*. Berlin: Erich Schmidt, 1987.

Schanze, Helmut. "Goethe: 'Dichtung und Wahrheit,' 7. Buch: Prinzipien und Probleme einer Literaturgeschichte des 18. Jahrhunderts." *Germanisch-Romanische Monatsschrift* 24 (1974): 44–56.

Scherpe, Klaus R. *Gattungspoetik im 18. Jahrhundert: Historische Entwicklung von Gottsched bis Herder*. Stuttgart: Metzler, 1968.

Schipperes, Heinrich. "Natur." In *Geschichtliche Grundbegriffe: Historisches Lexikon zur politisch-sozialen Sprache in Deutschland*, edited by O. Brunner, W. Conze, and R. Koselleck, 4:215–44. Stuttgart: Klett, 1978.

Schlegel, Friedrich. *Sich "von dem Gemüthe des Lesers Meister" machen: Zur Wirkungsästhetik der Poetik Bodmers und Breitingers*. European University Studies, vol. 928. Frankfurt a.M.: Lang, 1986.

Schmidt, Horst-Michael. *Sinnlichkeit und Verstand: Zur philosophischen und poetologischen Begründung von Erfahrung und Urteil in der deutschen Aufklärung (Leibniz, Wolff, Gottsched, Bodmer und Breitinger, Baumgarten)*. Munich: Fink, 1982.

Schneiders, Werner, ed. *Christian Wolff 1679–1754: Interpretationen zu seiner Philosophie und deren Wirkung*. Hamburg: Felix Meiner, 1983.

Schöffler, Herbert. *Das literarische Zürich*. Frauenfeld: Huber, 1925.

Scholl, Rosemary. "Die Rhetorik der Vernunft: Gottsched und die Rhetorik im frühen 18. Jahrhundert." *Akten des V. Internationalen GermanistenKongresses Cambridge 1975*, edited by Leonard Forster and Hans-Gert Roloff, 3(2):217–21. Bern: Lang, 1976.

Seeba, Hinrich C. "Lessings Geschichtsbild: Zur ästhetischen Evidenz historischer Wahrheit." In *Humanität und Dialog: Lessing und Mendelssohn in neuer Sicht*, edited by Ehrhard Bahr, Edward P. Harris, and Lawrence G. Lyon, 289–305. Detroit: Wayne State University Press, 1982.

———. "Literatur und Geschichte: Hermeneutische Ansätze zu einer Poetik der Geschichtsschreibung." In *Akten des VI. Internationalen Germanisten-Kongresses Basel 1980*, edited by Heinz Rupp and Hans-Gert Roloff, 3:201–8. Bern: Lang, 1980.

———. " 'Der wahre Standort einer jeden Person.' Lessings Beitrag zum historischen Perspektivismus." In *Nation und Gelehrtenrepublik: Lessing im europäischen Zusammenhang*, edited by Wilfried Barner and Albert M. Reh, 193–214. Detroit: Wayne State University Press, 1984.

Servaes, Franz. *Die Poetik Gottscheds und der Schweizer*. Strassburg: Trübner, 1887.

Shankman, Steven. *Pope's "Iliad": Homer in the Age of Passion*. Princeton: Princeton University Press, 1983.

Simonsuuri, Kirsti. *Homer's Original Genius: Eighteenth-century Notions of the Early Greek Epic (1688–1798)*. Cambridge: Cambridge University Press, 1979.

Solmsen, Friedrich. "Aristotle and Cicero on the Orator's Playing upon the Feelings." *Classical Philology* 33 (1938): 390–404.

Spaemann, Robert. "Genetisches zum Naturbegriff des 18. Jahrhunderts." *Archiv für Begriffsgeschichte* 11 (1967): 59–74.

Spingarn, J. E. *Critical Essays of the Seventeenth Century*. 3 vols. 1907. Reprint. Bloomington: Indiana University Press, 1957.

Spitzer, Leo. *Classical and Christian Ideas of World Harmony*. Baltimore: Johns Hopkins University Press, 1963.

Stahl, Karl-Heinz. *Das Wunderbare als Problem und Gegenstand der deutschen Poetik des 17. und 18. Jahrhunderts*. Frankfurt a.M.: Athenaion, 1975.

Stein, Heinrich von. *Die Entstehung der Neueren Ästhetik*. Stuttgart: Cotta, 1886.

Sühnel, Rudolf. *Homer und die englische Humanität: Chapmans und Pope's Übersetzungskunst im Rahmen der humanistischen Tradition*. Tübingen: Niemeyer, 1958.

Szondi, Peter. *Einführung in die literarische Hermeneutik*. Edited by Jean Bollack and Helen Stierlin. Frankfurt a.M.: Suhrkamp, 1975.

Torbruegge, Marilyn. "Bodmer und Longinus." *Monatshefte* 63 (1971): 341–57.

Trimpi, Wesley. "The Ancient Hypothesis of Fiction: An Essay on the Origins of Literary Theory." *Traditio* 27 (1971): 1–78.

———. "The Early Metaphorical Uses of ΣΚΙΑΓΡΑΦΙΑ and ΣΚΗΝΟΓΡΑΦΙΑ." *Traditio* 34 (1978): 403–13.

———. "Horace's 'Ut Pictura Poesis': The Argument for Stylistic Decorum." *Traditio* 34 (1978): 29–73.

———. "The Meaning of Horace's 'Ut Pictura Poesis.'" *Journal of the Warburg and Courtauld Institutes* 36 (1973): 1–34.

————. *Muses of One Mind: The Literary Analysis of Experience and Its Continu-ity*. Princeton: Princeton University Press, 1983.

————. "The Quality of Fiction: The Rhetorical Transmission of Literary Theory." *Traditio* 30 (1974): 1–118.

Tumarkin, Anna. "Die Überwindung der Mimesislehre in der Kunsttheorie des XVIII. Jahrhunderts: Zur Vorgeschichte der Romantik." In *Festgabe Samuel Singer überreicht*, edited by Harry Maync, 40–55. Tübingen: Sie-beck, 1930.

Ullman, B. L. "History and Tragedy." *Transactions and Proceedings of the American Philological Association* 73 (1942): 25–53.

Vetter, Theodore. *Der Spectator als Quelle der "Discurse der Maler."* Frauenfeld: Huber, 1887.

Vierhaus, Rudolf. "Wie erzählt man Geschichte? Die Perspektive des Histo-riographen." In *Historisches Erzählen*, edited by Siegfried Quandt and Hans Süssmuth, 49–56. Göttingen: Vandenhoeck & Ruprecht, 1982.

Wach, Joachim. *Das Verstehen: Grundzüge einer Geschichte der hermeneutischen Theorie im 19. Jahrhundert*. 1926. Reprint. Hildesheim: Olms, 1966.

Wagner, Fritz. "Herders Homerbild, seine Wurzeln und Wirkungen." Dis-sertation, University of Cologne, 1960.

Walzel, Oskar. *Das Prometheussymbol von Shaftesbury zu Goethe*. Leipzig: Teubner, 1910.

Waniek, Gustav. *Gottsched und die deutsche Litteratur seiner Zeit*. Leipzig: Breitkopf, 1897.

Wehrli, Max. *Johann Jakob Bodmer und die Geschichte der Literatur*. Frauenfeld: Huber, 1936.

Weinberg, Bernard. *A History of Literary Criticism in the Italian Renaissance*. 2 vols. Chicago: University of Chicago Press, 1961.

————. "Scaliger versus Aristotle on Poetics." *Modern Philology* 39 (1942): 337–60.

Wellbery, David E. *Lessing's "Laocoon": Semiotics and Aesthetics in the Age of Reason*. Cambridge: Cambridge University Press, 1984.

Wellek, René. *A History of Modern Criticism: 1750–1950*. New Haven: Yale University Press, 1955.

Wetterer, Angelika. *Publikumsbezug und Wahrheitsanspruch: Der Widerspruch zwischen rhetorischem Ansatz und philosophischem Anspruch bei Gottsched und den Schweizern*. Tübingen: Niemeyer, 1981.

Windelband, Wilhelm. *Lehrbuch der Geschichte der Philosophie*. 15th ed. Tü-bingen: Mohr, 1957.

Windfuhr, Manfred. *Die barocke Bildlichkeit und ihre Kritiker: Stilhaltungen in der deutschen Literatur des 17. und 18. Jahrhunderts*. Stuttgart: Metzler, 1966.

Wojtowicz, Tadeusz. *Die Logik von Johann Jakob Breitinger*. Paris: Maloine, 1947.

Wolff, Hans M. *Die Weltanschauung der deutschen Aufklärung in geschichtlicher Entwicklung*. 2d ed. Munich: Francke, 1963.

Wundt, Max. *Die deutsche Schulphilosophie im Zeitalter der Aufklärung*. 1945. Reprint. Hildesheim: Olms, 1964.

Zilsel, Edgar. *Die Entstehung des Geniebegriffs*. Tübingen: Siebeck, 1926.

Index

147

University of North Carolina Studies in the Germanic Languages and Literatures

For other volumes in the "Studies" see p. ii.

Send orders to:
The University of North Carolina Press, P.O. Box 2288
Chapel Hill, NC 27515-2288

Several out-of-print titles are available in limited quantities through the UNCSGLL office. These include:

81 ELAINE E. BONEY. *Rainer Maria Rilke: "Duinesian Elegies."* German Text with English Translation and Commentary. 2nd ed. 1977. Pp. xii, 153.

82 JANE K. BROWN. *Goethe's Cyclical Narratives: "Die Unterhaltungen deutscher Ausgewanderten" and "Wilhelm Meisters Wanderjahre."* 1975. Pp. x, 144.

83 FLORA KIMMICH. *Sonnets of Catharina von Greiffenberg: Methods of Composition.* 1975. Pp. x, 132.

84 HERBERT W. REICHERT. *Friedrich Nietzsche's Impact on Modern German Literature.* 1975. Pp. xxii, 129.

85 JAMES C. O'FLAHERTY, TIMOTHY F. SELLNER, ROBERT M. HELMS, EDS. *Studies in Nietzsche and the Classical Tradition.* 2nd ed. 1979. Pp. xviii, 278.

87 HUGO BEKKER. *Friedrich von Hausen: Inquiries into His Poetry.* 1977. Pp. x, 159.

88 H. G. HUETTICH. *Theater in the Planned Society: Contemporary Drama in the German Democratic Republic in Its Historical, Political, and Cultural Context.* 1978. Pp. xvi, 174.

89 DONALD G. DAVIAU, ED. *The Letters of Arthur Schnitzler to Hermann Bahr.* 1978. Pp. xii, 183.

91 LELAND R. PHELPS AND A. TILO ALT, EDS. *Creative Encounter. Festschrift for Herman Salinger.* 1978. Pp. xxii, 181.

93 MEREDITH LEE. *Studies in Goethe's Lyric Cycles.* 1978. Pp. xii, 191.

94 JOHN M. ELLIS. *Heinrich von Kleist. Studies in the Character and Meaning of His Writings.* 1979. Pp. xx, 194.

95 GORDON BIRRELL. *The Boundless Present. Space and Time in the Literary Fairy Tales of Novalis and Tieck.* 1979. Pp. x, 163.

Orders for these titles only should be sent to Editor, UNCSGLL, CB# 3160 Dey Hall, Chapel Hill, NC 27599-3160.

Volumes 1–44, 46–50, 52, 60, and 79 of the "Studies" have been reprinted. They may be ordered from AMS Press, Inc., 56 E. 13th Street, New York, NY 10003.

For complete list of reprinted titles write to the Editor.